Making the Cut

Making the Cut

An Unorthodox Love Story

Max Olesker

EBURY
PRESS

EBURY PRESS

UK | USA | Canada | Ireland | Australia
India | New Zealand | South Africa

Ebury Press is part of the Penguin Random House group of companies whose addresses can be found at global.penguinrandomhouse.com

Penguin Random House UK
One Embassy Gardens, 8 Viaduct Gardens, London SW11 7BW

penguin.co.uk
global.penguinrandomhouse.com

First published by Ebury Press in 2026

Copyright © Max Olesker 2026
The moral right of the author has been asserted.

This book is a work of non-fiction based on the life, experiences and recollections of the author. Names of people, places, and the detail of events have been changed to protect the privacy rights of others.

Penguin Random House values and supports copyright. Copyright fuels creativity, encourages diverse voices, promotes freedom of expression and supports a vibrant culture. Thank you for purchasing an authorised edition of this book and for respecting intellectual property laws by not reproducing, scanning or distributing any part of it by any means without permission. You are supporting authors and enabling Penguin Random House to continue to publish books for everyone. No part of this book may be used or reproduced in any manner for the purpose of training artificial intelligence technologies or systems. In accordance with Article 4(3) of the DSM Directive 2019/790, Penguin Random House expressly reserves this work from the text and data mining exception.

Set in in 11.7/14.2 pt Garamond Premier Pro
Typeset by Six Red Marbles UK, Thetford, Norfolk

Printed and bound in Great Britain by Clays Ltd, Elcograf S.p.A.

The authorised representative in the EEA is Penguin Random House Ireland, Morrison Chambers, 32 Nassau Street, Dublin D02 YH68

A CIP catalogue record for this book is available from the British Library

ISBN 9781529951721

Penguin Random House is committed to a sustainable future for our business, our readers and our planet. This book is made from Forest Stewardship Council® certified paper.

For Eliana, and for my dad.

Contents

1. Beginnings and Endings — 1
2. I, Jew? — 4
3. Growing Up, Melting Down, Stepping Out — 24
4. Ah... — 31
5. The Discussion — 43
6. Some Much Needed Respite in the Form of the End of the World — 55
7. On the Road Again — 66
8. A Series of Surprising Conversations — 78
9. Onwards — 96
10. A Letter of Intent — 103
11. Going Contactless — 109
12. The Minyan — 112
13. We'll Be in Touch — 127
14. The Diagnosis — 136
15. Lion — 141
16. Meeting the Beth Din — 149
17. Ohhh, You've Got the Wrong Soul Too? — 156
18. Round Two... — 165
19. Stairway to Hendon — 175

CONTENTS

20	A Series of Plot Twists	182
21	Coffee with the Bernsteins	187
22	The Area	195
23	A Walk in the Park	211
24	Pure Hendonism	217
25	Rosie Jones's Breasts (and Other Impediments to Conversion)	232
26	The March of the Living	242
27	Having a Laugh	249
28	The Weight of the Wait	257
29	Suddenly, Everything Happens at Once	284
30	D-Day	287
31	A Healing Experience	301
32	It Ain't Over Until the Fat Rabbi Sings	318
33	The Mikveh	326
34	Who Judges the Judges?	333
35	Totnes	337
36	Endings and Beginnings	350
Acknowledgements		357

CHAPTER 1

Beginnings and Endings

The Edinburgh Fringe. 2am.

She has red lipstick, and clear blue almond eyes which dance with mischief, and a sheer *confidence* that I have never encountered before. Uniquely, it doesn't seem fuelled by either insecurity or entitlement – by trying to achieve anything, or to prove anything. She just seems to exist more vividly than other people.

'Your show was really funny!'

'Thank you so much!'

'Would you like a drink?'

'Ivan and I have just bought a bottle of wine – would you like a glass?'

Somewhere across the bar, Ivan Gonzalez, my comedy partner, turns and gives a cheerful vague wave in the direction of whoever said his name.

'Nah', she says, 'I'm going out. Shots?'

She orders us both Jägerbombs – undrinkable, saccharine, poisonous things. Much later, we will realise that neither of us actually liked them in the first place – though our friends who were with us at the bar assure us that, that evening, we both drank them slowly, savouring each syrupy monstrosity as though it were a delicately aged Old Fashioned.

'Cheers. It's nice to meet you.'

Nestled between a group of loud French-Canadian circus performers and some extremely earnest student puppeteers, we are pushed closer together in the crush of the bar as she explains that, technically, we've met before. A previous summer, when working at the Fringe, she was assigned to run the front of house at a chaotic show in which comics become professional wrestlers – a show I produced, and a product of my misspent youth as a teenage grappler – and so, the first time we met, she was taking tickets and I was somersaulting off a ladder onto some comedians. Tale as old as time.

'Our double-act show has quite a different energy to the wrestling, hope that was OK?'

'I mean, I demanded a full refund because you weren't wearing your lightning bolt shorts, but otherwise very few complaints.'

She is sharp and whimsical and surprising and effervescent and self-possessed and spectacular.

Her name is Eliana.

'And I liked the Jewish jokes,' she says.

'Oh, it's OK,' I say. 'I'm allowed to make them.'

Her eyes light up.

And so it all begins. Because I am Jewish.

One year later. London. 3pm.

We have fallen deep into the ravine of togetherness. We have moved in together, organised surprise birthday parties for one another, given one another handmade cards, become part of one another's friendship groups, nursed one another through illnesses, argued furiously and reconciled passionately. We have fallen inescapably in love.

My suitcase is packed and waiting by the front door. There are more of my possessions piled on top, an unruly, unwieldy overspill of things – clothes, books, stationery – crammed hastily into spare rucksacks, canvas totes and, eventually, overstuffed plastic shopping bags. Yet more things on the floor. My coffee machine. My stupid folding bike that I love. My half of our life together.

We cook each other a sad beige dinner of steak and mushrooms, and we sit in silence and eat.

My face is grey. Tears streak Eliana's cheeks.

Eventually, a cab arrives. An XL, to account for, you know, all of the stuff.

'I'm so sorry,' says Eliana.

'So am I,' I respond.

We have broken up. Because I am not Jewish.

CHAPTER 2

I, Jew?

In order to best make sense of it all – the fateful meeting, the tear-stained separation, and all of the thermonuclear, life-uprooting chaos that followed – it makes sense to go back to the very start.

On 18 May 1987, a week earlier than intended and with the help of a pair of forceps, my oversized (and temporarily misshapen) head and I exit my mother and enter the world. I am the eldest of three boys, and we grow up in the centre of Portsmouth – a gritty, blustery, densely packed naval city on the south coast of England. 'Pompey' is small enough that you can walk everywhere; a place where everyone is no more than half a degree of separation from anyone else. It is an island, connected to the mainland by a single dual carriageway, and you can feel the restless energy of the city as you travel in on the Eastern Road.

It is a footballing city, with Fratton Park home to the beloved Portsmouth FC, a team passionately supported by its fans, known as the Blue Army, and, throughout my childhood, by the infamous and violent 6.57 Crew – our football hooligans being perpetually near the top of their league table, even if our football team rarely reach the summit of theirs. It is a drinker's city – at one time, Portsmouth was proudly home to 365 pubs, one for every day of the year. It is a city locked in an eternal, bitter rivalry with neighbouring Southampton (AKA 'the Scummers' – the hatred is ostensibly football-centric, but in practice extends to a mutual vague dislike and distrust between townsfolk that plays out in any and all social situations). And it is a city in which occasional glimpses of historic beauty – the elegant Victorian houses of Old Portsmouth, the thrilling sight of HMS *Victory* and *Warrior*, still afloat in the Historic Dockyard – sit alongside high-density urban areas of intense deprivation, which crackle and hum with low-level aggression. In my youth, whenever Portsmouth plays Southampton, chaos ensues – when we lose, our fans come back to Portsmouth and furiously trash the city. Later, when we win, our fans come back to Portsmouth and triumphantly . . . trash the city.

It is an unlikely surrounding for the eccentric, bohemian household created by my eccentric, bohemian parents. My mother is a unique combination of ceaselessly creative and formidably pragmatic. She set up her own community arts organisation whilst pregnant with me, taking a single day off to give birth, before promptly returning to work to finish constructing a Chinese dragon for the Paulsgrove Carnival. My father is a lecturer in English and Drama. In reality this is a cunning ruse, allowing him access to all the obscure books and archive materials he could wish for, along with the time and space to produce an endless array of songs, poems and plays – a great many inspired by the Yiddish folktales of Chelm, a mythical 'city of fools'. Together, they take a cheerfully experimental approach to parenting, and I am raised in an environment which is loving, supportive, and results in me arriving at school furnished with approximately zero of the requisite skills needed to navigate the realities of a Pompey childhood. I am different, I come to realise, in a host of ways.

I look different, for one, having been given the freedom to dress myself however I wish. Choosing one's own clothing is a noble act of creative self-expression – it is also one which sees me stand out a mile in my mainly school-uniform-wearing primary school, due to my approach of 'dressing entirely in whichever block colour is my favourite at that moment'. Is 'you should feel free to express yourself as you wish, and don't let bullies affect your judgement' a piece of inspiring advice for a parent to give a child? Absolutely. Does it, in practice, result in me immediately easing into my natural position as pariah of the Portsmouth school playground? But of course!

I am also armed with a completely different set of cultural reference points. Having grown up in a house in which my mother carefully limits our TV usage, and which certainly never stretches to anything as decadent as Sky or cable, there is instead my father's study – an endless, impossible trove of knowledge, stories, facts, myths and fables. Long before it is possible to dive into Wikipedia, I pose any and all questions to my dad, who generally recites a relevant quotation or three off the top of his head, before calmly retreating into the dusty chaos of his study, which is organised according to a unique anti-filing system understood only by him – some mystical combination of ley lines, fractal theory and instinct – returning minutes later with between four and twelve books on and around the theme of my question (and another three that have nothing to do with it at all, but he thinks I might find interesting nonetheless). So I become an omnivorous reader – immersed in multiple books at any one time, their rich fantasy worlds overlapping in my mind, often more real to me than the drabness of my urban reality. And whilst my obsessive interest in reading presents a clear point of difference from my schoolmates, what truly marks me out is my knowledge of popular music – which is precisely nil.

This is because my father's love of the creative arts, though seemingly limitless in almost every other direction, has an abrupt musical cut-off point somewhere in the mid-1950s. My mother, despite having grown up in the seventies and enjoying the music of Billy Bragg and Kate Bush and Ian Dury, clearly eventually gives up on there being any modern music in the house, given my dad's utter lack of interest in ever actually listening to it. So, whilst it is a thrill – aged ten – to discover on some forgotten shelf a cassette of a band named Queen, who seem to paint sound in glittering luminous colours, with a singer whose soaring voice bespeaks a world of roaring hedonism . . . until then, I know only the weird and wonderful ancient melodies and primal hymns my father has assembled on tape for my brothers and I; Appalachian mountain ballads, traditional English songs sung in the exquisite, eerie countertenor of Alfred Deller; the lilting Sephardic Ladino music of The Burning Bush; the raw, gut-stirring folk of Ewan MacColl. Haunting, beautiful stuff, sure. But have you ever attempted answering the schoolyard question 'Are you Blur or Oasis?' with 'I've never heard of them – but are you a fan of terrifying Scottish folk song "The Craw Killed the Pussy-o"?' Good luck.

And I sound different, too, because my parents are essentially self-invented. They are both only children, raised primarily by their mothers. My dad was born in Driffield, Yorkshire, but this was a quirk of wartime evacuation; after the war, he grew up on the outskirts of London, in a prefab dwelling which he shared with his mother. My grandfather, having been an Entertainment Officer for the RAF, then took a job as a travelling salesman, eventually knocking on a door in the north of England which offered him such a warm welcome that he never felt the need to return home. My mum, thirteen years younger than my dad, grew up in deepest rural Hampshire – firstly in a caravan in the New Forest, on the anti-property edict of her strictly communist father, and then, when he died of lung cancer shortly before my mother turned eighteen, in a house in Salisbury – my grandmother having quietly developed the opinion that she might more effectively bring about the socialist revolution from a premises with, for example, heating.

My mum's mum, Nana Beatrice, who lived with us in the last decades of her life, had grown up in a farmhouse in County Antrim, and spoke with a thick Northern Irish burr that she never lost. My dad's mum, Grandma Anne, who we'd visit in her retirement home in Eastbourne, had a broad London accent with the odd Yiddishism thrown in – she had lived in Seven Sisters, and worked for my Great-uncle Phil's busy garment factory on Brick Lane, sewing gents' trouser waistbands into the night ('Piecework, but no peace . . .', remembered my father, in a poem he composed for her funeral). But neither of my parents sound remotely like their mothers. As my mum and dad each took the pioneering step of departing for university, they both, perhaps as defence mechanisms, devised accents all of their own – versions of RP that seemingly had no grounding in either their parentage or the towns in which they were raised. And so it is a combination of those two fictitious accents that I first acquire.

Eventually, as I become a little more worldly-wise (i.e., eight), I learn to code switch, and slide into Pompey – the broad, surprisingly thick accent that's somewhere between old-school Cockney and rustic West Country ('Alroight, geeze? Gahn dayn tayn t'noight?' = 'Alright, geezer, going down town tonight?'), and comes with its own rich and glorious slang ('Oi, mushter, don't be a dinlo, let's get shanted!' = 'Hey, mate, don't be an idiot, let's get incredibly drunk!').

But when I start junior school, if you can imagine a slightly undersized seven-year-old child with an aggressive bowl haircut, clad entirely in red, wearing multi-coloured circular glasses (as a result of my obsessive reading-induced myopia) and attempting to engage suspicious classmates or bemused adults in overly confident conversation in a strange cut-glass English accent about the work of Robert Louis Stevenson or singing 'Brochan Lom', a traditional Scottish Gaelic nonsense song about porridge . . . you come close to painting a picture of the alternate dimension in which I exist.

And so, inevitably, for a time I am bullied vigorously. Lewis Daniels leads the charge. He is naughty, popular, wears branded clothes, plays football – my opposite in every way – and, having decided I am to be the object of his derision, attracts with little effort a band of willing subordinates to help him deliver a campaign of rapidly increasing spite. I doubt many of the perpetrators remember. I expect even Lewis, my great nemesis of 1995, barely recalls the part he played, during stolen moments in unseen stairwells and distant corners of the playground, in my emotional degradation. But I do know that, over the course of Year 5, what begins as part of the standard, priced-in rough-and-tumble of schoolyard life becomes more pointed, more vicious, and the concept of attending school begins to fill me with increasing horror.

Eventually, as the misery of the playground lunch-hour seeps into my entire school day, and then becomes a cloud of dread that follows me home, my parents – seeing me wake up weeping in the middle of the night at the prospect of another day of inescapable smirking violence – take a somewhat drastic step; they move me to a different school. Wimborne Junior, though similar in many ways to Craneswater – another underfunded inner-city Portsmouth state school – is intangibly but profoundly different. There is, somehow, an undercurrent of kindness – not only from the teachers, but, remarkably, from the pupils.

The alchemy of the classroom is subtly different, here. Achievement isn't scorned or mocked, and the two great social tribes of the era – the tracksuit-clad 'townies' and goth-inspired 'grungers' – seem to co-exist with a harmony unthinkable in the combative corridors of Craneswater.

Here, effortlessly, without having to try and contort into something I'm not, I find myself befriending people. The curious edges to my personality are met with warmth by my new friends, even as their gentle teasing teaches me to learn, for the first time, to assimilate into social groups – which I do with the delight of the perpetual extrovert. Long aware of the power of humour, for the first time I feel able to harness it – to use it to both shield and fuel me. I am still odd. But I am, in my own way, popular. And I am happy. I suspect, quietly, it is one of the great turning points in my life.

My year-and-a-bit of readjustment at Wimborne means that I arrive at secondary school equipped with the social techniques required to survive – now savvy enough to hide my eccentricities when prudent, to pretend to not care about reading as much as I do, to move amongst my natural enemies without unnecessarily inciting their wrath. I learn to protect myself, but to stand up for myself. To duck and weave and surround myself with friends, and pursue the things I love unashamedly.

I have become aware of my many differences. There are those I have mentioned. And then, in the background, there is something else.

Perhaps it starts with the Yiddish folk songs my father sings to me.

Or maybe the book of truly inexplicable Eastern European children's folk stories which I find on my bookshelf, uniquely spectacular for how very little actually happens (sample plot: a bird flies into a room through an open window. It leaves.)

Or the small, cigar-shaped *mezuzah*, embossed with enigmatic, flowing symbols, installed diagonally on the doorway to Grandma Anne's flat in her Eastbourne old-age home; or the memories of lit candles, placed in strangely shaped ornamental candlesticks, glinting in the dark in the kitchen of our family's first house in Margate Road.

At the same time that I become aware of anything, I become aware of my Jewishness.

And, once I start to read compulsively, and my parents deem me old enough to contend with concepts that are complex and disturbing – the best children's stories all containing flashes of darkness, in any case – I am given a copy of *Rose Blanche*. Illustrated by the Italian artist Roberto Innocenti, and translated from Christophe Gallaz's French text by Ian McEwan, it is the tale of a young German girl who watches in confusion as the men of her town go to war, as red armbands are enthusiastically donned and flags are waved by the excited, united populace – and as other families, and groups of scared young people, are rounded up by police and soldiers, and taken away. Rose, attempting to understand what is going on, makes her way to the forest, where she discovers, behind barbed wire, a group of emaciated children, clad in striped clothing. Secretly, she befriends them, learns their names, and comes to smuggle them food.

As the war ravages on, the morale of the town diminishes – the gung-ho jingoism dwindles to nothing, and eventually the armbands and flags are sheepishly discarded. Suddenly people all need to leave in a hurry as other troops arrive – the Russians, I will later come to understand – and Rose's mother loses her in the melee. The reader last sees Rose Blanche wandering through no-man's land when . . . *'Behind her were figures moving through the fog. Tired and fearful soldiers saw danger everywhere. As Rose Blanche turned to walk away, there was a shot, a sharp and terrible sound which echoed against the bare trees.'* Rose's mother never finds her again, and the book ends with the arrival of spring – *'another, gentler invasion'* – grass growing around the shattered wooden fenceposts, and flowers blossoming around the rusting barbed wire.

I find the ending almost intolerably sad. It seems unthinkable that this little girl, who had acted with nothing but curiosity and kindness, should be killed, and with each rereading of the book I strive to somehow save her, feeling an urgency that rises in my chest, futilely, with each turning of the page.

And as for the huddled groups of children, in their stripes . . . I am troubled by these images, and I ask innumerable questions of my parents. I learn that my father, born in 1942, entered the world at a time when there was a concerted effort to erase 'people like' him', and like his family – like Grandma Anne, and the grandfather I never met, and the smiling faces in the black-and-white photographs on our walls; *bubbe* and *zaider*, my father called them fondly. I learn that, due to an accident of geography, our family was immensely fortunate, and that many, many others were not.

Horrified by the senselessness of war, I solemnly resolve to be a lifelong pacifist, taking solace in the notion that, presumably, the rest of the world must feel the same, and that by the time I am older such things will have been surely consigned to the dustbin of history – a perceptive piece of forecasting, indicative of why today my insight into global affairs is so sought after on the world stage.

My mother and father, in their freewheeling way, don't decide in advance the extent to which their sons would have a Jewish 'identity'. They have always done things at their own pace, and in their own order – something I noted, aged seventeen, during the speech that my brothers and I all made at our parents' eventual wedding. Our Jewishness isn't something that is presented with any expectations or preconditions – it is simply a fact; a component of our heritage, and a facet of our identities that we can explore, should we wish to.

We grow up learning about the Jewish festivals, lighting candles, singing songs, and attending weddings of our French cousins at which we wear *kippot* – small circular hats, ours handmade by my mother – and dance to wild soulful music. A point is made of sitting as a family on Friday nights, of eating and singing together, and talking to one another. At the annual Passover Seder meal, a long, ceremonial dinner rich with symbolism, my father tells the ancient story of the Israelites' exodus from Egypt in a booming Shakespearean declamation, and when it comes to the story of the four sons – one wise, one wicked, one simple, and one who doesn't know how to ask about Passover – my brothers and I squabble under our breath over which of them we will each get to play.

'Why is this night different from all other nights?' one of us asks – as per the time-honoured script.

'Because Leo's doing the Fruit Walk?' someone responds. This is entirely off-script, though a regular feature of our family life – my brother having at some point in his childhood devised a piece of interpretive dance when travelling back from the fruit bowl to his seat at the table, which has grown over the years to become a ceremony in its own right.

But our unique familial traditions intermingle with those of the festival, and we leave out an empty chair for Elijah the Prophet, who fails to attend every year, although in fairness, as more or less every single Jewish family in the world is doing the same thing that night, he does have a number of invites to choose from.

Every so often, our Uncle Daniel – my father's half-brother – comes to visit, and we experience another manifestation of Judaism: Orthodoxy. Our uncle, with his full beard (like my father), his wide-brimmed black hat (unlike my father) and his meticulous religious observance (absolutely nothing like my father), brings a sense of the exotic to our English coastal town.

Portsmouth, believe it or not, was once – about 250 years ago – a thriving centre of Anglo-Jewish life, anchored to the city's naval port. Initially there was a community of German Jews, who arrived in the 1760s – some hundred years after Oliver Cromwell first permitted Jews to resettle in England, ending an expulsion that had been in place since 1290 – and who started off as pedlars. Then, in the late nineteenth century, they were joined by Jews from Eastern Europe, many of them tailors leaving London's overcrowded East End, who came south to the coast and worked for the navy – if not to take up arms, then at least to stitch them.

At this point in my life, in the mid-1990s, Portsmouth is not known for its sense of *Yiddishkeit*,* the dwindling handful of people who attended the local *shul*† having a median age of close to eighty. My parents take the view that if Judaism is to ever have a place in our lives, or resonate with us at all, then it would be via a community with members closer to our own age. And so they look slightly further afield, to a pleasantly ramshackle community of no fixed address, a diaspora-of-a-diaspora, which meets in various locations around the south of Hampshire.

The community is led by a charismatic, impressive rabbi named Orli – she leads with a gently sardonic wit, and a beautiful singing voice. It is a necessarily eclectic group, drawing in people from all ages and social backgrounds. Here there are kids our age for my brothers and I to befriend, scurry around with, hoard sweets with, and show off to. It becomes part of our childhood.

One day, I meet an old woman at a service who twitches and looks at me furtively and speaks strangely, under her breath. I,

---

* That is, 'a Jewish way of life'.

† A *shul* is a synagogue, and a synagogue is a *shul* – they can be used interchangeably.

grinning, approach my parents, ready to send her up with some crude, unflattering impression. 'Have you seen that woman?' I begin, 'She's like—'

My mother looks at me in a way that I have never experienced before. 'No,' she says. 'That's Vera, and we must be very, very kind to her.' She points discreetly to Vera's arm, and there I see the row of numbers, tattooed onto her long ago, on the orders of somebody who saw her as less than a person.

As the eldest child, I am perhaps uniquely free to embrace or reject, without precedent or comparison, the traditions and rituals I encounter. And, as I grow towards adolescence, I start to think about what my relationship to this pocket of my identity might be. Practically speaking, I have a decision to make: whether or not I will have a *bar mitzvah*.

I'm getting to the age, you see. In halls and function rooms scattered across Hampshire, I am starting to attend the *bar* and *bat mitzvah* celebrations of boys and girls a year or two older than me. Here, my mates are somehow transformed into something more than fellow hyperactive pre-teens. They take centre stage. They dress up smart. They are received as adults. They recite a fiendishly complex Hebrew portion directly from the vast Torah scroll in front of a rapt audience of loved ones. They make speeches. Speeches are made about them. And then, of course, they celebrate with a huge party. Leila Hershberg has the largest cake I've ever seen, in which she and her friends are immortalised as Disney princesses. Isaac Abelman enters his party by *skateboarding into the hall* to a huge roar of applause.

A *bar mitzvah* feels like a glamorous, exciting possibility – and, my parents explain, if it's something I am interested in pursuing, then the option is certainly there. 'But, of course, there's an awful lot of responsibility,' says my mother. 'Lots of work you'd have to do. In fact, that's sort of the whole point. The party's just a little bit of it.'

So it feels like I reach a natural Jewish crossroads. A point at which I have the opportunity to turn towards, or away from, this part of myself. I think about the songs and ceremonies that have echoed through the generations – all of these strands that have shaped my past, and brought me to my present. Of Vera, and the numbers on her arm. Of the joyful chaos of the dancefloor at our cousin's wedding, and the warmth and connection at our Friday night table. Of something ancient and vast, which I could embrace or reject.

I am also, to be very clear, hugely into the idea of having a massive party.

I decide that I will have a *bar mitzvah*.

This decision of mine precipitates a decision in my mother – something she'd always been meaning to do, but hadn't got around to: she converts. This isn't something my brothers and I had realised was a necessity; the South Hampshire community, an inclusive group, had long embraced my mother's attendance, where her unique combination of 'formidable administrative skills' and 'a compulsion to generate beautifully hand-drawn artwork for any and every occasion' rendered her participation valuable if not outright essential. What's more, so progressive is our community that the Jewish lineage is happily accepted as passed down via the father as well as the mother, meaning we three boys have been welcomed from the off, without caveat or murmurings about our 'status'.

But now, with the prospect of a Jewish life cycle event ahead of her, my mother decides the time is right to formalise her identity – and, by extension, ours. She studies, reads countless books, writes long essays, is invited to meet with senior rabbis in

London. It is a long, involved process, but one she seems to find enriching.

My parents' bed, with its frame designed and hand-painted by my mum, is a perpetual source of wonderment to friends when they visit our house for the first time; it is an elevated four-poster bed, floating above the floor, accessible via a mini flight of stairs which lead up to the grand entrance, through orange and red wooden pillars which extend up to the ceiling. It is like something from an intensely coloured Indian palace. Here, my mum studies for her conversion – she will spend long afternoons sat in bed, happily researching and writing, surrounded by books and papers. Her profound dyslexia means that her essays, although beautifully written, are full of spelling she describes as 'creative' ('Pffft, who wants to be constrained by a specific order of letters?' she shrugs), and so I will ascend the wooden stairs, collect her work, take it to the family desktop computer in the hallway and type it up, rendering it in more conventional English. She writes of the Jewish festivals, of the cycle of the Jewish year, of the evolution of Jewish thought and philosophy. Before long, her working knowledge of Jewish life is far greater than that of my father.

Eventually, my mother is invited to visit the *mikveh* – the body of free-running water into which the convert is immersed. And we three boys, children beneath the age of *bar mitzvah* – are invited into the *mikveh* too. I remember it as an exciting, joyful invitation; a further welcoming, a rubber-stamping of who we are. It does, however, bring about another slightly delicate discussion – the fate of my foreskin.

My parents, in their inimitably relaxed way, opted not to make the surgical impositions that traditionally befall an unwitting Jewish male at around eight days old. At this point I am thirteen, on the cusp of the great changes which inform one's path to manhood (the outer-outer cusp, it turns out – a hormonal betrayal which will see me undersized throughout Year 9, as my friends sprout upwards and outwards, suddenly and unfairly the same height as the girls we have looked up to, longingly, for the last year or so). I am asked if I would like to undergo this surgical procedure. I make it clear that, given any possible modicum of choice, I would under no circumstances like to have a piece of my penis removed. Although it is made clear that the overseeing rabbis really would prefer it if this traditional life-cycle milestone were honoured, the sensitive psychological and physiological challenges of adolescence are deemed sufficient reason to forgo the scalpel. And so, for the sake of parity, my brothers are spared too. Phew, I think, bullet dodged – an issue I'll never need to think of again.

So my mother, brothers and I all travel together from Portsmouth to Waterloo, and take the tube to north London.

My mother enters the *mikveh* alone, happily completing her journey. My brothers and I enter the *mikveh* together, floating around nude in the lukewarm water, swimming, splashing one another, dunking our heads, and giggling at the strangeness of it all. There is a trio of photographs in our family album taken of us that day; we are sat on the steps outside Leo Baeck Rabbinical College, damp-haired and squinting into the sunlight, my mum smiling and my brothers and I posing and mugging ridiculously, all of us proud of the journey we have completed.

My *bar mitzvah* study begins.

Rabbi Orli sets a date, and assigns me a Torah portion – it's a beast, a biggie, a double-sized monster. And, what's more, she suggests that I chant it, with the musical cantillation, as opposed to the more straightforward atonal reading that some of my older mates have opted for. Never one to resist putting on a show of some kind, I eagerly agree.

I begin to attend *cheder* classes – Jewish Sunday school – my parents driving me hours into deepest Hampshire to be introduced to the inscrutabilities of Jewish lore and law. I find these lessons by turns interesting and irritating – conflicting as they do with rehearsals for school plays, deeply important Nintendo 64-based social plans, and my most recent obsession, which is to become another trajectory-altering facet of my life: professional wrestling. Like so many of my contemporaries, I have discovered the glories of Stone Cold Steve Austin, The Undertaker and The Rock – in my case via a schoolmate with access to that most unthinkably exotic of luxuries, Sky television. This affords us ill-advised 1am access to the then-WWF's 'Monday Night Raw', a combative attitude-filled soap opera delivered in front of a roaring live crowd, to which I swiftly become addicted. However, unlike most of my contemporaries, I take my obsession one step further than administering the occasional Stone Cold Stunner in the playground to an unsuspecting friend. By sheer chance, Europe's leading wrestling school opens up in Portsmouth, a mere twenty-minute rollerblade journey from my house, and so I don't just watch wrestling – twice a week I start training to become one.

This means that *cheder* often feels like an imposition, competing as it does with my rehearsals for school plays, my marathon through-the-night *Goldeneye* tournaments, and my ongoing quest to transform myself into high-flying grappler 'Max Voltage, The Human Dynamo'. But these Jewish classes also afford me something strange and nourishing; experiences and perspectives I can't find elsewhere, a window into a hidden world – at least, when I'm paying attention.

'Concentrate, Max,' says Orli.

'I am!' I protest indignantly, despite the fact that I have been entirely focused on drawing myself as a wrestler leaping off the top rope, and trying to work out what my wrestling gear should look like.

'OK! Then you'll be able to tell me what this Hebrew letter sounds like?'

She points to a 'ע', and looks at me. My face reddens and I attempt to style it out.

'. . . y?' I venture, optimistically and unimaginatively.

'No, it's silent.'

'Oh, come onnnn! How was I supposed to know that?'

'Possibly by listening.' She leans over and looks at my doodling. 'Also, I'd lose the mask. You look like a Power Ranger.'

I do, eventually, learn to read Hebrew – my father sitting with me and teaching me with books from his study, some dating back to his own *bar mitzvah*, many decades before. The mysteries of the lettering start to reveal themselves to me – and the dots and lines that float above and below the letters dance before my eyes as I try to pin down their meaning, and retain their vowel sounds and their glottal implications.

I receive tutoring from a kindly older woman in the community, who starts to teach me my Torah portion, and I somehow locate an obscure website offering an audio download of the chanted Hebrew, albeit broken up into approximately sixty low-res .wav files. I download them on our family's crackling early-2000s modem, a process which takes around a week and presumably costs my parents about £10,000.

With the date of my *bar mitzvah* approaching, I have a further decision to make. Do I tell my regular schoolmates? My secondary school, Priory, is an oversubscribed, underfunded state school in inner-city Portsmouth. It's not entirely lacking in warmth – I have successfully located a pleasant group of friends, and found means of survival despite my unashamedly flamboyant love of theatre, comedy, and wrestling – but it's still a tough place. In a playground where achievement is smirked at, effort is frowned upon, and differences stamped out (figuratively and, on the rare occasions that Ricky Kennet isn't suspended, literally), there has always been a careful balance to be found – keeping one's head below the parapet as much as possible, trying not to seem *too* different.

And inviting my mates to my *bar mitzvah* will mean 'outing' myself. Conceptually, my classmates already know of my Jewishness. It is, seemingly, a reason that Louis Moore headbutts me in Year 8, an act preceded by the phrase 'Come on, Jew-boy' – although, knowing and befriending Louis as I come to in later years, I can also well believe the excuse he gives in detention that morning, almost Zen-like in its elegance; namely, that he simply 'felt like headbutting someone'. However, my classmates have never seen me *doing* anything 'Jewish'. I've never lit candles with them at Chanukah, attempted to explain the intricacies of a Pesach dinner, or worn a *kippah* (that's the singular of *kippot*), or recited a Jewish blessing in front of them. This would change all that. But also, if this event is to mark the next stage of my development, my ascendency towards adulthood, then I wish to do so in the presence of my friends. So, with trepidation, I invite them all to come and share in this weird, easily mockable part of my life. And, to my delight and terror, they all say yes.

It is the day of my *bar mitzvah*. Nerves raging – a potent combination of the pressures of delivering my musical Hebrew centrepiece, and the ever-present spectre of possible shame and ridicule that seems to cloud every moment of that precarious phase of early adolescence – I step forward and, with ill-fitting suit and cracked voice, I read aloud my Torah portion. My brow furrows with effort. My mind contorts to make sense of the ornate text – which, as per ancient tradition, is handily free of any of the vowels or punctuation that ordinarily appear when the language is printed in less exalted settings (sure, wouldn't want reading Biblical Hebrew to be *too* easy).

'*U'mikneh rav haya livnei Reuven u'livnei Gad atzum me'od; vayiru et eretz Ya'zer v'et eretz Gil'ad, v'hinei hamakom makom mikneh . . .*'

('The children of Reuven and the children of Gad had an abundance of livestock,' I am chanting, tentatively. 'And they saw the land of Ya'zer and the land of Gil'ad . . .')

My parents flush with pride. My mates are baffled and fascinated. My cousins – who have flown over, from France and Switzerland – beam. My rabbi applauds. An elderly Chinese man waves and smiles (we're in a community centre for Chinese Elders).

I finish my portion. I make a speech, drawing on the themes of the portion – I talk about responsibility and commitment, about leadership and negotiation, and also about goats (there's really quite a lot in the verse about goats). And then we cross the road to our house, and feast on homemade sandwiches and salads and bagels.

My Uncle Jacqui, an impossibly suave and charming Parisian, demonstrates how to do chin-ups on the garden climbing frame whilst wearing his tailored suit. And, in fact, sparing myself decades of analysis in years to come – it's pretty clear that this encounter, in a nutshell, is more or less my origin story, and a high I've been chasing ever since.

My father stands on a stool and sings a song he has written, replacing the words to the folk song 'Roumania Roumania' with his own lyrics, which culminate in a chorus of 'Wrestlemania Wrestlemania', and my friends double over with laughter – both at his lyrical contortions, and at the wild, uninhibited extroversion of it all – of Jewish celebrations, and of life in the wayward Olesker house.

My friends are having a wonderful time. Rene Langley heroically smuggles in some warm gin in an empty plastic Panda Pops bottle and we all swig from it and profess to really like it, actually. Becky White gets off with Danny Chadbourne and then throws up down the side of the radiator (actually, that might have happened the other way round, but either way everyone's happy enough).

When it gets dark, we are led out to the car park of the school opposite, where the sky is lit up by a classic more-or-less-legal fireworks display. Operations overseen by 'neighbourhood man who reckons he pretty much knows how it all works'? Check. Bucket of sand? Check. Absolutely no further safety precautions? Check!

We celebrate. I am, officially, a Jewish man. It is a status I will happily and unthinkingly hold until roughly twenty years later, when a series of events happen that take my identity and blow it up spectacularly – like the firecrackers, rockets and Roman candles which explode above us on that warm summer evening, lighting up the Portsmouth night sky as I stand in the midst of my family and friends, waving a sparkler, giddy with anticipation at the endless possibilities of my adult life.

CHAPTER 3

Growing Up, Melting Down, Stepping Out

Powered by the examples of both my parents – and my own innate sense of baffling optimism – as I tumble into adulthood I build a life for myself based entirely around my passions.

I excitedly escape Portsmouth and make a break for university on the fringes of London. Here, in a freshers' week audition for a piece of Highly Serious Theatre, I meet Ivan, immediately bond with him over our shared love of comedy when we're supposed to be preparing our Deeply Emotional Audition Scene, and promptly form a comedy double-act which consumes most of our waking life. Then, shortly after graduating, an application letter of mine is randomly lifted from a slush pile and I'm offered an internship at *Esquire* magazine, which, via my relentless keenness and the magazine itself being horrendously understaffed, I manage to parlay into a full-time job. When I eventually leave, it is purely to accept the offer of performing at a comedy festival in Australia that Ivan and I would otherwise have had to turn down.

And so for some years I cheerfully and unwisely divide my time between the equally reliable worlds of 'freelance print magazine journalism' and 'double-act comedy', with occasional forays into 'producing increasingly large-scale one-off events combining comedy and professional wrestling'. I am, like an inverse Liam Neeson in *Taken*, a man with a very particular lack of skills. And yet what my vocation lacks in 'any form of financial stability or the ability to seriously plan one's life', it makes up for with constant novelty and, when the stars align, a deep sense of job satisfaction. For many years, it proves remarkably possible to forge a life this way. Until, suddenly, it doesn't.

A series of things happened in short order, which resulted in me arriving at the Edinburgh Fringe that year an emotional wreck.*

First, I had broken up with a beloved girlfriend. Then, the day before I set off for Edinburgh, the largest project of my career – a TV show that Ivan and I had worked on painstakingly for years – had been de-commissioned by the same man who had commissioned it. It broke my heart, and I wept on the phone to the only other person in the world who'd known about it; my newly ex-girlfriend, who had lived and suffered through the torturous commissioning process, and who – in her eternal kindness and extraordinary magnanimity – still found it within her to console me.

I was personally and professionally lost. And I felt bereft – incapable of anything positive, as though everything I cared about, and attempted to cultivate, was certain to turn to mouldering dust.

As any comedian will attest, it's a mark of how badly things were going in my life that performing at the Edinburgh Fringe made me feel *better*. But it did.

Edinburgh, and the festival, offered a haven.

Suddenly, at my lowest point, I was back enveloped in a world that I loved. Performing each evening with Ivan – a fizzy,

---

* If anything, this simply made me slightly more efficient than most performers, who tend to hit that point about three days into the second week.

warm-hearted romp about friendship and the overly-elaborate stag night I'd arranged for Ivan – lifted my spirits and gave a focus to my days. And then, after the first show of the festival, I met Eliana, which gave an exhilarating new focus to my nights.

I had landed in Edinburgh feeling emotionally and professionally hollowed-out. But, suddenly, I had a song in my heart – and a completely different set of problems.

Our Jägerbomb-infused encounter in Edinburgh, it transpires, is also Eliana's birthday, and so I am invited to join her on a night out with both of her siblings and their respective partners, who had all come to the show – an arrangement so strangely wholesome it makes me question whether or not her interests extended beyond the purely social. I would later learn this was, in fact, a quintessentially 'Eliana' approach; 100mph and entirely direct – 'Here's what you could win! Want in?' The next morning, clinging to the remnants of my humanity, and with last night's Red Bull sloshing malevolently in the pit of my stomach, I stagger to a theatre venue to watch the play Eliana has written and directed, as I solemnly promised I would the night before (a conversation that took place at 3am whilst in a conga line led by her brother, in a gloriously sticky-floored makeshift venue overseen by a majestic Essex drag queen). The play is fantastic. It's sharp and witty and perceptive and unpredictable, and as my hangover evaporates in the heat of the tiny theatre space, I feel as though I am falling into Eliana's world, and I don't want to leave.

The festival continues, and suddenly we are a part of one another's lives. Eliana seems rocket-fuelled – she watches show after show each day, fiercely opinionated, hungry for more, always fascinated to experience the new. And, at the end of each frenetic day, we meet in some packed bar or heaving events space, and it is as though we have instantly resumed whatever conversation we were in the midst of – the hours ticking by effortlessly, our discussions curtailed only by the eventual moment the venue closes and we're kicked out, at which point we find somewhere else, because in Edinburgh in August there's always somewhere else. The bars change, and the drinks in our hands change, and the friends around us come and go, but we remain delightedly, animatedly, in conversation.

She is hugely impulsive – 'I may have tried to fight a bouncer because I thought he was being sexist,' she explains, recounting a recent, disastrous, night out, 'but it turns out that my friend was actually just being an arsehole' – but also extremely cautious. 'I love writing more than anything,' she explains one evening, 'but I don't want to have to rely on it as my *job*, because I think it would make me hate it, and I want some actual stability in my life.' I stand, nodding, from my safety-net-free position surrounded by the smoking wreckage of my last 'project', and it sounds like the wisest thing I have ever heard.

Eliana has the most singularly expressive face. As she experiences joy, or distaste, or whatever, every scintilla of sensation is writ larger than life across her features – her glittering blue eyes widening and her red lips contorting, completely in thrall to her emotions, without a hint of vanity. It is as though she experiences a constant tidal wave of feeling. She has a low, husky voice, like a jazz singer, and when she laughs it is with a purity and a strength of feeling that causes the rest of my world to fade into total insignificance.

She is irreverent, and razor-sharp, and completely unguarded in a way I have never before experienced.

I've now met all her siblings, and she wants to know about mine, and so I tell her about my family, and paint her a picture of my journey from Portsmouth – an exotic destination she's never visited – to east London – an almost equally exotic, equally undiscovered location to Eliana, who I soon learn is a proud inhabitant of northwest London, somewhere that I, in turn, am almost entirely unfamiliar with.

It somehow doesn't seem enough to be spending the present with one another – it is as though we are hungry for one another's history.

'So, as you can see, I've always been pretty talented,' says Eliana, as we emerge from yet another bar, and she shows me a video on her phone: a digital capture of a grainy VHS video of an old family holiday, with an infant Eliana delightedly waddling around announcing to her family that she has 'taught herself to belly dance' – puffing her stomach out and proudly patting it with her hands.

'Wow,' I reply. 'I didn't know you were dance trained.'

'Even more amazingly – that was all instinct.'

We buy appalling crepes from the appalling crepe stall that never closes, and eat them together in the street, animatedly talking about nothing and watching the world go by, standing in a never-ending slipstream of wide-eyed tourists and overexcited stand-ups and ambitious self-congratulatory young actors and the weary, black T-shirt-clad, Leatherman-toting, hard-working-and-harder-drinking roadies, techies and production crew who make festivals a reality.

We walk across the Meadows together at 5am, and sit on the swings and just keep talking.

And eventually, as the sun starts to rise, I walk her to her flat, and we kiss at the front door. Just like in the movies.

When the festival ends we take a leap, and meet back in London, in the Real World. Even without the strange magic of Edinburgh surrounding us, each encounter feels impossibly exciting – an exhilarating blur of discovering one another.

At the first available instance, I invite her to my flat to meet both of *my* brothers and *their* partners, whom she embraces warmly, and I make (a shambolic) dinner for us all.

London feels as though it opens up to embrace us; the Soho Theatre, my home from home when performing with Ivan, becomes our nightly destination, as we devour all of the comedy and theatre that we were unable to watch in Edinburgh – and then next door to Quo Vadis for cocktails, or onwards to a press dinner at some glistening new restaurant, or to a spectacularly grotty bar for a friend's birthday, or the chaos of a house party . . . The destination is fairly immaterial – whatever we are doing, wherever we are going, feels supercharged by the fact that we are together.

We each begin enthusiastically cooking meals for one another – neither of us realising or revealing that this is not something the other previously had the remotest skill or interest in. With an attempt at casualness, I ask my youngest brother, a borderline professional cook, for the recipe for an elaborate Vietnamese salad that he once made, and I then spend the better part of a full working day painstakingly assembling it, in order to casually produce it from the fridge that evening when Eliana comes round. ('Oh, this . . . ?')

Eliana, too, off-handedly mentions I could 'Come by for a bite' if I fancy it – I arrive to discover a four-course extravaganza, lovingly handmade, with her best friends, siblings and partners all sat around the table, equal parts excited to eat and amazed by Eliana's unexpected swing towards domesticity. 'I'm totally shocked,' one of her best friends tells me, as she passes the tuna tartare. 'At university Eliana lived primarily on mulled wine, which she realised you could both buy and drink all year round and not just at Christmas – something she considered a "life hack".'

We assemble lists of films that neither of us have seen and

begin ticking them off, one by one, over the course of endless indulgent Sunday afternoons, eating popcorn in bed.

Our worlds begin to merge. Spare toiletries, just in case, begin to creep into our respective bathrooms. The days of the week that we see one another rapidly start to outnumber the days that we don't. However long we spend talking together – it is as though there is never enough time.

And, just as I start to feel the pull of enormous possibility – the sense that I have found myself in a relationship with no perceivable limitations, something propulsive and vital, that might carry us onwards together, off towards the horizon, as far as the eye can see – I begin to discern the makings of a catastrophe.

I have known from the start that it is incredibly important for Eliana – essential, even – that her partner is Jewish. That much, from our first fateful, barely drinkable drink together onwards, was abundantly clear. But as the months have rolled on, as we are drawn ever closer to one another, I become aware of two troubling things:

1. There are many people in the world who do not believe or accept that I am, in fact, Jewish.
2. It is very, very likely that one of those people . . . is Eliana.

CHAPTER 4

Ah . . .

This is how the realisation starts to stir.

Eliana and I are sat in her kitchen, chatting about our previous relationships. I've never had a Jewish girlfriend. It's never been a problem, I've never given it a second thought. Eliana's never had a Jewish boyfriend. But for her, by definition, that means those relationships were never serious.

'My boyfriend at university was furious,' says Eliana, 'because I explained my parents' view, which is "Look, we'll meet him if he's *halachically* Jewish – otherwise, forget it." He said it was basically racism.'

'Wow,' I say, astonished (and making a mental note to look up the word '*halachically*'), 'I mean – I can . . . sort of see where he's coming from. But then I suppose' – I say, thinking of my mum – 'he could have converted?'

'Ugh, I'd never make anyone not Jewish do the Orthodox conversion,' says Eliana. 'It's the hardest conversion in the world.'

Ha! I sympathise. Ha! I laugh. Ha. I smile, flush with relief, relaxing in the comfort of my 100 per cent incorrect interpretation of this exchange.

How could I have known, there and then? Given how we'd met, given how we'd connected? There was so much I didn't know. But, crucially, that conversation was the moment I realised that Eliana was Orthodox. Not the staid, traditional-looking, and, crucially, *easily-identifiable-via-visual-signifiers* Orthodoxy of my uncle, and the characters in *Shtisel*, and the hurried men and women rushing up and down the street if you reach the end of Stoke Newington's cortado oasis and keep going into Stamford Hill. No, in Eliana – she of the dazzling red lipstick, the fishnet tights, the audacious miniskirts, and the play she had written which contained a hugely explicit and very, very funny sex scene, but who also kept kosher, and had never used technology between sundown on a Friday and sundown on a Saturday in her life – I had discovered Modern Orthodoxy.

Prior to this, I had already known that there are many different strands of Judaism, and 'types' of Jew, in the world; that when it comes to Jewish traditions, there is a *smörgåsbord* – or more accurately a *kiddush*. That is, a snack-filled buffet, a sort of pre-lunch lunch one hoovers up in synagogue, before returning home for one's *actual* enormous lunch, subsequent mid-afternoon nap, and then large dinner – this culinary arrangement being one of the reasons Jews worldwide are so renowned for their physical fitness. I knew that my family were part of the progressive Reform movement – which happens to be the most popular denomination in the USA, and the tradition of choice for millions of Jews around the world. And, whilst it's not the *very* loosest, hippie-dippiest interpretation of Judaism (Liberal Jews, please wave your tie-dye *kippot* now), I've always been aware that the South Hampshire Reform Jewish Community's approach to Judaism is one that some might consider . . . less traditional. Our rabbi? A woman – not only that, but a proudly gay woman! Our community's approach to observing the Jewish sabbath? Flexible! (It's fairly difficult for people to 'refrain from technology' when the vast majority will need to drive approximately twenty miles to get to the synagogue – 'synagogue' being a word which, in practice, could actually mean community hall/

someone's front room/on a few occasions a Quaker Meeting House, weirdly.) The quiche that community member Damian once absentmindedly brought along to a group meal? Bacon-topped! (When realising his culinary faux-pas, he hurriedly hid it in the boot of his car, produced something salmon-based from a nearby shop, and everyone expertly pretended nothing had happened.) And I'd always known that not every synagogue accepted, as ours did, equilineal descent – that is, the notion of Judaism being passed down via either parent, as opposed to purely the mother – though of course my mum had now converted, and, in fact, given that my brothers and I entered the *mikveh* too, technically so had we.

I also knew that the most rigid expression of Judaism, and its largest religious group, is Orthodoxy – which, as well as emphasising keeping kosher, favours strict abstention from technology during the sabbath, only has male rabbis, has yet to accommodate gay marriage, and sees men and women sit separately in synagogues. But Orthodoxy was something I had always associated with black hats and long beards – again, my Uncle Daniel's flavour of choice. In fact, when coming to stay with us, Daniel would literally travel with his flavours of choice, always bringing with him a supply of mysterious kosher food – the strict vegetarianism of my mother's kitchen not providing the culinary sureties he required. What I didn't know about, until Eliana and her siblings conga-danced into my life, was the existence of the Modern Orthodox – a community with, somehow, both feet in both worlds. Modern, forward-thinking, immersed in the twenty-first century – and yet, impossibly, still passionate observers and custodians of Orthodox traditions and rules stretching back across thousands of years.

And these were far more than just 'rules', I discovered that night – when, in one of the most consequential Google searches of my life, I looked up the word *halachichally* – they were laws.

'*Halacha*' is a Hebrew word.* It means 'Jewish law, as derived from the Torah'. For the observant Orthodox Jew, it is immutable, binding – part and parcel of their identity, the undergirding to their lives.

For other manifestations of Judaism? Well, the further across the spectrum you go, the less fundamental *halacha* is deemed to be. It's there, but it's there to be modified – a jumping-off point for further traditions and customs. And this is a major point of difference which divides Orthodoxy and Reform.

Now, this doesn't mean that Orthodoxy would fail to recognise someone as Jewish due to their being a member of a Reform synagogue. But it *does* mean that their definition of 'who is a Jew' relies entirely on *halacha*. And so, to the Oleskers . . .

My father is 110 per cent *halachically* Jewish. Of this there is no doubt. He was born to two *halachically* Jewish parents – my Grandma Anne, and her husband, Percy – and that attendant status means that, although my father would never consider himself religious, he is a fully kosher Jew wherever he might be in the world. Of additional benefit is the fact that, with his ample white beard, strong nose and even stronger array of hats, he looks as though he might be a popular-if-wayward rabbi. But my mother, Northern Irish on her mum's side, and of thrillingly unknown parentage on the other (Romany Gypsy, she suspects) – is undoubtedly *not* of Jewish descent. And, whilst she converted to Judaism, she did so via the Reform movement.

---

* And by the way, the 'cha' isn't the hard 'ch' of 'change' or 'chimichanga', it's the guttural, throat-clearing soft 'ch' at the end of 'loch', or 'Bach' – an utterance technically known as a 'voiceless velar fricative', for those optimistically prepping for an upcoming as-yet-unconfirmed *QI* appearance.

And this, I discover, is the issue.

Reform conversion is anathema to the Orthodox. It's not just frowned upon, not just disputed; it is rejected outright, considered entirely invalid according to *halacha*. The Reform mindset is permissive; inherently slightly woolly. But Orthodoxy deals in absolutes. They absolutely require a Jew's mother to be Jewish. And they absolutely do not accept my mother as Jewish. And, thus, they absolutely do not accept me.

Picture a Venn diagram. To millions of Jews in the world, I am considered Jewish. To many others, I am someone they might *personally* consider Jewish, but they might nonetheless attend a synagogue where my status would be unacceptable to the in-house rabbis, and thus, with a mournful shrug, there would simply be nothing they could do about it. Oy. And to the millions of observant Orthodox? I am definitively, unequivocally, not. And thus, at the age of thirty-two, I learn something new about the world, and about myself. I discover I exist in the schismatic cracks between 'types' of Jew – the intractable ravine between different denominations. I am Schrödinger's Jew.

In many ways, it seems bizarre that I didn't know this crucial fact about my identity. But, then again, why would I? My rabbi, for instance, strangely hadn't seen fit to mention it when I celebrated my *bar mitzvah*. My kindly uncle hadn't chosen to deliver a thunderbolt theological judgement on behalf of his Orthodox community. My parents, weirdly, hadn't opted to share this opinion ('Of course, son, to many people your very identity is rejected! And your mother's conversion? Deemed a hollow charade! Pass the *challah*.'). The vast majority of my life had been spent amongst non-Jews. The remainder had been spent amongst Jews who accepted me.

I had always known that I was a 'different' sort of Jew. And I was perfectly prepared to be thought of as a terrible Jew. But

I hadn't realised that, to some, I am no sort of Jew at all; I am a nothing.

It is a breathtaking, maddening, revelation.

To the Orthodox, if my *mother* had been *halachically* Jewish and my *father* had been converted Reform, or not converted at all, I'd have been deemed to be Jewish – even if we'd foresworn our identities, even if I'd been an enthusiastic attendee of an ashram, or an ordained Catholic priest, or a leading importer of artisan hand-cured bacon. None of that would have mattered; to them, I'd be kosher. But because it happens to be the other way round – because the 'wrong' parent is Jewish, and because that parent converted via the 'wrong' community . . . my identity is vaporised.

One weekend, when I return to Portsmouth, I look in the family album at the photos of my mother, my brothers and me outside the *mikveh*, and I read the handwritten caption beneath, in my mother's looping hand; 'Now nobody can say we are not Jewish.'

I feel my throat tighten, and my eyes dampen, and I smile ruefully at my damp-haired childhood self, sat with my brothers and my mother, happy and together.

At this point, my unpicking of this issue is a closely guarded secret – I'm barely able to acknowledge the situation to myself, let alone discuss it openly with others. But, as I am looking through the photo album, my mother walks into the room. And so, without disclosing my reasons for revisiting these memories, I talk to her about her decision.

'You chose to do it once I'd decided to do my *bar mitzvah*, right?'

'Oh no,' my mum explains, 'I'd known from the day you were born that I would one day convert.' She tells me a story.

As the midwife held me in St Mary's Hospital, Portsmouth, she asked my mother what I was to be named. 'Max Jacob Henry Olesker,' said my mother.

'You sure?' the nurse winced, disapprovingly. 'Sounds a bit Jewish.'

'Well, he is!' my mother replied, indignant. And then, with a look of distaste, the midwife hurriedly handed me back to my shocked mother, and left. 'I knew then,' my mum told me, 'that this would never be something you'd be totally free from – even if you had no interest in Jewish life at all. But I also knew that I had the opportunity to stand with you, and your father, and be on that journey with you. And so of course I knew I would.'

As I attempt go to sleep that night, I turn the issue over in my mind. It is excruciating. It is a new reality that I feel punched in the stomach by – over and over.

What's more it feels doubly, triply unjust, because, as a child, I naively thought we'd addressed any queries; not only had my mum converted, my brothers and I had even gone to the *mikveh* too, to double-stamp our identities! And the thing that burns the most – the abject fuckery of it all, the hardline stupidity, the utter infuriating bullshit of it, is that this distinction has nothing to do with blood, or DNA, or even how 'good a Jew' I might be – it's not a value judgement on my comprehension of Hebrew text, my aptitude for saying certain prayers, my enthusiasm for participating in organised religion or keeping kosher. I've been snookered by a piece of theological bureaucracy.

If you want to get right into the weeds of it – as I do, scouring the furthest reaches of the internet for a scrap of hope, opening tabs upon tabs until my laptop starts to burn into my thighs – I am deemed, by Orthodoxy, to have a non-Jewish soul.

*

I could, of course, just walk away from the whole thing. Or else raise the subject in an indignant fury, flip over a table, and storm off, slamming the door behind me, never to return.

The only problem being I am falling in love. I am being drawn inexorably towards someone, finding it increasingly implausible to *not* spend time with this person. And, in those moments when I am not spiralling into panic – attempting to suppress, or fend off, these hideous, hurtful concepts bombarding my sense of self – I am having the absolute time of my life.

Eliana and I are constantly finding excuses to message one another, excitedly recommending books to one another, and then follow-up books to those books, going to the theatre together, making one another experimental cocktails, dancing around the kitchen to the soundtracks of ancient musicals (a mutual guilty pleasure we indulge in without a modicum of guilt), meeting one another's friends – and, happily, instantly getting on with one another's friends. We are beginning to confide in one another, and to rely on one another. And so – though I am realising, with increasing urgency, that I have found myself in an unsustainable situation – walking away simply doesn't feel possible.

I hold the issue up to the light. Rotate it, carefully, watching it glint. Trying to make sense of it. Searching for ways of solving the puzzle.

There is a famous, entirely true, aphorism: 'two Jews, three opinions'. Whilst I now know that, according to the black-and-white, the *halacha*, of it all, I am not considered Jewish, I don't know for a fact that this is how Eliana sees me. I don't know for certain that this will be a dealbreaker, that she considers me a non-Jew, a non-viable partner.

There are glimmers of hope; unlike the various disappointed undergrads from Eliana's Manchester University-era, I *have* met her parents!

'Hello, darling, so lovely to see you!' says Eliana's mother, Katy, as I join the family for another Sunday lunch at another lovely London restaurant. Both she and Eliana's father, Maurice, are nothing but warm, welcoming, entirely generous, and I slot myself in next to Eliana, and her siblings, and their partners, as the bread is served.

'Mm, so Eliana tells me you're a historian?' says Maurice.

'No, Dad, I said he's writing for *Horrible Histories*, it's a TV show!'

'Oh, how wonderful,' says Katy, 'history was my favourite subject – I wish I'd read it at Oxford instead of Law.'

'But then you might not have met *me*,' says Maurice, adoringly, tucking into his bread.

Katy rolls her eyes indulgently and turns back to me. 'So what period of history are you writing about?'

'Erm – embarrassing illnesses,' I say, with as much gravitas as I can muster.

'How wonderful!' beams Katy.

The Bloody Marys arrive, and as we sip them Katy enthusiastically – and disarmingly – asks me about my family tree. But is that because she knows I'm Jewish? Or because she believes I'm not?? Or possibly because she's just really into family trees?! I leave the meal pleasingly full, and gently buzzing on cocktails, and completely unclear on where things stand.

Elsewhere, there are further shards of doubt; the fact that, after several months, we haven't defined the 'what' of who we are. Are we an item? Might we be? Is such a thing even possible? Whatever it is, it's by far and away the most intense non-relationship of my life.

Another recurring warning signal; on Friday nights, Eliana disappears. Her phone is turned off, and she retreats into the world of Shabbat, and Friday night dinner with her family, and, though it's entirely unspoken, it feels like this is something that cannot be breached – that it wouldn't be possible for me to be with her, or for her to be with me.

But the most telling thing, the thing that makes it seem increasingly likely that this is all a non-starter, is this: throughout the thousands of hours Eliana and I have spent together, and the countless conversations we have had on every conceivable topic, the subject of whether or not Eliana actually views me as Jewish is the one subject we have, very eloquently and very exhaustively, Not Discussed.

'Ugh, I'd never make anyone not Jewish do the Orthodox conversion.' I replay the conversation in my mind, over and over. 'It's the hardest conversion in the world.'

I am sat with my laptop gazing, inevitably, at the requirements for an Orthodox conversion. They are, as Eliana said, horrendous. It requires scaling a vertiginous wall of obligation – far too much stuff to even consider it. And, even if I were to attempt to navigate that path, there is a key unavoidable horror at the end of it: circumcision. I immediately shudder in terror at the thought of the senseless surgical destruction of a cherished part of my body, thus ending one of the most fruitful relationships of my life. It all adds up to impossible. And, logistics aside, there's the other point that keeps thundering back into my head: *I'M ALREADY FUCKING JEWISH*. I close my laptop.

It is a strange thing to become aware of, during the first flush of romance, a burgeoning comprehension that, no matter how blissful or carefree or *right* your relationship might feel, it is, actually, possibly, completely and utterly fucked.

It is a possibility which I find genuinely unthinkable, but cannot stop thinking about. I have pushed forward, wilfully ignorant, for as long as I can. We have danced together in the gap of plausible deniability, but the walls are closing in. The pressure has become unbearable. If we do have a future, I want to know. And if we don't, I *need* to know.

On the day that I resolve to finally raise the issue, I go to speak with Bernard Kops. In his mid-nineties, Bernard is a mischievous playwright and poet, a contemporary of Harold Pinter and Arnold Wesker, still writing and ranting in his flat in Haverstock Gardens, just off the Finchley Road, where he lives with his beloved wife Erica and their imperious apricot cat, Mish Mish. I first met them via my father, and they have become friends of mine (actually, Mish Mish views me as a subject, at best). They are wise, they are witty, and they are Jewish – as contentedly irreligious as you could find, but indisputably Jewish to their very core, from the *mezuzah* on their door to the creative heartbeat of every one of Bernard's plays, poems and novels.

I start to explain — and Bernard and Erica immediately understand the implications of it all.

'She's an Orthodox girl, she's not going to change!'

'Oh, but he's in *love*, Bernard! He'll want to find a way!'

'Is she beautiful?'

'I'm sure she's very beautiful, Bernard, but that's not the point—'

'No, the point is she's very Jewish. But then – you're still Jewish . . .'

'Yes, but not the way they want! You know . . .'

I walk with them in their communal garden. Bernard, full of elliptical wisdom and mystical tangents, holds forth on a great many subjects – with a few songs thrown in for good measure, including several he wrote as a teenage songwriter in Tin Pan Alley, and a couple that he simply makes up on the spot – but eventually settles on the subject at hand. 'You must approach the matter carefully,' says Bernard, 'slice gently into it.' And by the time I have left, Bernard has proffered the perfect phrase with which to begin this conversation I have no desire to have and no way to avoid.

I hear it thumping in my head at 1am, replaying it over and over again, as I lie next to Eliana, drowning in the silence. Eventually, I slowly sit up, and I gather the courage to begin the conversation that is set to torpedo our relationship.

'. . . I don't want to believe that this is impossible,' I begin. (It's a great opener – thanks, Bernard.)

'I feel so incredibly content when I'm with you . . . but that feels dangerous. Because to me this has already grown into a grander and more wonderful thing than I thought it ever could. And the thought of it going away makes me feel terrible.'

Eliana – who usually doesn't have time to take a breath before launching into a response – stays very, very quiet. Eventually, she looks up at me sadly.

'I've put this off three times,' she says. 'It's crossed out in my diary. Do you want to talk about it?'

No. I don't. But we do.

CHAPTER 5

The Discussion

We talk until 5am, and then we spend the next two days sat in the bath, where our conversation continues.

At some point, presumably, we leave the bath – I have vague memories of eating something, sleeping fitfully, possibly going and performing comedy somewhere – but mainly we soak in the water, as the bubbles slowly pop around us, and cold reality begins to seep into our carefully constructed alternate universe.

For the first time, we are both sat looking at the issue face on.

'You've known from the start,' she says, 'that it's incredibly important to me that my partner is Jewish.'

My face flushes. 'Right. And you just . . . don't believe I'm Jewish.'

'It's not that I don't believe – it's that . . . according to Orthodoxy, according to *halacha*, you're *not* Jewish.'

I've sensed this was coming, obviously. But, hearing those words aloud, I feel a gut-punch that I'm unprepared for. What *am* I, then?

Eliana is speaking with a focus, a certainty, I've never seen from her before.

'It's a line I just can't cross,' she says. 'And, even if I *did* want to cross it . . . it would destroy my family.'

*

Eliana is, I discover, more religious than either of her siblings. This isn't unusual. Religion, which is at once absorbed from one's surroundings and emanates from one's inner life, rarely spreads itself homogeneously across families, and it is perfectly commonplace for a Jewish dinner table to contain family members of all levels of religiosity, from the piously devoted to Hashem* to the squarely secular, and for everyone to rub along perfectly agreeably – whilst loudly bickering, of course, about absolutely everything else. In this, they might be no different from, say, a Catholic family (save for the texture and flavour of the guilt, which is less predicated on Original Sin and more on not spending enough time with one's grandmother).

And what's more, it's entirely possible that an individual Jew's relationship to their *own* Jewish practice might fluctuate enormously over their life. 'Oh, I was black-hat *charedi* [ultra-Orthodox] for ten years,' someone might say, cheerfully, 'and then I was non-religious for a while. And now I'm more Modern Orthodox.' Viewed from one angle, it's confusing, contradictory behaviour. But, from another, it makes perfect sense; people change, and what is right for them changes.

Regardless, wherever they happen to be on the spectrum, it is more-or-less a truism that every Jew privately believes that anyone even fractionally more observant than them is a raving religious nutter, and anyone *less* observant than them is a godless heathen – they alone having achieved the correct balance. However, given that it's commonly understood that everyone *else* holds this exact opinion also, people tend to happily coexist in a state of agreeable-disagreement, without the slightest interest in imposing their personal values – enlightened though they undoubtedly are – on

---

* 'Hashem' is one of the more frequently used ways Jewish people refer to the divine, whose name is often written 'G-d', as a mark of reverence.

the person they happen to be arguing about school catchment areas with across the dinner table.

But, as I now come to understand, the strands that bind Eliana to her identity are densely interwoven; stretching back across generations, and rooted in far more than just religion. That is a huge, deeply felt part of it, of course, a core component of her life, something she is nourished by. But beyond her Saturday synagogue attendance, her adherence to the laws of *halacha*, her keeping Shabbat in the face of all modern temptations, there is something else; the ever-present memory of her grandfathers. They were, both of them, Holocaust survivors, and their stories have come to shape the contours of her family's life.

Eliana's maternal grandfather, Charles, has only recently died, and Eliana's mother is still within her year of mourning – a period of ritual and reflection in which observant Jews recite the *kaddish*, a prayer for the dead, thrice daily. During the war Charles and his family, who were Belgian, had fled to Switzerland, where Charles's father had ongoing business, and which they hoped might be a safe haven. Instead, they were promptly handed back over to the Nazis (the scrupulous Swiss even making the family pay for their own taxi to the German border). Charles's parents were immediately sent to Auschwitz and murdered. Charles and his sister were earmarked for the same journey, but, in a grotesque stroke of luck, the train carriage for children was already too full. Instead, they were bundled off to an overcrowded building full of other children waiting to be processed. There, one of the leaders of the UGIF, a French organisation established by the Vichy regime to manage and monitor the Jewish population, took a sinister shine to Charles's fifteen-year-old sister, and offered them both highly conditional 'protection' in and out of hiding in Paris. And thus they were able to survive the war.

But it is the story of Eliana's paternal grandfather, a man also named Max, which perhaps looms largest over the Ostro family. My namesake died almost ten years before I might have had the chance to meet him. In later life he was a warm, chuckling presence with wild wispy eyebrows, a knack for dealmaking, and an engaging if cryptic turn of phrase (it was said he spoke nine languages – and was completely indecipherable in all of them!). But the fact that he had a long, colourful life, and lived to be surrounded by his children and grandchildren, is entirely astonishing, given what he endured.

Max began his life in Shidlovitz, a bustling *shtetl* (a small Jewish town) in the Polish-Lithuanian region of Galicia. Here he learned the basics of business, working in his parents' shop, and he grew up in the orbit of the Ostrovtza Rebbe, Rabbi Meir Yechiel, a renowned and charismatic religious leader whom Max and his family revered, and who infused within Max a sense of deep warmth, spirituality, and love of Jewish life.

The Shidlovitz of Max's memory was a vibrant, joyous place – often impoverished but coursing with life and chatter, with families rushing back and forth through the uneven streets and narrow alleyways, with shoemakers and button factories, and with three crowded markets on Wednesday afternoons full of elderly women selling their vegetables, bakers offering fresh bagels and loaves of bread from wooden huts, and roving blacksmiths shoeing the horses of travelling merchants. Of the 10,000-odd population, around were 80 per cent Jewish, and so Shidlovitz boasted a profusion of synagogues and *yeshivot* (places of Jewish study). In the mornings the townsfolk were awoken with a roar from the bearded town crier, Bunim the Beadle, who roamed the streets in the early hours with a lantern in hand urging the populace to 'Arise to serve the Creator!', an exhortation which Max's father followed enthusiastically, studying the Torah with passion throughout the day whilst sat in his shop, often at the expense of the customers who entered, misguidedly hoping for some sort of service.

It was a world which Max loved beyond all measure, and by the end of the war it had been completely and permanently destroyed.

The Nazis turned Shidlovitz into a ghetto, a place where swathes of the Jewish population from around Poland were rounded up and sent to. From there, they were transported onwards – initially to work camps, and then, as the war progressed, and other countries closed their doors, to death camps.

Order broke down, and the Nazis began to openly massacre the townsfolk of Shidlovitz. Vast swathes of the population were systematically murdered, and the rest rounded up. Max, his parents, and his brother, Yeheskel Benjamin, were all herded into a cattle cart, on a train bound for the death camp of Treblinka. Here they were separated forever from Max's oldest brother, Chanina-Aaron, who was forced to remain in town to bury the bodies – a task generally rewarded upon completion with being shot.

As the train hurtled towards its appalling destination, a gap was prised in the side of the cattle truck; the bars and barbed wire were pushed apart, creating an opening just large enough to clamber through. Max's parents, people of immense faith, drew strength and solace from a passage of the Torah in which Jacob, when being pursued by an enemy, divides his family into two camps, maximising the chances that at least one half might escape. They drew from this an unwavering certainty that if both of their sons were to escape, at least one would survive. They told Max and his brother that they had no choice but to each jump from the moving train, and then attempt to find one another and make a break for freedom. And so they did. The fourteen-year-old Max leapt from the train to Treblinka, narrowly escaping knocking himself out when his head struck a wooden sleeper (his hat falling behind him in mid-air and cushioning his fall; the first of what Max would come to view as the many miracles that kept him alive). He scrambled across no-man's land, dodging gunfire. Though he painstakingly walked back along the route they had both agreed upon, Max never saw his brother again.

Now entirely alone, Max knocked on houses near the train tracks, in search of refuge and directions home. Nobody answered, so Max, now suffering from typhus, slept overnight in the snow. The next day, a door he knocked on finally welcomed him in – at which point he was lunged at by the inhabitants, Polish Christians, eager to claim the financial rewards being offered for handing in Jews. Max escaped the house, and fled as best he could, but his pursuers chased him down on a sleigh, and he was captured. (As the police officer who took delivery of a battered and bleeding Max noted wryly, there was no additional reward given for *assaulting* the Jew – that had been an act the group had carried out due to sheer enthusiasm.)

The policeman recognised Max from his hometown – another sliver of a miracle, and one which gave Max enough credibility to hastily negotiate with him. In the end, on the promise of a bribe Max had no idea if he could honour, but solemnly agreed to nonetheless (even, in a moment of audacious inspiration, haggling with the policeman on the price – on the basis that this would make it seem far more believable that he might one day ultimately pay him), Max was able to secure being sent not to a concentration camp but instead to a work camp. Here, there was *merely* starvation and gruelling labour instead of near-instant annihilation, and Max intuited that claiming a skilled role might help preserve him – so he volunteered his services as a metalworker, learning on the job to mask his lack of any relevant skills whilst plotting his escape. Eventually, along with a group of fellow inmates, they picked their moment and broke out – an immensely dangerous midnight charge under the fence into the Polish countryside, where the men dispersed.

Max found sanctuary on the farmland of a Polish worker – a paid employee at the factory in which Max had been forced into slave labour. It was a fraught, precarious financial arrangement constantly on the verge of falling through – the worker being well aware that he was risking not only his own life but that of his entire family if Max were to be discovered.

At first, Max hid in the barn, until the day that it was raided by the Nazis searching for escapees – Max recalled a Nazi officer stopping, looking directly at him, standing close enough that he felt his breath on him, and then . . . moving on. Did he somehow not see him? Did he choose not to? Another miracle, surely.

After that, the barn being deemed too risky, the farmer dug what amounted to a shallow grave beneath a hen house. Here, for over two months, Max existed; lying in the dirt and the darkness, subsisting on water and the occasional burnt potato.

And, throughout this, Max was sustained by his faith. His beloved Ostrovtza Rebbe came to him in his visions, sang to him – and Max would sometimes sing too, wild affirmations of hope and positivity that drove the farmer mad with panic. At times he would lose his nerve, and demand that Max leave – to which Max responded that he couldn't; if he left he'd be dead, but if the farmer wanted him gone he could shoot him if he wished. And each time something within the farmer would buckle, and he'd relent, and let Max stay.

And so Max survived. The war came to an end. Poland was liberated.

He returned, briefly and uneasily, to Shidlovitz, only to discover a sparsely populated shadow of the hometown he remembered, bereft of the Jewish community that was once its lifeblood. He visited what used to be his family home; a stranger opened the door.

Instead of staying in Poland, Max went out into the world. He married late but swiftly – meeting Maureen whilst on a business trip in the Far East and proposing after only two days, with the curious reasoning that he was very taken by her mother. Though it was not an easy marriage (Maureen not being as identical to her mother as Max might have hoped for), they had two children – a son and a daughter.

Max's son, Maurice, had lived in a dozen countries by the time he was fifteen. In amongst this chaotic childhood he inherited two things from Max: the same deep, warm love of Judaism which had sustained his father in the coldest hours of the night, and an ability to talk his way in and out of any situation – including a place at Oxford University, where he was accepted for a fast-track degree after audaciously knocking on a college porter's door, asking to speak to the admissions tutor, and conjuring an ad hoc interview out of thin air, despite his lack of anything as prosaic as 'the necessary grades'. It was here that he met a beautiful Law student named Katy, whom he enthusiastically pursued (so regularly did Maurice hold open the library door for her that for some time she thought that was simply his job) until she finally agreed to go on a date with him.

Katy was the daughter of Charles, who had moved to the UK after the war as a refugee, and had married an immensely glamorous woman known universally as 'Lion' for her shock of dyed red hair and her capacity for fierceness. Katy was taken both by Maurice's easy charm and by the uncomplicated warmth and love with which he approached Judaism. It was a counter to the fractious, intense relationship that Charles had developed with religion – after the war, in a radical shift in personality which would now likely be recognised as complex PTSD, the previously unreligious Charles suddenly manifested an abrupt, oppressive zealotry, which appeared overnight to the shock and dismay of his wife and the confusion of his young children.

Maurice, by contrast, found peace and strength in the same traditions that had sustained his father. Max, who remained Maurice's closest friend until his death, had passed on more than just a specific religion; it was a reminder of the lost world Max carried with him, and an attitude of unceasing positivity which had held strong in the face of the immense, incomprehensible tragedy which had swallowed up so much of Jewish life, yet which – but for a series of occurrences so unlikely as to be indistinguishable from miracles – had somehow spared him. And it was this worldview, this guiding philosophy, that became the bedrock for Maurice and Katy's relationship.

'There is an important, recurring, Jewish phrase,' Eliana tells me; '"*L'dor Vador*", which means "from generation to generation".' In the face of inconceivable adversity, Max had been able to pass down his values to the next generation. To Eliana's parents, the continuation of this unbroken chain is their everything. Eliana feels it too. How could she not? And so she cannot break the chain. How could she?

Soaking in the bath, I feel the passion and the urgency with which Eliana tells her family story. I can see, looking into her eyes, that the things I first learned about when reading *Rose Blanche* are, to Eliana, far more immediate. Not just the awful mistakes of the past – these are things that happened to two of the people in her life that she was closest to. And it is incumbent upon her to preserve and continue that which was so very nearly destroyed.

I understand that.

But there is a complicating factor; I do, also, exist. I am a real person.

Eliana's beliefs do not, *cannot*, cancel out my identity, or that of my family. The meaning I have derived from being Jewish throughout my life, the sense of my past and of who I am – it doesn't all simply disperse, floating away like ash in the breeze, just because I have discovered that there are those who view me differently.

What's more, as I hear Max's story I feel acutely aware of a bitter geographical irony – the Oleskers, too, came from Galicia, the very same part of Eastern Europe as the Ostros. The people on our wall, my father's *bubbe* and *zaider*, originally descended from the town of Olesko, a tiny rural settlement which gave us our surname.*

The air around me feels leaden, weighted with the relentless pressure of a series of simultaneous impossibilities. We are the same: neighbours, born from the same patch of Eastern Europe and both flung into the English diaspora. And yet we are entirely at odds: we exist in alternate dimensions, entirely unable to ever coexist. This person opposite me is the person I feel closest to in the world. And yet they are the person I feel most distant from in the universe: it is through them that I have experienced a profound, existential uprooting of my identity, a denial of who

---

* As children, my brothers and I discovered to our excited astonishment that this far-off town of Olesko a) existed, and b) somehow boasted its own castle. We harboured grand dreams of one day being triumphantly welcomed back to our hometown and reinstalled in this vast and spectacular building – until our parents, having finally got round to making a long-promised pilgrimage to visit Olesko, came back home to report that a) the 'castle' is in fact more like a large house, which now contains a not particularly interesting museum, and b) our ancestors were almost certainly not aristocrats but potato farmers, and would have never been allowed inside in the first place.

I know myself to be, and a diagnosis of my categorical unacceptability as a partner – they make me feel not only distant from them, but distant from myself.

I try to push through the fug of it all, and find the right words. Or, failing that, any words at all.

'. . . I didn't know that it would all come to this.' I say, eventually. 'I suspected, but I really didn't know.'

'I knew from the very start,' Eliana says. 'From Edinburgh. And I came back home and told my mum, instantly. I said, "I've met this man. I feel more for him than I've felt for anyone. And either he's utterly right for me, or I'm going to get my heart broken. But whatever happens, I know it feels too important to walk away from."'

'So accept me as I am,' I say. 'Just accept me.'

And now Eliana's face flushes.

'I can't.'

'You could. Of course you could.'

'By asking me to accept you, you're asking me to reject what I believe.'

I'm not asking that. *I'm not*.

I try a different tack.

'I don't understand. If this was never going to work . . . I've met your parents . . .?'

'And they think you're wonderful.'

'And what do they think about this whole . . .?'

'I think . . . I think my mum's actually found it a lot more difficult than when I've had non-Jewish boyfriends.'

'Because I'm Jewish?'

'Because this is different. With the others, it was clear; it was never going to last. Whereas this . . .'

'It feels arbitrary,' I say. Eliana nods, doesn't push back.

'And in a way it is,' she says. 'But everyone draws arbitrary lines, and then lives according to them. It doesn't mean they're not important.'

'It feels . . . horrendous,' I say. 'To have been deemed unworthy, a non-starter, because of an arbitrary line you have drawn.'

And I finally scratch at the thing that has haunted me since I learned about it.

'You're saying that I have the wrong sort of soul.'

'I'm not.'

'You are. That's what you're saying. That's what this all means.'

A long silence.

'I'm so sorry,' says Eliana. 'The last thing I want is to cause you any pain.'

The conversation wends back and forth in an endless, exhausting loop, until I sense Eliana step outside of it. Her expression softens.

'Have I said anything that shocks you?' She asks the question calmly, kindly.

In a sense, no, she hasn't; this is the exact end of the road – the dreaded but seemingly inevitable worst-case scenario – that I had been bracing myself for. But, in another way, I do feel shocked; by Eliana's immutable force of feeling. The intractable, diamond-hard certainty that underpins her set of values. Something that means we can never be together.

'I do believe this is the right thing for me. I do.'

She does.

And then, finally, there it is. The kicker.

'If you wanted to consider conversion . . .' she says, 'It's not something I'd ever demand of you. But it would mean we could be together.'

I cannot believe what I am hearing.

Eventually, one of us pulls the plug, and the water seeps out from around us, slowly.

CHAPTER 6

Some Much Needed Respite in the Form of the End of the World

Having finally addressed the awful, unmentionable subject of our total incompatibility, we both then do the sensible thing and completely ignore it.

Well, actually, a series of things happen. Firstly, we both exhale. The tension, inexorably building for months, has finally been pierced, and though we haven't even begun to think about addressing the subsequent, even larger and more impossible issue that looms in the distance – 'finding any sort of resolution that doesn't make us both exceptionally miserable' – even the act of clearing the air and acknowledging, with an agonised shrug, the doomed-ness of it all feels like an achievement worth marking with half a breath of respite.

Secondly, the world ends.

In March 2020, life as we know it temporarily comes screeching to a halt. The novel strangeness of our predicament is superseded by the novel coronavirus, which rapidly mutates from 'nothing anyone's ever heard of' to 'everything anyone can think about'.

In the newspapers, sinister graphs containing evil-looking arrows and unpromising numbers suddenly proliferate. Televised 'daily briefings' from slightly hollow-eyed politicians stood next to panicked healthcare professionals thrust unwillingly into the glare of the spotlight quickly become the norm. And on social media accounts around the world, people's second cousins, distant uncles and least-stable former schoolmates roll up their sleeves and, as one, commence a rigorous daily schedule of posting increasingly unhinged bollocks. It's clear that everything is changing.

The upshot is that, whilst Eliana and I find ourselves at a relationship crossroads, tasked with making a decision about our future, it isn't the decision we thought it might be.

'They're saying there might be a lockdown. A sort of quarantine.' I'm lying on Eliana's bed, reading the doom-laden headlines on my phone with fascinated disbelief. 'Three weeks to "flatten the curve".'

It has been six months since Edinburgh and Jägerbombs and conga lines. Just a few weeks since the bath and the Conversation.

'Wow. Do you think they'll do it?' says Eliana.

'It seems mad. But then it's also sounding... quite "imminent".'

'So we couldn't see each other at all?'

'Don't think so. I think travel would be totally out. Don't think I'd be allowed to get the tube here. And, even without a lockdown, it's not been a *super*-regular occurrence you coming to my place in the Docklands...' (As the saying goes: 'You can take the woman out of NW3... with great, great difficulty.')

In short order, the inevitable question jokily bounces its way into conversation.

'So, do we quarantine together? Haha!'

'Haha, maybe?'

'I mean, it's just for three weeks, I guess, you know? We may as well...'

Had we been dating for just a few weeks less, or had we not had the Conversation, it's entirely possible it might have felt too much, too soon, and we might have gone our separate ways. But instead . . .

'Yeah, three weeks! Sure, why not?'

Which is how I end up living with Eliana and her family for seven months.

All of a sudden I am transplanted – from my ragged corner of industrial east London to fragrant, genteel Primrose Hill. It is a leafy, picture-postcard village in the heart of the city; the stuff of implausible dreams and even less-plausible English romcoms. It is also a ghost town. As a particularly warm and enticing springtime softly envelops the city, the streets are almost entirely empty; the residents (of whom I, unaccountably, am now one) all barricaded indoors, nervously avoiding the mystery virus and each other.

I experience a little of Primrose Hill in the brief window that constitutes my Government Mandated Daily Walk Of No Longer Than One Hour, but the vast majority of my new reality is indoors, in Eliana's beautiful family home at the edge of the park, where, alongside her parents, siblings and their partners, we form our 'bubble'.

Ever since I first gently percolated into their lives, Eliana's parents had never been anything other than warm towards me – ever-keen on updates about my comedy career, and the shows that Eliana and I had seen, and the pretentious bars we had visited. But the family's existence on Friday nights through to Saturday evenings – the Jewish Shabbat – had always lain beyond an invisible barrier. It had always been another world, the mere acknowledgment of which risked shattering my and Eliana's carefully constructed reality.

But now, with the planet in freefall, her parents unhesitatingly and unquestioningly welcome me into their home. And, with reality as we know it placed in a state of suspended animation, the previously unthinkable happens: I am invited to Friday Night Dinner.

'So, what sort of thing should I expect?' I say to Eliana nonchalantly on Friday afternoon, whilst, beneath the table, I urgently google 'Frday niffht dinnre Reform/Otrthfdx difffrences'.

'It's very relaxed,' she says. 'We sing *shalom aleichem*, and *eshet chayil*, and there's *bensching* at the end.'

'Cool!' I say, as I attempt to comprehend any of the specifics she has just mentioned, whilst my mind helpfully offers up nothing but a wall of white noise.

'Honestly, don't stress.'

'I'm not stressing!' I shriek.

Shakily, I wander off to the utility room, where I iron four different shirts (I packed too many shirts), quietly panic about which suit to wear (because I am incapable of *not* overdressing, I also packed too many suits), and vividly visualise the various ways in which I could get things wrong.

Due to unthinkably bizarre global events, I have been welcomed into the inner sanctum of Eliana's family life, something I thought I might never experience. It now feels important that I don't utterly disgrace myself.

My panic was out of place – as, arguably, was my floral suit. Friday night dinner at the Ostros turns out to be something both entirely new and utterly familiar.

Just like the meals of my childhood, there are blessings of candles, and wine, and bread. Many of the melodies and phrases are exactly those I remember. Some moments are similar, but delivered with additional ornate flourishes. And some elements I have never encountered before – like the ceremonial hand-washing before blessing the *challah* loaf, and the lengthy, elaborate, musical after-blessing that formally rounds off the meal, replete with numerous different call-and-response elements (this, it transpires, was the '*bensching*' Eliana had mentioned).

But beyond these differences – the intricacies of which I am at no point expected to know, and which I am guided through tactfully and generously by those around me – it is everything I recognise. It is a meal eaten by a busy, bickering family, exchanging gossip and insults, talking over one another, cackling with laughter, eating too quickly, and unpacking the stresses of their week.

There's Eliana's brother Michael, the eldest, who works in finance, talking animatedly about his latest deal, slinging around business jargon that nobody understands – some of which it seems quite possible he's simply made up.

Sat next to him is his girlfriend, Talia, studying for her degree in nutrition, recently gluten-free, and discreetly tucking into some gluten-filled *challah*.

There's Eliana's older sister, Tamara, who has been known to describe herself, unbidden, as 'a bit of a character' and 'conventionally hot' – the latter perhaps being an indication of the former – and her boyfriend, Julius, both lawyers.

Julius is as extrovert as they come, much to the constant and visible dismay of Tamara, who is generally engaged in the (doomed) task of reining him in. In another life Julius would have been a wedding singer; in *this* life he is in the midst of an ongoing crusade to join the synagogue's professional choir via sheer force of willpower and the time-honoured technique of 'standing nearby and singing very loudly'.

There's Eliana's father, Maurice, a preposterously high-flying businessman, who is nonetheless rendered childlike with happiness at the very sight of the evening's food, and who launches into long, winding stories – mercilessly heckled by his children as one tangent becomes another – before gently falling asleep at the end of the table.

And there's Eliana's mother, Katy, ethereal yet utterly alive to the needs of those in the room, constantly aiming to ensure there's enough food for everyone (there absolutely is) and drink for everyone (there really is, honestly, but thank you so, so much).

Conversation is . . . vibrant.

'So, Max, what are you writing at the moment?' says Julius.

'Well, I'm working on a sitcom—'

'Oh! Is it difficult to get a sitcom made?' says Tamara.

'It can be – it's quite a precarious industry, and—'

'Darling, would you like any more soup?' says Katy.

'Oh, no, that's so kind, thank you—'

'And what's it about?' says Julius.

'It's about wrestling,' says Eliana.

'Dad, did you see that article in *The Week* about the yen?' says Michael.

'Wrestling? Like Mike Tyson?' says Tamara.

'Mmhm, I did,' says Maurice. 'Ungh, these ribs are *incredible* . . . but this is my last one, everyone, OK? OK?'

'Darling,' says Katy, 'I think perhaps not everyone else is as fascinated by your plate as you are.'

'No, Tams, that's boxing,' says Eliana.

'Oh my *goddddddd*, Tamara, I can't believe you don't know the difference!' says Julius. 'That's so embarrassing, haaah!'

I cling to my seat and try to keep up as impossible-to-follow conversational strands come and go – Julius and Tamara are getting a cat! Or are they? – and plates are passed back and forth, and occasionally the spotlight suddenly swings back to me.

'You were saying, Max?' says Talia. 'Making the show has been quite difficult?'

'Oh – well, it can be quite up and down—'

'Mhhm. Yes, exactly, the yen has been going through a rough patch,' says Maurice.

'Max isn't talking about the yen, Dad,' says Eliana.

'We've been looking at Scottish Fold kittens,' says Tamara. 'They're definitely the best.'

'Right, but this is exactly why it's a great time to invest!' says Michael.

'You think so?' says Maurice. 'OK, look, I'm having one more rib.'

'Also, d'you know, I think I'm very close to being invited to join the *shul* choir,' says Julius.

'He was talking about the sitcom he's writing,' says Eliana.

'You're really not, Julius,' says Tamara, 'they asked you to sit down.'

'Oh, darling, are you writing a sitcom?' says Katy. 'How wonderful! What's it about?'

'Well—'

'You know, that reminds me,' says Maurice, 'I was speaking to Richard Hoffman after *shul*, or rather, we'd been speaking before *shul*, because you know, we're on that committee, and actually it's funny—'

'No, Dad, please,' says Tamara.

'. . . the committee was supposed to convene last week, and it didn't, and I'd been speaking to Baroness Hayes at an event the week before, well, not at the event, after the event, because we were in a queue, in this sort of corridor—'

'Dad,' says Michael, 'with a gun to my head I could not tell you what you you're talking about, and I think if you're being honest with yourself not even *you* know.'

'Darling, are you *sure* you won't have any more soup?'

And so it goes.

And my greatest fear, the one lurking beneath my surface-level worries about mispronouncing Hebrew words and putting my elbow in the soup, proves unfounded; there is not a glimmer of reservation from Eliana's parents about my sudden attendance at their table. No undercurrent of pushback, no hint of distaste, no suggestion that I am in any way an intruder. I am welcome.

It sets the tone for our lockdown.

In a fragrant pocket of northwest London, as a deadly virus sweeps the planet, Eliana and I fall in love, become an item, and officially become exclusive – all in that bizarre order. The complications of our situation had, until now, rendered those initial stages effectively impossible, but in our new lawless world everything happens – effectively in reverse. 'By the way, I'm not seeing anyone else,' Eliana confides to me, deadpan, weeks after we have declared our love for one another – reassuring, given that her only options at this point are either her own immediate family members, or a fairly aggressive garden fox.

In the outside world, things are chaotic, and sad, and terrifying, and occasionally insane – it is the era of mass brawls in supermarkets as shoppers attempt to stockpile toilet paper – but, inside, Eliana and I are free to uncomplicatedly be together. Because why not? Because if the world is falling apart, if we don't know what the next day will have in store, let alone the next month, why shouldn't we?

*

Months pass. My family and friends shrink to squares on a screen, and my new bubble world (the Covid Crew, as our group-chat is inevitably named) becomes all I know.

We eat together. We exercise together. We watch films together. When a sacred Ocado delivery slot can be secured, we diligently and misguidedly spray down the groceries with cleaning vinegar, wipe them dry and leave them in the sun.

We all celebrate each other's birthdays – finding ever more elaborate and tenuous ways to 'surprise' one another. Eliana has a powerful and unquenchable love of table football in all its forms, and I discover an eccentric collector of vintage foosball tables who agrees to deliver some to the house when I take Eliana out for a carefully timed walk, thereby facilitating a retro arcade-themed birthday celebration. When my birthday comes around, Eliana goes to great lengths to acquire a pink suit I once wore for a Prom-themed show with Ivan, leaving it on the bed with instructions to put it on and come downstairs . . . where a gloriously tacky balloon arch has been constructed, a makeshift dancefloor prepared, and her entire family have dressed up in seventies Prom attire – Maurice wearing one of the classic white wide-lapelled suits he wore as a young man in the nightclubs of Miami, and demonstrating impressive muscle-memory for every one of the dance moves.

In a bid to ward off lockdown insanity I attempt to improve my primitive piano skills, and when it comes to the birthday of Eliana's grandmother, Lion, who lives just down the road but we daren't visit in person, we diligently prepare what we advertise to her as a 'concert', and she appears on Zoom – wearing a string of dazzling pearls and coral lipstick – to listen to our whole household enthusiastically blunder their way through an eclectic setlist ranging from assorted songs from *Les Miserables* through to Robbie Williams's 'Party Like a Russian'.

'Any other requests, Lion?' asks Eliana, bright-eyed.

'I think you've played all the songs I like,' Lion responds, diplomatically.

I am immersed in a world of warmth, generosity – and of Modern Orthodoxy. Eliana's parents, it's clear, delight in their Judaism. It supports and defines them in a tangible, ongoing way. It is the drumbeat which marks out the passing of their days, from the Friday night dinners to the Saturday Shabbat lunches – which are prefaced with our own approximations of a synagogue service led by Maurice, who extemporises an explanation of the weekly Torah portion, and enthusiastically encourages us as we each attempt to read out a short passage from the accompanying reading known as the *Haftora* (with my adolescent *bar mitzvah*-era Hebrew creakily reactivating, I do battle with the fear of being outed as a fraud and an interloper, and try not to sweat through my shirt). We celebrate the Jewish festivals together, and I feel a sense of familiarity, hearing the echoes of the rhythms of my youth – albeit delivered with a fluency and flair that is entirely new to me. I remember old traditions and am welcomed into new ones.

And then, gradually, incrementally, the world starts to recover.

The pandemic subsiding is, I am very aware, unarguably a good thing. The awful graphs ticking downwards, the flickers of hope on the faces of politicians; it all speaks to a world in which normality might return. Life as we knew it might spring back. The double-act sketch-comedy industry might even right itself, I think (a sentiment shared by dozens of others across the world). It does, however, mean that my ever-present cognitive dissonance – *the world is going to hell, yet I'm so happy!* – starts to tilt in the other direction – *things are improving, which means . . .*

As the restrictions in the real world start to loosen, the walls around Eliana and I start to close in. The things we previously failed to solve . . . remain resolutely unsolved.

As talk begins to spread of the world cautiously reopening, it becomes clear that lockdown has functioned for me like the demo level of a computer game – a vivid, enticing sample of a future I don't yet have. 'This is what you could win . . .' This could be your partner. This could be your family. This could be your life.

One afternoon, after yet another sensational lunch, Katy finds me in a corridor and, to my surprise, tackles a subject she's never mentioned before with characteristic Ostro directness.

'Max, my darling, I just want to say that we love you so much. Whatever happens, it's been so wonderful being with you. And if you thought that converting was something you might be able to do, and that might be right for you, we would be so delighted, and we would support you however we could.'

We do, it seems, still have a decision to make. One that it's quite clearly impossible to make whilst ensconced in the heart of Eliana's life, surrounded by a family whose values could only ever pull me in one direction. And, given that the only plausible way forward involves me converting, something I'm not remotely certain I can agree to, there's only one possible next step. We must break up.

A few nights later I pack my things, we eat our miserable steak dinner, I order a cab, and Eliana and I are no more.

CHAPTER 7

On the Road Again

'Even by your standards', says Lou, 'this is top-tier "your life is a mess" stuff.'

As is invariably the case, Lou has a point.

I have known Lou since university. She has had an unenviable front-row seat for the various relationships and break-ups which have shaped me – and she has offered generous, irritatingly perceptive counselling at every turn.

She and her husband Josh are consummate hosts, effortless company, and flawlessly reliable shoulders to cry on and/or prop oneself up against whilst singing raucously at two in the morning, or indeed six in the morning, depending on what the occasion calls for. In short, the sort of friendships that one's life is sustained by.

And now I am sat in the living room of their flat in Highgate, explaining everything that's happened.

Josh, who happens to be Jewish (observant? Not remotely! *Halachically* Jewish? Sure is, lucky bastard), understands it all in a heartbeat, and shakes his head, slowly. 'Fucking hell, mate.'

Whilst this was presumably a reaction to my convoluted tale, it might equally have been a comment on my general state of being at this point; I am sat cross-legged on their floor, wearing my ancient and slightly moth-eaten blue silk dressing gown, hacking into an extraordinarily decadent cheeseboard I have curated and purchased myself, and drinking an extremely large glass of red wine whilst talking loudly, intensely, and at great speed. It's not behaviour which speaks, overtly, of 'stability' – which is unfortunate for Josh and Lou, given that I've just moved into their flat.

My time in the Docklands was short-lived – a bewildering whirlwind of unpacking, wild-eyed reunions with much-missed old friends (each relieved that the other is no longer confined to the grainy corner of a Zoom window), and work days spent attempting to will various comedy projects into existence with Ivan. And then, fairly swiftly, lockdown 2.0 loomed on the horizon. This presented an issue.

Of all my under-developed adult skills (and there's a long list), the thing I am least capable of is, without doubt, spending time in my own company.

This has been the case since childhood – something which made me hilariously easy to discipline, as the threat of being made to 'stand in the corridor' away from human company was terror-inducing enough to ensure I was immediately and entirely biddable. And it's a condition that has persisted. Left to my own devices, I can amble through a morning happily enough, and I can just about grit my teeth and make it through to lunchtime. But when forced to spend anything longer than half a day alone, my urge for human contact becomes genuinely overwhelming. The prospect, therefore, of entering another lockdown, but this time on my own, without Eliana *or* the protective safety net of the supportive group of people in our social bubble, felt akin to being made to stand alone in the world's largest, emptiest corridor. It simply wasn't viable. Luckily, as I look at the familiar, sinister graphs on the TV screen, and panic rises in my stomach, my phone rings.

*

'Basically, the theory would be – this way Lou doesn't have a meltdown, and you don't have a meltdown', is how Josh straightforwardly sums up the logic behind me moving into their flat. Josh works in TV – one of the few industries that has worked out a means of remaining quasi-operational in the face of pandemic chaos – and has been offered a job that will mean he'll shortly need to be in deepest rural Wales for an extended period of time.

In a bid to curb Lou's anxiety, which is always heightened when Josh is away for long stretches of time, and has been, reasonably enough, exacerbated by this period of relentless global chaos, the couple have devised two plans. The first involves them buying a beautiful and ridiculous-looking Chow Chow puppy named Iggy. The second involves me being installed in the spare room, so Lou and I can rattle around the flat together and – the hope would be – prevent one another from truly falling off the face of the planet.

By the time Josh has finished speaking, my bags are fully repacked and a taxi is on its way.

And so, as the world shuts down once more, I find myself in a different part of north London, in a very different frame of mind, consuming six different types of cheese and trying to make sense of my future. We'd actually managed to avoid the topic for much of the day – Iggy the puppy being a magnetic presence, capable of doing almost nothing yet doing it extremely charismatically – but as evening begins to fall, conversation inevitably returns to the baffling one-man soap opera that my life has become.

'. . . and that's basically it,' I say, my monologue eventually stuttering to a conclusion. 'We've split up and gone our separate ways. It's game over.'

'Unless you did this conversion, right?' says Lou.

'Well . . . yeah.'

'And that's . . . on the cards? Not on the cards?' Lou's instinct for knocking off the necessary emotional scab and examining the wound beneath is perceptive to the point of being irritating, actually.

'It's . . . not even about it being on the cards, really – it's that even if I wanted to do it, it's basically impossible.'

'Basically impossible or properly impossible?' says Josh, the pragmatist.

'To be honest, I looked it up a while back and it was all so . . . much, that I sort of blocked it from my mind. Tried not to properly think about it.'

'So, come on then,' says Josh, 'Talk us through it.'

I sigh, open up my laptop, and fire up the website.

These are the things I would need to do, in order to convert to Orthodox Judaism in London.

'For starters, there'd be going to synagogue,' I say.

They nod. Makes sense.

'Quite a lot of synagogue,' I continue.

'How much?' says Josh.

'Every day.'

'Every *day*?'

'Yep. Well, more, actually. Three times a day, eventually.'

'Jesus.'

'Not masses of him. But yeah, lots of synagogue.'

'Fair enough. It's different, but . . . I'm sure you could hack that. What else?'

'There's keeping kosher.'

'Yeah, obviously,' says Josh. 'No pork, no shellfish, all that.'

'Sure, that's where it starts – but it's more than that. Everything you eat can't just not be "non-kosher", it has to be certified kosher – does that make sense?'

'Certified – as in, there's an actual certificate?'

'Exactly. Called a *hescher*. Everything has to have a *hescher*.'

'Right.'

'And I think by the end you wouldn't be able to eat a non-Jew's cooking. Which to them would include my mum.'

'. . . Right.'

I scroll down.

'And then there's keeping Shabbat. That's no technology after sundown on a Friday, 'til sundown on a Saturday. No phone, no taking the tube. And no work.'

For the first time, a flicker of concern registers on Lou's face.

'But, mate, you work in comedy.'

'Yeahhh.'

'Doesn't quite a lot of that . . . happen on the weekends?'

'Yup.'

We sit in silence for a moment. I keep scrolling.

'Then there's a series of meetings with a court of judges.'

'You what?'

'Yep. You get grilled – a sort of inquisition. They check in on your progress, ask you questions about Jewish law. It's quite intense – you need to prepare for them with months of lessons with a tutor.'

'Judges? Sorry,' says Lou, 'I thought it would be a rabbi?'

'Oh, the judges are also rabbis. Very senior rabbis. They're called the Beth Din.'

'The Beth Din. That doesn't sound un-stressful.'

'This is mad,' says Josh.

'It gets madder,' I say. 'I'd need to move into a religious family's house.'

Josh puts his head in his hands. 'What?'

'Yep. It's . . . quite integral to the whole thing. They want you to be totally immersed in the process, and for that to happen they feel you need to live with a family.'

'Right. But that could be Eliana's family, right?'

'. . . I don't think so, no.'

'But they're—'

'I know, I know. And, look, perhaps they would let me live there. But, firstly, I'm not sure they'd be deemed religious *enough*. They seem to want you to live in deeper north London – Hendon, Golders Green, that sort of thing.'

'So you'd just be living in a new neighbourhood, with some religious family that you don't know, as a sort of lodger?' says Josh.

'Basically, yeah.'

'OK, that . . . might be weird,' says Lou. 'But, honestly? All sorts of weird shit tends to happens to you, and you seem to be . . . generally fine.'

I look up from carefully assembling my fourth plate of cheeses and nod, gratefully.

'And, look, it'd be a mad adventure and you'd be having it together.'

'Ah, well, that's another thing,' I say. 'I'd very much be staying there on my own.'

'Wait, what?'

'I would not be allowed to live with Eliana, or indeed have any physical contact with her, at any point in this entire process.'

At this point, Josh actually bursts out laughing.

'Fuuuuuucking hell, mate. Are you serious?'

'I am. In religious communities, men and women don't touch before they're married.'

'I mean. What? No touching at all?'

'None.'

'What if you were, like, holding hands?'

'Pretty sure if we were caught holding hands in Hendon, it would be game over.'

'This is blowing my mind,' says Josh. 'I actually don't believe these people.'

'Joshy!' says Lou. 'You can't say that.'

'Course I can,' says Josh, 'I'm Jewish! And, to be fair, so's Max!'

'How long does it all go on for?' says Lou.

'Amazingly, there's no set length of time,' I say. 'It takes as long as the Beth Din decide it takes.'

I close the laptop.

Lou takes a deep breath, and sums it up. 'But other than totally reorganising your working life, spending more time in a synagogue than out of it, not being able to eat your own mum's cooking, moving into a random religious family's home on your own for an unknown amount of time, and not being able to touch the woman you love, there's not really much to it?'

'Yep, pretty much. Just that, and getting a bit of my penis cut off, really.'

In the end, the final word on the matter comes from Iggy, who makes a fairly messy statement on the carpet which seems about as eloquent as anything else there is to say.

Each morning I open my eyes only to discover that the Big Question has already smashed itself, sledgehammer-like, into my consciousness; to convert, or not? It is a stark decision – the unavoidable dilemma I am faced with the millisecond I wake up, find myself grappling with constantly throughout the day, and attempt to unpick in my fitful dreams.

The entire subject still feels entirely overwhelming and completely unanswerable. But it does, at the very, very least, feel fractionally more plausible a thing to tackle than it did when Eliana and I were together.

I'm not sure if you've ever tried to gain perspective on the topic of 'whether or not you should embark on converting to Orthodox Judaism' whilst at the same time living with your Orthodox Jewish partner in her Orthodox Jewish parents' house. In the unlikely event that you haven't, take it from me, whilst there are many things you will find in that environment – doting anecdotes about school play performances; endless, almost scary, amounts of food; and substantial amounts of footage of your partner's father waterskiing on various family holidays – if you're on the hunt for 'any sense of distance and perspective whatsoever' you're in entirely the wrong place.

But here, in Highgate, accompanied by an old friend willing to offer sage advice, and a slobbering, overindulged puppy who offers a unique brand of wisdom of his own,* I at least have room to breathe – to try and regain my bearings.

Was this entire episode, this journey to the brink of a potentially vast and surreal life choice, simply a manifestation of pandemic-induced mania? These have famously been Unprecedented Times™ – so was this just my unprecedented response? An example of the desperate lengths I might go to in order to avoid that most dreaded, unthinkable of all eventualities: being on my own? In short, is it Eliana that I want to be with, or is it, in fact, just . . . somebody?

There is a possible means of answering this, and it is one suggested by Eliana herself, as I lie on the bed in Josh and Lou's spare room, phone in hand. 'Date other people!' she says.

The logic is undeniably sound.

For one thing, I have spent the last year growing incredibly

---

* NB: This is a lie – Iggy is, respectfully, a simpleton.

close to Eliana, living deep within a world constructed according to her and her family's values, to the point that I've found myself very seriously contemplating a decision that, mere months previously, would have been totally unthinkable. Perhaps, if I were to spend time with *other* people, it might put things in perspective – either the concept of the conversion would somehow come to make sense, or else this whole mind-boggling almost-decision would retreat into the mist, to be looked back on in years to come as nothing more than a half-remembered glitch from a year when the world went mad.

And then there's also the fact that, despite my and Eliana's intense, constant, daily communication – a heady mixture of continued in-jokes, important updates on her sister's ridiculous Scottish Fold kitten (Tamara and Julius did get their cat, in the end) and tense, granular, theological debates – we are now both, although it feels easy to forget and strange to remember, single.

Nonetheless, the idea of responding to this suggestion with full-blooded enthusiasm seems . . . risky. Plus there's a throwaway casualness to her delivery that makes me think she must, surely, be joking? But, no, with her distinctive, nuclear brand of self-confidence, she's serious. 'Honestly, go for it! I think you should. Work out what's right for you.'

'God, she's impressive,' says Lou that night, over a sushi dinner which, in a further expression of my lockdown-and-meltdown-induced culinary mania, I have haphazardly constructed by hand, a process which has taken four excruciating hours and resulted in us sitting down to eat at 11.45pm. 'She's right, too. This is obviously a decision you need to make with some semblance of sanity. And, to be honest, if she hadn't said it, I would have. Get out there.'

I nod, and attempt to finish my Hinge profile. Lou glances over at my screen. 'Ugh, don't use that pic. Makes you look like you'd be into close-up magic.' I delete the picture from the app. And my phone.

And so it comes to pass – making the most of my new status as a free-and-single (in utter crisis and emotional free-fall) man about town (that town being 'a wet, wintry London in which it is still quasi-illegal to meet with a stranger'), I date other people.

There are pints ordered in sterile, socially distanced pubs with Mollie (works in advertising and loves her dog); tinnies consumed on park benches with Reena (insurance, outwardly quite strait-laced but secretly went to old-school garage raves once a month until the world shut down); a bottle of wine shared with Alice (journalist and painter, documentary obsessive) whilst sitting in her garden and trying not to think too hard about whether or not this action makes one or both of us criminals – it's not, to be honest, one of the great times to be single in modern history.

Nor – and I'm sure this is down to my own total unsuitability to be dating anyone at this point, or else the fault of substandard app-algorithms – are any of these dates anything other than *absolutely fine*. But they do, at least, shake me out of the bubble that had become my world during the first lockdown. They reopen my horizons, and allow me to at least place the conversion – this immense, drastic choice – within the context of the world's myriad possibilities. 'Look, see?' my internal monologue can now say, moderately reassuringly. 'You don't need to panic – perhaps things could work out with Claire?' (art gallery curator, aggressively into running). 'Or, you know, perhaps not Claire if we're being honest', (way too into running), 'but whatever happens, just statistically, it seems *fairly unlikely* you will die alone?'

But, of course, the Big Question doesn't vanish beneath this sea of perfectly pleasant, slightly identikit evenings. Somewhere, in the distance, is Eliana (well, I say 'somewhere' – she's ensconced in

Primrose Hill with her mate Pippa, who's moved in for lockdown 2.0, a period they've decided to spend focused on the ambitious yet wholesome pursuit of 'learning about every country in the world' via a series of handwritten Post-It notes they add to an ever-growing cloud on the wall).

I am, I realise, completely incapable of walking away from the possibility of navigating this alien process and being with Eliana until I am certain that I can't bring myself to go through with it.

The thought of the conversion (and I am able to think of little else) presents a dense forest of implications – logistically, professionally, personally, religiously, logically, surgically – all of which are intertwined with vine-like tendrils of doubt, misgiving, bewilderment, furious disagreement, curiosity and fear. Wherever I am and whatever I'm doing, during this period of my life I am, at some level, engaged in the perpetual task of identifying each strand of thought, painstakingly extracting it from the thicket of surrounding worries, and tracing its path from start to finish in order to work out how I truly feel – with each 'completed' thread affording me a further glimmer of comprehension. Some of my conclusions bring me closer to a sense that the conversion might be possible. Some make it all feel more out of reach than ever. But I am determined that, if I *do* walk away, it won't be because the whole thing was just too difficult to comprehend – I want to disentangle the impossible Gordian knot of it all, to *know* that it's wrong for me.

I am, by necessity, reading far and wide throughout this period of soul-searching, 'soul' being the operative word in my case, given that I am, I suppose, searching my soul regarding the possibility of *changing* my soul. And how, for that matter, might that work? Would I be having a new soul installed? Or would I be seeking to upgrade my existing soul? Is it a new lick of paint or a straight swap? And if it's the latter, is my old soul simply discarded, or can it at least be recycled, and offered as a donor soul to someone who works in venture capital or TV comedy commissioning?

I have purchased books. I have read articles. I have trawled conversion-related websites long into the depths of the night, poring repeatedly and fruitlessly over the same pages, reading and rereading, searching for answers, staring incredulously at the glowing screen, before finally, inevitably, giving in to exhaustion, closing the laptop, and lying in bed – mind whirring, nerves frayed, no closer to knowing what the hell I should do with my life. I realise that my reading can only take me so far. To go any further, to actually find the answers I seek, I'll need to talk to people who truly understand the process.

CHAPTER 8

A Series of Surprising Conversations

The thought of speaking to a rabbi feels like a strange one. Not strange as in 'makes no sense' – indeed, when it comes to discussing esoteric Orthodox Jewish matters, talking to a rabbi feels about as straightforwardly sensible a starting point as there could possibly be – but strange as in 'entirely out of my comfort zone'. It feels like a step closer to a rabbit hole (a rabbi hole? No, almost certainly not . . .) that I'm still not at all sure I wish to travel down.

'I'm not going to push anyone,' says Eliana, diplomatically, 'but, if you did want to speak to a rabbi, I know who I think you'd properly get on with.'

Later that week, a genial, twinkling-eyed South African rabbi named Avraham appears on a Zoom call, sat serenely in front of a towering set of shelves laden with Jewish books. Avraham leads the Beit Shalom community, and is Eliana's family's long-time community rabbi – 'And also, more importantly, friend,' he says, smiling. I explain my predicament, and he listens intently.

'Firstly, you should know that this is a very important decision,' he says. 'It is one which will shape the contours of your life.'

I nod. He has a gentle, powerful sincerity – a curious combination of 'beloved children's TV presenter' and 'wise king'. 'Secondly, you should know that if you were to undergo this process in London, it is a gold-plated conversion. It's the Rolls-Royce of conversions; the best in the world. But you wouldn't be making it easy on yourself. Here, it is impossible to say how quickly it will take, but it will be a question of years. There are places in the world where you could be rushed through the process in a year, maybe even less. But it's very likely that would leave you open to scrutiny in years to come – and, more importantly, it wouldn't give you the satisfaction of knowing you'd done it properly.'

I nod again. 'And where, haha, where would these other quicker conversions be?' I say. In my mind.

Rabbi Avraham, who radiates warmth and calm, says that he's here to speak further should I wish to, and that it's important that I do what's right for me. He doesn't give the process the hard sell – in fact, quite the opposite; 'Remember,' he says, 'if any of it's not right for you, you can just . . . stop.'

Now I've broken the seal – I've spoken to a rabbi. It's a conversation that has left me with more questions than answers (and this, I will come to learn, is one of the key indicators that you've been speaking to a rabbi) but, as a result, I am emboldened to keep speaking to people. For one thing, what about these other conversions, elsewhere in the world? Yes, it feels absolutely implausible to suddenly be contemplating the possibility of decamping to Jerusalem or Antwerp or Montreal, but then again, *everything* feels implausible at this point, so why not? Before long I find myself fielding calls from assorted rabbis around the globe – each more certain than the other of their views, all of them offering vastly differing, bluntly expressed opinions about where and how it is best to complete a conversion. At one point one of these rabbis announces that he is involved in the running of a *yeshiva*. He invites me to join it for taster lessons on Zoom, and I sign up on the spot. As a result, my mornings now begin abruptly at 6am, at which point I must prise open my laptop and take my place in a digital classroom amongst a sea of other floating heads, and groggily attempt to participate in the ongoing collective endeavour that is understanding, refining and debating the finer points of some 3,000 years of Jewish thought; doing my best to keep up as an excitable bearded man takes some passage of Talmudic text I only dimly understand and informs me urgently that – no, actually, I don't understand it *at all*.

It's a schizophrenic, clearly unsustainable phase; a period in my life in which, at any given second, the message flashing up on my phone might equally be from a Hinge date in Finsbury Park or an Orthodox Rabbi in Hungary.*

But I can't stop speaking to people at this point – not until I've answered the Big Question. And it becomes increasingly apparent that, whilst it's all well and good having endless phone calls with rabbis encouraging me to move to South Florida or Sydney or Stamford Hill, the people with a genuine insight into this process are, actually, those who have made the choice to experience conversion for themselves.

'Hello, nephew,' says my Uncle Daniel, with a chuckle, when he responds to my lengthy message with a phone call. 'Now this is something of a surprise.'

Yes, despite my Uncle Daniel being a bearded, black-hat-wearing, *tzitzit*-sporting, religious Jew – and identifiable as such from the moon – he is also, though it seems extraordinary to me, a convert. You see, Daniel is my dad's *half*-brother. After Percy, my grandfather, began a new life in the north of England, there, unbeknownst to my dad, he fathered a new family – it was only as

---

* NB: in this scenario, it's incredibly important to make sure you're responding to the right person.

my dad grew up that he began to hear rumours of half-siblings, and they, for their part, heard rumblings of an extrovert, mercurial man with an encyclopaedic knowledge of obscure folk music and a penny whistle that he was unafraid to play, if the need arose, with his nose.

And my grandfather's new wife was non-Jewish. Meaning his children – well, I won't go into it again.

Uncle Daniel is the first of around half a dozen men I speak to who have all navigated some form of Jewish conversion process, somewhere in the world. Each story is unique, and each man underwent the journey for their own reasons – be it love, an inner compulsion, a familial connection, a longing for community, or some combination of the above.

There's Woody, who did a Reform conversion in order to marry his wife. 'It was pretty demanding, but I don't think it's anywhere near as hardcore as your one sounds,' he says.

There's Matthew, who took the exact same path I'm staring warily at – converting via the Orthodox London Beth Din. 'Before that I was devoutly Christian,' he explains (perhaps, I wonder, he's just 'really into religion' . . .?).

There's Archie, whose father was Jewish, and who, over the course of a decade, underwent *three* conversions; firstly Reform, then Masorti, before finally finding the meaning he was seeking in Orthodoxy. 'It felt like a natural progression each time,' he says, 'although I realise that it's, you know, fairly unusual.'

My Uncle Daniel, for his part, had a series of encounters which drew him closer towards Judaism – strange coincidences, meaningful conversations – and, ultimately, he felt compelled to pursue an Orthodox conversion. And this meant then – as it does now – making contact with the Beth Din.

'So I went along to see them – this was long before the internet,' he says. 'And I knocked on the door and this little hatch opened, and a man on the other side said, "Name?" and I said, "Daniel Olesker". And then he shut the hatch, and I heard him moving around the office, and then a minute later it reopened, and the man had a folder. He said, "Yep, we have your file here." They knew who I was already!'

Mysterious. All-knowing. As my understanding of the Beth Din begins to take shape, this is the image of them that grows in my mind.

And, as Uncle Daniel stresses, dealing with the Beth Din during a conversion process is no ordinary transaction. 'The important thing you need to know is . . . you're used to being a Western consumer, with Western consumer rights. With the Beth Din, that's not the case. You're a supplicant.'

This is a sentiment echoed, in various formulations, by other converts I speak to. 'The Beth Din want you to be their bitch,' says Matthew.

We speak, at length, about the total control with which they oversaw his entire conversion, about the strangeness of it all, about the time he spent living with a religious family – 'By that point, you can't even really cook your own food, because it would make their kitchen utensils un-kosher.' (*what?!*) – and about the periodic in-person meetings with this daunting group of men that mark out the various stages of the process.

'Those meetings are very, very intense,' he says. 'You end up prepping for days, weeks. But they control things from afar, too, when you don't see them.'

In the tone of Matthew's voice, I feel the weight of the Beth Din's presence. It is a presence that, I start to realise, exerts a gravitational pull over the entirety of Orthodox Jewish life in the UK, dictating the ebb and flow of decision-making – marriages, divorces, financial arbitrations, the certification of kosher food.

As a court of judges answerable only to themselves, their office is, effectively, both unaccountable and, within their community, all-powerful. And if I am to try to navigate this process, it will be entirely on their terms.

I begin to realise how truly alien this process would be. I think about some important, hard-won gigs that Ivan and I have lined up across the year – pulled back from multiple lockdown-induced cancellations and carefully rescheduled – and what might happen to them if the conversion began. 'What if I were to perform, just once or twice, on a Saturday?' I say, with a sinking feeling, knowing in my heart of hearts what the answer is likely to be.

'Oh – if it were during Shabbat? That would be it,' says Matthew. I feel a chill in the pit of my stomach. 'The process would be over. And there'd be no way back.'

Whilst panicking deeply about the implications on my professional life, there is another worry – borderline irrational but no less keenly felt – which I am suddenly gripped by.

'Could I keep my Jewish name?' I ask a new-found friendly rabbi.

When I had my *bar mitzvah** I was given a Jewish name; Jacov ben Shmuel bet Miriam – 'Jacob son of Shmuel and Miriam' – which are the Jewish names of my parents.

I am perfectly content at the thought of that name being underlined and rubber-stamped with approval by an Orthodox bureaucratic body; but the thought of having a different name imposed upon me for some reason, as part of this process of redefining my identity, fills me with great unease. My worries are waved away, lightheartedly, by the cheerful rabbi.

---

* Actually, 'became *bar mitzvah*' is the odd-sounding but grammatically correct phrasing.

'Yes, of course you could. Not a problem.'
I feel flushed with relief. Another piece of the puzzle.

The notion of intentionally making it harder to do something which is, simultaneously, my job, my passion, and an already exceptionally precarious career at the best of times, is something that feels borderline impossible to even think about, let alone accept. But I try to find ways to make it make sense.

I pace around my office, monologuing to Ivan. To be clear, that happens most days – it's essentially our creative process – but on this occasion I am explaining my fraught and conflicted thinking. My circling closer and closer to this unthinkable eventuality.

'And if I *did* do it, then things would change in the way we work. And obviously that would affect you, and I don't feel comfortable with that . . .'

Ivan has been silent for a few minutes, listening to my ramblings, and thinking deeply. Eventually he speaks. 'We weren't supposed to tell people for a while, but I think now is probably a good time; Andrea's pregnant.'

I burst out laughing with delight, and hug him.

Things are changing. Maybe everything's changing.

And, in amongst all this, whenever I can, I meet with Eliana. We sit together in cafés and have strange, intense lunches where, with a combination of heightened emotion and detached, coolheaded analysis, we attempt to parse with forensic accuracy the life we could lead together. Number of children. Schools they might go to. Synagogues they might attend. It's extraordinarily strange and difficult – attempting to carefully construct a hypothetical future together, at a moment when we're entirely apart.

Heatedly, we deconstruct the differences between the traditions we each grew up with – firing back and forth from our respective entrenched positions of comfort and understanding.

'Why can't men and women sit together?' I say.

'It's tradition', retorts Eliana, 'and actually it creates a nice, focused atmosphere! I *like* being sat with women!'

'You're a feminist – how can you accept an institution in which women can't be rabbis?'

'Look,' says Eliana, 'I think they will, one day, but by definition "Orthodoxy" is about preservation of tradition – things move incredibly slowly!'

'And how do you justify being part of a religion that doesn't accept gay people?'

'. . . I struggle massively with this,' says Eliana. 'But . . . look . . . it's not that gay people aren't "accepted" . . . there are plenty of gay people in my community, there are a bunch of Orthodox organisations that are specifically designed to *support* LGBTQ people in the community. It's just the basis for Orthodoxy is a text that's thousands of years old, and it's obviously incredibly traditional, and it's focused on procreation! Are there lots of rabbis who don't support gay people? I'm sure there are! Is that shit? Yes! But there are a bunch who *do*! The reality is so far from what's written down!'

Which – of course it is. But, right now, I'm having to try and find a way to commit to the bits which are written down.

'And you have to remember,' she continues 'I'm trying to preserve something; my family is trying to preserve something that was almost wiped out. They say it takes two generations for traditions to totally disappear! Say what you like, but Reform Judaism is just less likely to preserve the things that are important to me!'

These are knotty, urgent conversations – we are locked in an ideological tug-of-war, each desperately trying to pull one towards the other, in a bid to find a patch of common ground stable enough to become a base upon which to build our lives.

The way it feels to me, I say, is that in order to justify an identity that I already have, I am being forced to contemplate subscribing to a series of things that I profoundly disagree with.

Eliana presents a different view. It's like having citizenship of a country, she says. That country might have done things you disagree with – in fact, it almost certainly has. So does having citizenship mean you subscribe to everything about that nation's philosophy, or embrace their worst excesses, or embody the views of their most hawkish or corrupt politicians? Absolutely not. Does joining a certain religion mean you are irrevocably allying yourself with everything its most hardline exponents have uttered? Or does it mean you've found something of value within that way of life, something you have connected with? Aren't there contradictions and flaws to be found in every institution we're a part of – in almost every decision we make, for that matter?

At times I feel like Eliana and I are entirely suited to one another; different manifestations of the same person – such as when, for instance, she comes round to the flat on the important mission of 'witnessing Iggy in person', and we spend an hour playing with the puppy together and our lives, in a brief state of suspended animation once more, feel blissfully simple. At other times, it feels like we exist in two different circles of a Venn diagram that just barely overlap, and we are obstinately attempting to cram the lives we might lead together into that thinnest of intersections.

Sometimes it all just feels so glaringly illogical. And perhaps it is. But at that point, I remember the words of Rabbi Avraham . . . 'This decision cannot be based on logic,' he said, on our Zoom call. 'It's something higher than logic.'

Even at the moments when it all feels entirely out of reach, the one thing that is clear to me, the single thing that cuts through all the worry and the agonising moral wrangling and the fear and the frustration, is Eliana. The woman who has blazed into my life, and whom, even as we argue across a café table, it doesn't feel remotely odd to imagine being married to. Which – although it frequently gets lost in the morass of destabilising conversations and fruitless arguments – is actually, ultimately, the future we're talking about. The future we want.

If I could bring myself to undergo the conversion for any reason, it would be for love.

Except, it transpires . . . that's not allowed.

To add to the Orthodox conversion process's stratospheric list of requirements, a bleary-eyed rereading of the website reveals yet another potential roadblock; one cannot convert in order to get married. Love is not deemed an acceptable reason.

Now, in true Talmudic fashion, there are, also, acknowledgements that being in a relationship with a Jewish partner is frequently the reason someone might find themselves at the starting line of a conversion process. But the Beth Din wish to be satisfied that there's more to it than that – that, were the relationship to fall apart, the prospective convert would keep going.

Even as reading these sentences makes me want to melt into the floor with exhaustion, I understand – begrudgingly – where they're coming from. It's entirely understandable that, in a process such as this, sincerity would be deemed of paramount importance. But it also makes me question myself.

I, clearly, felt that I was Jewish before I met Eliana. Now, entirely due to our relationship, I have found myself navigating a treacherous and often painful path in which I must seek to redefine the nature of my own existence, in order to allow myself the mere possibility of being with the woman that I love.

So where does that leave my motivations? My feverish research and ceaseless phone calls? Am I doing any of it for the right reasons?

And, say I *were* able to commit to starting the process – how would I then approach the immense series of obligations, the vast changes to my lifestyle, which would be integral to the conversion?

Because, I discover in this same sitting, someone who converts isn't expected to be as observant as other Jews; they're expected to be more so. I reread this passage, in mild horror, assuming I've misunderstood. But no, there it is: 'The London Beth Din is aware that the standards it requires for conversion create an anomaly insofar as converts are expected to be more religiously observant than the majority of the mainstream Jewish community, who tend to be more traditional than observant.' I would be, yet again, an anomaly.

There is a world in which I do the following: just pretend. Treat the whole thing like a game. Commit to completing the process, but give nothing of myself to it. Make all the right noises in these terrifying meetings; rattle off a series of crowd-pleasing buzzwords I've learned by rote, until my interlocutors start stroking their beards in approval.

And as for all these new forms of observance – keeping kosher, abstaining from technology during the hours of Shabbat – I could simply nod and smile when learning about them, and then carry on living my life in private entirely as normal.

There are multiple reasons why this approach feels wrong to me.

Firstly, I haven't got the slightest interest in leading a double life. I am a horrendous liar – or rather, whilst I'm capable of carrying off a lie plausibly enough,* the act of having lied invariably leaves me wracked with anxiety and writhing with self-loathing. The thought of taking on an entirely new lifestyle full of fiendishly complex rules is challenging enough – the thought of taking on that lifestyle in public and then immediately flipping back to a different set of rules in private, of cauterising my brain and holding two realities in my head at once, and having to move seamlessly between them . . . the knots of stress in my stomach feel physically solid.

Secondly, if I am to embark on a quest of extreme difficulty, increasing intensity, and totally unknown length, I don't *want* to just skate through it at a surface level. I want to truly engage with it. To try and find some sort of meaning in it. For me, I decide, that meaning – and this is a glinting, double-edged sword – comes in the form of connecting the process to my Jewish identity. Leaving to one side the question of how Jewish I already am – a point the Beth Din and I seem unlikely to ever agree on – there is no doubt that this would send me far deeper into the waters of Jewish life than I had ever previously swum. Centuries of thought and practice to discover and engage with, and – whether or not I take to it all – at the very least try to understand. It feels, to me, like another incidence of arriving at a crossroads in my life, the way I did when I was thirteen – the decision to become *bar mitzvah* or not, but infinitely vaster in scale. A chance to turn away from my identity, or towards it.

---

* That Drama & Creative Writing BA Hons (1st) from Royal Holloway University didn't earn itself.

And so I resolve that, if I *am* to take on this monstrosity of a challenge, I will do so as wholeheartedly as I can.

One by one, I unpick my forest of doubts. Every worry and concern I hold, I am able to contextualise, process, justify in some way.

Except one.

The concept of being surgically altered. It is a notion so terrifying, so strange and preposterous, that it clearly can't be real. But it is also, simultaneously, inescapable.

And so, it inevitably emerges as a question at the end of my long, garden-pacing phone calls – a 'one more thing' that it feels outrageous to ask about, but that I can't not.

And each and every man I speak to, with exquisite generosity, answers in immense detail.

Uncle Daniel completed his conversion in Jerusalem, which is where, some five decades ago, he received his *brit milah*, his circumcision ('A *brit* for a Brit,' he says with a smile), an experience he seems to have been wholly unperturbed by (and, following which, he successfully went on to have approximately twelve children).

Woody got it done at the end of his Reform conversion – *oof, you could have just written them a strongly worded letter! I think . . .* – and then, astonishingly, discovered that he hadn't needed to convert at all. 'Just after I finished, I found out my mum was Jewish already, she just hadn't realised!' Matthew claims to have healed in just a few weeks, and that the only difference in sensitivity is that, when he goes swimming, he is slightly *more* sensitive. 'Plus you feel this sense of . . . religious arrogance.'

Archie, he of the multiple conversions, was circumcised in infancy – but as a result he did experience the equivalent ceremony designed to mark the arrival of an already-circumcised man into the Tribe: the '*hatafat dam brit*', a ceremonial drawing of blood via a pinprick on the tip of the penis.

But the headline, which I cling to desperately, is that nobody I speak to reports having had a hideous experience. Again, I think, humans adjust.

When I meet up with friends, and we go on long, meandering, lockdown-y walks, and talk about life, I inevitably end up holding forth about my convoluted situation – a subject which, invariably, boils down to circumcision chat.

A surprising number of them reveal they've been snipped at some point in their adult life – albeit all of them due to phimosis, which is tightness of the foreskin. Once again, to my relief, the upshot is that everyone reports that it was unpleasant but, basically, fine – with the exception of one friend who gleefully tells me a story about his infected wound that is so horrendous it causes me to lie awake attempting to scrub the anecdote from my memory, via the sensible technique of thinking about it constantly.

At one point I end up speaking on the phone to a cheerful *mohel* – that is, professional circumciser – from Stamford Hill, who volunteers to come to my house and perform the procedure for approximately £100 cash, at which point I realise with blinding clarity that the type of circumcision I wish to have – if I am to have any at all – is *an expensive one*.

And I am inevitably pulled into the swirling madness of the internet, where I read the furious screeds of the 'intactivists', those who deem circumcision to be genital mutilation, and use weights and stretching techniques to optimistically attempt to regrow the flesh they have lost. As unhinged as some of their (extremely detailed) posts are, I have nothing but sympathy for their sense of indignation. Irrespective of outcome, what absolutely cannot be denied is that these people did not have a say in the matter.

I find myself spending far, far, far too much time on *r/circumcision*, a subreddit full of helpful gentlemen happy to post photos of all descriptions, and even more happy to check in and message you privately to ask how things are going (it's not a sex thing, the mods are very clear about that).

I learn about the 'shang ring' method (neat scar line but a longer healing time – popular in sub-Saharan Africa); the various merits of glue vs stitching (glue can leave a neater scar, but it takes longer to heal, and is *far* more likely to tear); I search in vain for clinics offering the procedure via a laser, a technique which allegedly exists but appears borderline mythical.

And then I discover that, once you've selected your method (freehand scalpel, I finally, wincingly, decide, would be the least-worst option), you can choose your 'style'. That's right. Did you not know there are various 'styles' of circumcision available? From 'high and tight' to 'low and loose'? OK, fine, let's really get into it; if the scar line is closer to the head of the penis, it is considered 'low'. If it's further up (or down, depending on your angle, and that of the shaft for that matter), then it's considered 'high'. And the tightness or looseness depends on the amount of skin removed – if there's 'spare' skin, for that casual, comfy look, then you've gone 'loose'. If the appearance is more sleek and streamlined, you've opted for 'tight'.

I am, of course, going mad.

I've been speaking to my parents about my decision a great deal, as might be expected.

And, of the two, whilst it is my father who has grown up steeped in Jewish tradition – the stories, the songs, the slang – it is my mother who, because of her journey, has far more perspective on the subject.

For my dad, being Jewish isn't something he's ever had to think about – he just *is*. For my mum? She knows what it is to love someone, and to take on a series of new elements, reshaping your life, in response to that. So her advice from the off has been astute, thoughtful and considered.

One afternoon, as I am cycling through London, my mum calls me.

'Darling, I've been thinking. I know how much you're struggling with this. It's very strange, obviously. But also . . . I can see why you're drawn to it. It offers many of the things that you do love, and that you need. I'm not saying do it. I'm saying, just . . . don't rule it out.'

And then, finally, cursed algorithms be praised, I go on a fantastic date (Tatiana, therapist, into rock-climbing and 'horny French disco music'). She's bewitching. Gregarious, fascinating, Russian-Swedish, she's even technically Jewish – though she couldn't care less about that designation. 'But if that's what you're looking for, your mama will be proud of you,' she smiles. We spend an evening in Hyde Park drinking negronis out of plastic cups until we get locked in, and then we climb over the fence together, cackling with laughter, and escape off into the night. It is an 11/10 evening – as engaging, adventurous, positive a date as I can possibly imagine.

And yet I wake up the next morning with the same hollow, inescapable feeling. The certainty that I should be elsewhere.

That I should be with Eliana.

Fuck.

Eventually, it all comes down to a phone call from the dick doctor. I have composed an email, incredibly carefully – the exact wording has been signed off by a kindly rabbi, to ensure that this display of individuality isn't forwarded to the Beth Din as evidence of my seditious, subversive, rabble-rousing (rabbi-rousing?) tendencies.

This is a genuine fear. When I spoke on the phone to Matthew, he spoke at length about the degree to which the Beth Din sought to clamp down on perceived dissent of any sort. 'A friend of mine, doing the conversion at the same time as me, he was on the right path. He was keen – a star student, really. And then he went and got himself circumcised – but by the wrong *mohel*. A surgeon that the Beth Din didn't approve of.' And they came down hard on him? 'Emotionally, I don't think he ever recovered.'

My agonisingly prepared email even contains – that's right – diagrams. Could I please look like *this*, as opposed to like *this*? It's amongst the more unhinged emails I have ever sent. I take a deep breath, and I press send. And, less than a minute later, my phone rings.

[UNKNOWN CALLER ID]

'Hello, Dr Strasser here.'

He has a measured, reassuring voice. And he has read my email.

'Yep, that's all perfectly standard. We can do that style for you. Remind me of this phone call in a few years' time. Good luck.'

. . .

And that's it. My final question, answered.

I am no less terrified by the concept. No less thunderstruck that this might actually be a reality I consent to. But I have identified the way through that feels . . . least unacceptable.

There is a throbbing feeling in my temples, at the surreal notion that I am committing now to an elective surgery at an unspecified point in my future. But I cling to the knowledge that, if it happens at all, it will be the final stop on my journey – I will have made it to the other side. And I remind myself of what Rabbi Avraham said, reassuringly, on our first call, when we discussed the possibility of the process; 'If you don't like it . . . you can just stop.'

So that's it, then. I'm . . . going to embark on the Orthodox Jewish conversion.

What to do next?

Firstly, I decide to phone my parents. It feels right to me that they should know first.

They respond to their eldest son's strange, long-agonised-over announcement with love and support, and the merest dash of astonishment that this might really be happening (same), and by wishing me all the luck in the world.

Secondly, I message Eliana. 'I'm in if you are?'

She phones back, even more swiftly than Dr Strasser.

'Right,' she says, 'what time shall I pick you up?'

CHAPTER 9

Onwards

Given that Lou and Josh have housed me, fed me, counselled me, and frankly put up with me for the entirety of my drawn-out period of soul-searching, I am relieved at having given them, at least, the satisfaction of a conclusion to this episode of the soap opera.

'You're doing it!' says Lou. 'I can't believe it!'

'Neither can I!' I say.

'Mazels, mate,' says Josh. 'I mean, is that what you say for something like this?'

'Hah,' I respond, 'I have literally no idea.'

I spend my final night at their flat, packing my stuff yet again, amidst a flurry of wine and toasting the end of this curious era.

The next day, Eliana comes to pick me up – there are hugs and warm farewells (in Josh's case, shaded with mild resentment at the fact that, due to his prolonged work-related absence, Iggy the puppy now seems to believe that I am his father) and we drive off together, reunited and jubilant, towards the beginnings of whatever comes next.

It's an extremely odd feeling, preparing to tell the people in my life that I'm about to embark on a religious conversion. It's the sort of announcement that I instinctively feel it might be necessary to take a slight run-up to, to dance around or contextualise in some way – the subtext being 'I haven't lost my mind, haha! Genuinely, though, I haven't.'

But then, of course, Ivan – who walks into our office moments after I've finished talking to Eliana – has long seen this coming. He's relieved on my behalf, ready to help reshape our double-act as necessary, and – as is his usual approach to life – generally more relaxed about things than seems entirely sensible.

I break the news to my brothers – a group call, because it doesn't seem right to phone one before the other. Our conversations are usually a Dadaist patchwork of convoluted running gags, bizarre tangents and other unspecified meaningless gibberish, but here, momentarily, we find ourselves all speaking to one another sincerely.

'Wow, brother – you're going on a spiritual journey,' says Leo. 'Love that.'

'I actually think it could be something you really benefit from,' says Huw. 'The way it sort of gives shape to your life.'

It isn't for a second something either of them might ever contemplate for themselves, but they can see, and understand, how I've got here. They are reflective, and understanding, and I am immensely grateful for their kindness.

. . .

'So, I guess at the end of all this you'll be cutting off your *schmeckle* for the big guy in the clouds, eh?'

'Oh, he'll be cutting that *schmeckle* for the man upstairs, no doubt.'

'*"Hey, Moishe! We're gonna need a smaller knife!"*' Aaaand we're back.

'Aha, so you're becoming more of a Jew?' twinkles Bernard, when I visit him and Erica in Haverstock Gardens. 'You'll be using the juju to make you a Jew-Jew?'

'He's doing it for love, Bernard!' says Erica.

'Well, we must do these crazy things for love, young man. I still love Erica like mad – she drives me mad!'

'You've always been mad, darling.'

I venture onto the group-chat populated by my oldest schoolmates, bracing myself for some level of ridicule or incredulity. I am met instead by a heartening, unexpectedly loving outpouring of support.

'Congratulations, broskiiiiii'

'Amazing news'

Heart emojis and fist-bump emojis and good-natured messages of encouragement.

I spend a long afternoon in the pub with Callum, my old university housemate – one of those friends you see all too infrequently, but then when you're together you immediately relax back into their company, as comforting as a warm bath.

As one does in these sort of timeworn friendships, we've inevitably reached back into our collective past, relitigating old victories and ancient heartbreaks, each formative stepping stone of early adulthood, tracing a circuitous path through to the present day of our thirties.

He beams with delight at the notion that I've somehow found a way of making my relationship work, but then his expression clouds a little.

'I dunno, mate – I'm feeling protective of you,' he says. 'Not sure how I feel about you having to get your penis chopped.'

We sit in thoughtful silence, sipping our pints.

'I mean,' he says, eventually, 'I will ask to see it.'
I nod, understandingly. 'Yeah, fair enough.'

And, Eliana tells me, there has been happiness and celebration at our reunion amongst her friends, who – I later discover – had told her in absolutely no uncertain terms that her 'let Max date whoever he wants' plan was a terrible idea.

'Girl, he can theoretically see literally whoever on this entire planet,' said Tara, Eliana's right-hand woman and formidable *consigliere*. 'He could date someone of any religion, probably a broader age range than you 'cos he's older. You can date, what, 0.00001 per cent of the population? Plus, you're picky as hell. Do not do this.'

Eliana smiled and shrugged and put another Post-It note on her wall of facts (Honduras. Capital city: Tegucigalpa). 'If it's going to work, it's going to work.' She has faith.

Interestingly, the one contact I might have expected to leap with joy – my Uncle Daniel – gives a distinctly muted reaction. At first I wonder if something's wrong. Have I somehow offended him? But, no, I discover, his reaction is entirely in keeping. Judaism is not traditionally a proselytising religion – it doesn't seek to recruit people – and so it is deemed inappropriate to react to news of a prospective convert's intentions with wild excitement, or even encouragement. One simply acknowledges that person's decision and then, should they make it to the *mikveh*, congratulates them on the other side.

However, that's not to say that there is indifference or aloofness amongst Eliana's parents. Instead, there are hugs and tears and an incredible sense of collective relief and delight as I return, once more, to the Ostros' family home – a place I thought I might never again revisit – for Friday night dinner. I am greeted like family.

At the start of the meal, Maurice – as he does every week – blesses each of his children. And then he turns to me.

'Tonight we wish a very special blessing to Max, who is beginning something extremely important to us, and to our family. And we wish you strength along the way for the challenges you may face, and we give blessings and love to Eliana too – may you support one another, and give one another strength, because this is something you will be doing together.'

'Darling,' says Katy, 'You have made us all so happy.'

When telling my parents of my decision, the one reservation my mother had raised, quietly, was this: 'The Ostros won't think we're . . . lesser than them, will they?'

'Absolutely not, Ma,' I said. 'I know why that might be a worry, but, weirdly, they're not remotely concerned about anyone else's levels of anything, and they're incredibly welcoming. They've just got this thing that's incredibly important to them, and their family . . . and it's this. But they won't look down on you, or anything. In fact, I really think you'd get on.'

And before long, this proves to be the case. In this brave new world, the previously unthinkable happens: Eliana's parents extend a Friday night dinner invitation to my entire family, and a full, chaotic quotient of Oleskers descend *en masse* to northwest London.

Before supper Eliana and I walk with my parents up to the Primrose Hill viewpoint, and I notice that my father is walking a little more slowly than usual. I see that, as he carefully navigates the branches and potholes in his path, Eliana has taken his hand, and is gently supporting him by the arm. They are joking and chatting together, entirely happily and naturally. I find myself watching the unaffected care and tenderness with which Eliana helps lead my father to the top of the hill where they stand, looking out across the city, silhouetted by a rich bruise of a sunset.

Surely, I think, there can't be any other way.

Friday night dinner with the Ostros and the Oleskers is a heady blend of professionals and unprofessionals, business and bohemia, that seems at once both unthinkably strange and completely natural. We gather around the dinner table, animatedly chatting and singing and talking over one another and inhaling endless quantities of food and drink.

'I mean, I've gotta say, it's pretty astonishing,' says Michael, awestruck by my dad's boundless capacity to eat.

'It's the famed Olesker appetite,' says my mum, shaking her head, as my dad tackles his fourth plate.

'He taught us everything we know,' says Huw, a similarly impressive plate loaded high.

'Yeah, big Papa O's just warming up!' says Leo.

My dad, smiling, his mouth full, briefly addresses the table with a contented thumbs up before returning to the task at hand.

'And you're so *slim*,' exclaims Talia.

'Oh, don't,' says my mum. 'It's quite irritating, he never puts on any weight at all.'

'I wish I could say the same,' says Maurice mournfully. 'I'm at my biggest ever weight right now,'

'Nobody cares, my love,' says Katy, firmly.

'So, Huw,' says Eliana, 'what have you been up to?'

'I've just got back from gigging in Bavaria,' says Huw.

'OK, I'm just going to have one more lamb chop,' says Maurice, 'and then no one let me have any more.'

'Huw, that's so cool!' says Julius. 'You know, I'm something of a singer myself—'

'And is there dessert . . .?' asks my dad, finally surfacing for air.

It all feels like a vision of a possible future, there for the taking if I can only grasp onto it.

All of which is to say: despite my trepidation at sharing this news with the people in my life, I am, in fact, swept into the beginning of the conversion on a huge wave of positive energy – which, it transpires, in the months and years to come, I will need to draw deeply on. But, right now, I bathe in happiness and swim in excitement, the soft candlelight of Shabbat dancing in Eliana's eyes as she smiles at me and holds my hand.

CHAPTER 10

A Letter of Intent

When getting into Orthodox Judaism, one requires a sponsor. It's a little like managing other addictions, only in this case their role is to ensure you're likely to *stay* hooked.

Specifically, before presenting oneself to the London Beth Din with the intention of converting to Orthodoxy, one cannot simply press an 'apply' button, or download a form. Instead, one first requires the endorsement of a sponsoring rabbi, who must write a letter attesting to one's good character. This must be accompanied by a letter written by the prospective convert, explaining their reasoning, all of which must be sent to the secretary of the conversions department, who must forward it to the co-ordinator of the conversions department, who then passes it on to the Beth Din themselves, at which point it will be read by the Dayanim – the judges – who make up this court. It's really as simple as that.

It is this arcane process, shrouded in formality, which I am seeking to a) understand, and b) begin, when I find myself standing awkwardly in the foyer of Regency Square synagogue, awaiting a personal meeting with the young community rabbi who I am hoping might be my sponsor.

This quest of mine has already been met with a number of what the showbiz industry euphemistically refers to as 'polite passes'. Over the course of my many lengthy conversion-related conversations, I have gradually built up a small circle of rabbis across the world who I feel some affinity with, whose company and conversation is pleasant, and who seem broadly sympathetic to my cause. However, when I gently broach the possibility of any of the more locally based rabbis becoming my sponsor, I experience their immediate retraction; whilst they each quietly offer me their ongoing advice and support, it is qualified with the caveat that, as it happens, it might be better if they were to keep themselves at arm's length – their outlook on the world not being deemed 'acceptable' by the Beth Din.

'They just don't like the way I operate,' one mutters.

'I'm happy to help you,' says another, 'but it will run a lot more smoothly for you if you don't mention my name.'

To be clear, there is nothing remotely subversive about this group; they are, each of them, Orthodox rabbis, men who do everything by the book (or the scroll). But it becomes clear that the levels of control exerted by the Beth Din extend beyond keeping would-be converts on a tight leash. There are political undercurrents, it seems, that run through the entirety of Orthodox Jewish religious life.

So my search continues. Whilst I may have the support of a Rabbinical A Team (The 'Oy' Team?), I still require someone willing to actually endorse me.

'I reckon Rabbi Yossi's your man,' says Eliana's brother, Michael. 'He's young, I'd genuinely go for a beer with him. Go for a chat.'

Which is how I find myself in Regency Square synagogue on a blustery winter's afternoon. I feel furtive, out of place – unattuned to the bustling rhythms of the building. I also realise I don't know what Rabbi Yossi looks like, and so I start smiling warmly at each passer-by I suspect might potentially be him – which is approximately 70 per cent of the people I see. Within thirty seconds I have managed to overthink my attempts at 'smiling warmly' to the point that I feel like an alien impersonating a human being.

He's late. Perhaps he's testing me? Then I suddenly realise, with a sinking sensation, that I haven't brought a *kippah*. Argh. Have I been offending everyone who's walked past me, as well as simply unsettling them? With relief I spot a vast pile of spares, hurriedly place one on my head, and wait.

And then Rabbi Yossi rushes over – late from one thing, clearly *en route* to another, but, quick, let's chat for a minute – a whirlwind of apologies and wisecracks.

'Hey! Good to see you. Sorry, it's always crazy. And oh – you know Bernard Kops, yes?'

'Ohhh, of course, we know Yossi,' said Erica, to my astonishment, earlier that morning.

'Eh?' says Bernard.

'Yossi, dear!' says Erica.

'Ahhh, of course, I knew Yossi,' says Bernard. 'Yossi? Yessy!'

Bernard and Erica have lived vast lives. They lived in Soho in the sixties, where they crossed paths with Francis Bacon and Lucien Freud, befriended Quentin Crisp, and were contemporaries of Peter O'Toole. Then, later, when they wished to start a family, they moved to Haverstock Gardens in Hampstead – a leafier, quieter enclave from which Bernard could still write poetry day and night, and plays and novels when they came to him, and rage colourfully against the literary establishment which he'd never quite been a part of (and which, paradoxically, he'd never have wanted to be a part of, even if they'd let him). In the ramshackle splendour of his garden flat, surrounded by posters of his plays and copies of his books, all covered with handwritten dedications to his beloved Erica, Bernard would hold forth, flamboyantly, to roomfuls of rapt students, who would share their work, and hear it read aloud by professional actors, and have it critiqued by the master. And, at one point, one of his students was a young man named Yossi, who had dreams of being a comic writer.

Perhaps it was too uncertain a profession. Perhaps it was merely a passing phase. Or perhaps one day the clouds parted and the call of Rabbinic life suddenly swept aside all other concerns. But Yossi soon became Rabbi Yossi, the smiling, bearded, hyper-energised young rabbi who beckons me to sit with him at the back of the *shul*.

'So, you want to convert, yes?'

Rabbi Yossi listens to me tell my well-worn story intently – somehow focusing in on my words despite the almost constant buzzing of his phone, and the ceaseless background hum of colleagues and community members popping their heads in, attempting to pull him into what appear to be fifteen simultaneous meetings at once. Rabbi Yossi screens it all out, nodding and smiling encouragingly as I speak, and jumping in the second I have finished.

'Sure thing, *boychik*. I get it. You're credible. Look, do me a favour, start coming to synagogue a few times, yeah? Then, when I write to the Beth Din, I will have properly seen you around.'

So you'll be my spon—?

'Absolutely. OK – I need to run. Speak soon – message me, yes?'

A few weeks pass. In that time, I make my first blundering evening appearances at the synagogue – invariably turning up at the wrong time, opening the wrong book, reading the wrong page, and understanding less than nothing about what is going on. Rabbi Yossi invariably nods and smiles when he sees me, gives me a thumbs up, and then rockets off to his next appointment. During this time I am also, with immense care, writing the letter that will eventually be sent to the Beth Din (via their secretary's secretary, and so on).

This period is also a final beat of calm, prior to what Eliana and I both realise will be a period of vast change. The moment that letter is sent off, alongside Rabbi Yossi's endorsement, then the cogs of the conversion process will slowly begin to turn. The laws that govern my life will shift. And for the entirety of the process I will become – as Uncle Daniel warned me – a supplicant. So, before all that, these weeks are a period where, with slightly less denial than before, Eliana and I can pretend that things between us are simple. Sure, there's the small matter of actually *doing* the conversion (or even being accepted on the process, for that matter), but there is a warmth and security in the knowledge that the decision has been made.

There's also the question of what the letter will say, as it pertains to Eliana and me.

Simply put, if I inform the Beth Din that we are in a relationship, it will mean Eliana has to effectively go through the whole process with me – attending the gruelling meetings, likely having lessons with a tutor – and if I *don't*, then she is entirely exempt.

'So, you know – you both split up in order to make this decision . . . maybe you're *still* split up?' suggests a friendly *shul*-goer, in a quiet chat. 'It will be a lot easier for her.'

Yes, you could argue that – and we toy with the notion of doing just this – given that the viability of our future has clearly proven to be contingent on my conversion to Orthodox Judaism, we're effectively *not* in a relationship until such time as my conversion is eventually ratified.

There are a few problems with this. Firstly, this argument is, obviously, a load of bollocks – we absolutely *are* in a relationship. The next issue is that Eliana has no interest in sitting back and leaving me to tackle this theological assault course alone – not just because it seems vanishingly unlikely that our relationship would withstand that approach, but because she is acutely aware of the onerousness of the challenge, and is determined to lift the burden however she can. 'If I could do this instead of you,' Eliana says, 'I would.' She can't. But being a part of the journey, undertaking it alongside me, is the next best thing.

Eventually, 757 of the most meticulously assembled words I've ever written later, the letter is ready.

> Dear Dayanim,
>
> I write to you under the auspices of Rabbi Yossi of the Regency Square *shul*, to communicate my hope and intention to convert to Orthodox Judaism under the London Beth Din . . .

I lay everything out in the letter. My relationship with Eliana, our break-up, our reuniting, my aim to connect this process with my existing Jewish identity. And, once it is ready, I message Rabbi Yossi – the man who is now, officially, my sponsoring rabbi – who fires off a message that I will never see, commending me to the Beth Din. With my heart in my mouth, I attach my letter to an email and fire it off into the ether, for the eventual attention of the men who will judge my soul.

CHAPTER 11

Going Contactless

What I would have liked to happen, upon having made this momentous decision, is to have immediately experienced some sort of dramatic, exciting, seismic sea-change in the way I experienced the world. For my sending of the email to have been accompanied by some sort of stirring orchestral score, beginning subtly and quietly (just the woodwind section, perhaps) and gradually swelling with a grand sense of purpose (horns, strings, maybe an organ) before blossoming into a vast, climactic overture; the sense of a man beginning a quest.

Instead, the first thing that happens is this: I move round the corner, and Eliana and I are no longer permitted to touch.

Yes, I've known this was coming. But there's a difference between knowing something and feeling it. And, as I sullenly move my things (yet again) into my new home (yet again), I feel it keenly. To say my thoughts on this subject are complicated would be a lie. I absolutely hate it. Not a single thing about being separated from my partner seems in any way positive. It makes me, immediately, miserable.

And yet, at the same time, I am aware that I am experiencing this situation in as gilded a manner as possible; whilst I have been exiled from Eliana's family home, the place I move into is – thanks entirely to their generosity – approximately twenty metres away. Which means Eliana and I can be together, even though we can't.

So I hold numerous truths in my head simultaneously. I have the support of my family and my friends. I am living down the road from my girlfriend in Primrose Hill. I am preposterously lucky in so many ways. All that's true. But what's also true is that, for an unspecified length of time, I am completely forbidden from touching my partner, and this makes me feel like absolute shit.

'It's unusual,' says a rabbi, 'because keeping couples apart is actually very un-Jewish.'

This is true; highly religious Jews move with astonishing directness and unsurpassable speed from first date (hotel foyer, chaperone nearby) to proposal (within a few months), to wedding (as soon as is practicably possible), to babies (many). And, although there are many ancient and baroque laws related to when couples are and aren't allowed to be intimate, Orthodox Judaism has, on the whole, a positive attitude towards sex; husbands are obliged to not just procreate with their wives but to satisfy them. It actively encourages couples to be together. Usually.

'So, yes,' says the rabbi, 'it's an unusual quirk of the conversion.'

The sheer fact of how close we are to one another simply highlights the absurdity of our being apart.

In a sense, it would be easier if we were far away. If we were in a long-distance relationship. What Eliana and I are now in is a short-distance relationship. Separated by twenty metres and the Ten Commandments.

There is a powerful weirdness in the air as I finish unpacking my things and go out to meet Eliana, to say goodnight.

We stand in the street, a foot away from one another. Eliana's breath turns to steam in front of me, curls of warm air floating towards my face.

Her expression is a strange mix of sadness and sympathy and slight embarrassment.

'So . . . sleep well . . . ?'

'Yeah, you too . . .'

Instinctively I go to hug her, and then immediately stop myself. Eliana flinches, then looks up and down the street furtively. At this – the notion that us embracing is something that could in any way be deemed a negative, or, worse, is now a transgression that we could be 'caught' at, and word of which might spell our doom – I suddenly feel sick with fury. For a second I'm frozen on the spot, completely unsure of how to end our interaction, and in the end I just turn around and walk away.

'Night,' I manage, as I shut the door.

Miserably, I walk through the darkened house and climb directly into bed, where I try and fail to find comfortable positions in which to sleep, constantly rearranging pillows and shifting sides, for hours and hours and hours.

CHAPTER 12

The Minyan

Seemingly seconds after I've finally tumbled to sleep, the ominous sound of my alarm drags me back to the surface.

'6:30am: ✡ Go to synagogue'

With my eyes sore and my head heavy, I shuffle around ineffectually in the pitch-black, gathering my things and stumbling out of the door.

It is cold and dark as I huff my way through the north London streets, making my way towards Regency Square synagogue – an alien start to an alien routine. My natural setting is nocturnal; ever prone to sleeping in and staying up. But this, I am learning, is entirely incompatible with the lifestyle of the Orthodox Jewish man, in which one must, as one rabbi explains, 'rise like a lion' from bed first thing in the morning, and head 'with alacrity' to the nearest house of prayer. I haven't managed alacrity, only a lack of sleep, but I suppose it's a start.

I approach the synagogue, and discover the outer gates are locked. As I attempt the door handle, a huge, shaven-headed security guard emerges from a sentry box and looms over me.

'I'm here for . . . synagogue?' I say, inanely.

He stares at me impassively, and then gives a stoic, almost imperceptible nod. I hear a click, and realise the door has been unlocked. Presumably he has pressed a button, or activated a remote, but I haven't seen him move; in the bleary half-conscious morning dark, I feel like I'm in the presence of some sort of retired Soviet super-soldier bred to have telekinetic powers.

I scuttle past gratefully, and make my way into the small bright hall. It feels like my first day at a new school.

Inside there is a small gathering of men, chatting with an easy familiarity to one another as they prepare to begin the service.

I nod and smile, and I take a seat at one of the wooden pews that seems unlikely to be occupied, trying my best to appear as though I belong. With a deep breath, I reach into my bag and produce my bag of tefillin.

If you've seen imagery of religious Jews at prayer you'll likely have seen them wearing two small black leather boxes, one worn just above the bicep, affixed by a leather strap wrapped tightly around the arm seven times, the other worn on the forehead – and these are tefillin. It's a fairly arresting image. It's also another new facet of Judaism for me – the Reform movement, given to thinking outside the (leather) box, generally views the scriptural requirement to bind tefillin to one's body as metaphorical rather than literal, and whilst there are plenty of Jews of all liberal stripes who are keen tefillin users, it's a far less integral part of daily practice, and never figured in my teenage studies.

As part of my stuttering Orthodox debut, I have made timid appearances at afternoon and evening synagogue services, but by tradition those proceedings are tefillin-free. For the weekday morning service, though, that's how it all begins.

I acquire my own set of tefillin a week prior to my first experience of early-morning *shul*, when I visit my parents in Portsmouth. It is before their first dinner with the Ostros – the first time I've seen them since I phoned to tell them about the conversion.

'Ahhh, the rabbi is here!' My dad smiles and hugs me. 'Well,

well, well, my son the *frummer** . . .!' says my mum, giving me a kiss on the cheek, 'Who would have thought it!'

We sit down for dinner and, before we eat, my mum places something on the table.

'We wondered if you might want these,' she says. 'They were your Great-uncle Phil's.'

Carefully disinterred from some archival box, in a small, frayed bag, she presents a set of ancient tefillin.

'And now they can be yours.'

As I take the bag, I feel the connection of generations – to Phil, my Grandma Anne's brother, who was in the rag trade and ran a garment factory – a *schmatte* factory, to use the old Yiddish – in Brick Lane, and would come to our family events with his 'friend' Mimi, a glamorous mistress who had been a dancer in the Bluebell Girls. And the notion of these tefillin being liberated from their forgotten corner in an attic, and being used once more for their intended purpose, feels a little like a spark of something dormant being brought back to life, like a bellows fanning an ember.

'We thought your father might have had some of his own, but if he did then he lost them years ago.'

My dad – who is, naturally, already happily eating medically-impossible quantities of food – nods and shrugs contentedly.

So now is my first attempt at wearing tefillin – or 'laying tefillin', to use the technical term – in a synagogue. Much like every single time I have ever worn a bow tie, I have been prepping for this moment via the repeated scrutiny of a plethora of contradictory YouTube videos.

I unzip the bag, bring out the tefillin and, affecting an air of competence, begin to put them on. Immediately, the specifics

---

* That is, one who is *frum* – or religious.

of my YouTube boot camp dissolve from my mind. Which way round did the box on the bicep go? And in what direction am I pulling the straps? I'm wrapping it – wait – how many times? Great, and now the arm box is slipping off – but also aren't I supposed to be putting the head one on, and how do you even adjust that bit, and where exactly on the head – and, of course, just to really make the whole process as straightforward as possible, there are also some passages of Hebrew I should be intermittently reciting at the same time as all this. Perfect. It doesn't go 'well', in the conventional sense. However, after what feels like a protracted hour of adjusting and wrapping and pulling and knotting, I am, sort of, wearing my tefillin. Having a leather box strapped to my forehead and another strapped to my arm does not, immediately, seem natural. But for the men around me, to whom all this is second nature, it somehow does; it appears part and parcel of who they are, these exotic adornments becoming a natural part of their outfit.

With the tefillin tenuously attached to my body, I open the *siddur* – the Jewish prayer book – and attempt to find my place. And then a man approaches me.

He asks me who I am. He asks what has brought me here. He listens to my answer. He informs me that I should take off my tefillin, and that, later in the conversion process, it may become appropriate for me to wear them again. And then he proceeds to the front of the *shul* and takes his seat.

I have had my first encounter with Dayan Horowitz. He is the senior rabbi of Regency Square synagogue. He is also a member of the Beth Din.

The fact that by joining Rabbi Yossi's community I would also fall into the orbit of a key member of my eventual judging panel was another reason Michael suggested I aim to begin my journey in Regency Square. It makes total sense; it means that, although I have yet to formally hear back from the Beth Din as a collective entity, my existence will become a reality to at least one of them. My daily endeavours will be apparent, as will my sincerity. I'll be more than just some words on a page – I'll be a human being.

What it also means, and I only realise this as I nervously remove my tefillin, wrap them up and pack them back away, is that my every action will take place in full view of a member of the Beth Din. It raises the stakes, and the stress, exponentially. Every second I am in the same room will feel like an audition – auditions being an environment in which, as my agent can ruefully attest to, I do not tend to thrive. But, for better or worse, there's no backing out now – I've shown up, and all there is to do is keep showing up. My attendance at Regency Square synagogue's *shacharit* – morning prayers – is now a part of my daily routine.

Each morning, I walk or cycle over in the dark and join the small group of men who, over the course of my first few days, I soon begin to distinguish from one another.

These are the men of the *minyan*.

You might know of the Muslim tradition of praying five times a day. For practising Orthodox Jewish men the obligation is three times a day, at specific windows of time, but – and there's always a but – if at all possible it must be with at least nine other Jewish men, without whom certain key prayers cannot be recited. This critical mass of ten people is known as a *minyan*, and it is a concept that makes up the bedrock of every synagogue – where, in effect, without a minyan a service cannot truly begin.

Observers might note that this edict, though derived from numerous Biblical sources, also happens to be ideal for community-building. The need for a minimum of ten people to congregate in the same spot means that Jewish life is, immediately, highly likely to consist of people living within walking distance of a synagogue – and, thus, in close proximity to one another. There is an instant interconnectedness, a knitting-together of the public and the private, and the creation of spaces where people can, yes, commune with the Almighty, but also schmooze and talk business and enquire as to whether that nice new family who've moved to the area might have any daughters interested in dating their eldest son who's actually looking very handsome now that the acne's clearing up and he's cut his hair, but, look, regardless, why don't you all come round for Friday night dinner and we'll just sit them near one another and see what happens? Religious rules which just so happen to have pragmatic benefits, particularly as pertains to preserving community and a sense of identity; there's a lot of that in Judaism.

Gradually, I become attuned to the rhythms of the Regency Square minyan. I start to learn where everyone sits, and who likes who, and who doesn't, and who's loud and chatty and who's studious and quiet – like a school classroom, except with a median age of around seventy. There's a cheerful Hungarian, who specialises in whipping up scrambled eggs in the kitchen at periodic communal breakfasts; there's a natty, moustachioed, Einstein-like figure, who wears tailored suits, drives in in a spectacularly flash sports car, and gives learned disquisitions on each week's Torah portion; there's a belligerent heckler, dazzlingly word-perfect when called upon to read Hebrew aloud, but also stunningly, hilariously rude about everyone else's attempts; and there's a lovely retired solicitor, a devoted Tommy Cooper fan, who mutters 'just like that', chuckles to himself, and prays in a rich bass voice. As I slowly find my place within the minyan, he becomes my neighbour, and I start to take a seat at the pew next to him each morning. The Regency Square regulars tend to be men of a certain vintage because, even though there are plenty of Jews in the neighbourhood, devotional daily observance is less in vogue in this part of town; it tends to be the older generations who begin their day this way. So this group of (mainly) jovial elderly men are the hard core, keeping their community afloat. There are, approximately, nine of them, which means that if everyone's in attendance, plus the rabbis, then a minyan is to be had. If not, then things could get tricky. However, there is another group that bolsters the daily attendance: the grieving.

The Jewish approach to death is one which is steeped in practicality. I remember this from the traditions I learned of as a child, when relatives died – the funeral, held as soon as can be arranged, bringing people together in an act of commemoration and mourning; the *shiva*, a week-long period directly afterwards, where the closest relations of the deceased sit, and receive guests, and begin to process the loss of their loved one; and the *yahrzeit*, the anniversary of the death, which becomes an eternal fixture in the calendar, a time when a long-burning candle is lit, and that person is remembered.

A year after the death of my father's mother, Grandma Anne, we lit a *yahrzeit* candle in her memory, and it burned a permanent black circle into my parents' beautiful wooden dining table. Perhaps we could have had the mark removed, but it seemed appropriate to keep it, and it is there to this day – sitting, elegantly, in the centre of this circular table, still a part of our family life.

Grief in Judaism isn't ignored or suppressed or brushed under the carpet, to be alluded to only in hushed, faintly embarrassed tones. It is tangible and real; something that is worked with, as practically as the *challah* dough that is kneaded and braided into shape, ready for the Friday night dinner table.

Integral to the mourning of the dead is the recitation of the *kaddish*. It is amongst the most important prayers in Jewish life – a series of utterances so fundamental that it almost supersedes prayer. There is a ponderous weight to the ancient Aramaic words; its cadences echo back across generations. Its recitation, in some form or another, is central to all strands of Judaism.

In Orthodoxy, mourners recite the *kaddish* daily for eleven months following the death of a loved one – as Eliana's mother is doing, in honour of her father, Charles. And for Orthodox men, the obligation is to recite it three times a day, at the appointed prayer times, as part of a minyan.

So in Regency Square's daily battle to reach ten men, these mourners represent the cavalry. I soon learn to identify them; they tend to be younger than the regular gang, often middle-aged men who have lost a parent, and they generally arrive looking slightly ragged and worse for wear – there being a prohibition on shaving for an initial stretch of the mourning period.

Again, the sense behind the ritual feels apparent – these men are simultaneously obliged to mourn and obliged to resocialise. They may not exempt themselves from society and drown alone in their grief, but nor can they leave their sadness unacknowledged and press on with their lives. Each morning of mourning, they spend time processing their loss, whilst surrounded by those who wish them a long life, and offer them unaffected sympathy, and support, and occasionally scrambled eggs, as they work towards reintegrating into the world.

So these become my people – the men I nod to each morning, at what comes to feel like daily registration. They come to understand my reasons for going brazenly tefillin-free, and soon stop offering to lend me theirs or, in the case of the heckler, stop loudly and repeatedly demanding to know why on earth I am refusing to wear any, until he is eventually shushed into silence by his irritated neighbours.

Very gradually, I begin to find my way through the service. The repetition (for there is much) helps me start to recognise key moments and pick out where I should be – or, at least, where I should have been when the person started speaking, only they're now inevitably some three pages ahead.

Orthodox prayer, to me, feels like the people leading it are speeding down a motorway, speaking at 100mph. It seems close to a garbled hum. Perhaps it's because there's so much of it, I think, and because people know it so well. The mere act of starting a paragraph activates the meaning in their mind, and so they can tear through each blessing without much focus on the words themselves.

Comparatively, in the services I grew up attending, there was far less prayer, much of it was in English, and it would all be said far slower and more deliberately. This was partially because, although the South Hampshire Reform Jewish Community has many distinctive strengths – including immediate warmth, an easy informality, and a couple who both play classical recorder and occasionally give impromptu recitals – a deep familiarity with the intricacies of a service is not chief amongst them. Also, because when the congregation gathered from across (South) Hampshire, it would tend to be for something of an event – if not a festival then at the very least a Friday night, or a Shabbat afternoon – so the blessings would be delivered with a certain sense of occasion.

But those moments, I suppose, represented a Jewish community at the peaks of its observance. The morning blessings in Regency Square, on a gloomy Tuesday morning, are a very different thing: the day-to-day ticking over of a practice that is far more rigorous and ingrained; the mundane daily endeavour of seeking connection with the eternal.

*

Another truism of Jewish life is that every Jew who goes to a *shul* also has at least one '*shul* we don't go to'. Spectacularly, at Regency Square, the *shul* that people don't go to . . . is the same *shul*.

The building is home to two different communities, each with their own distinctive flavour and approaches, and each of whom have a bracing and (quasi) affectionate disdain for the other. During the week, for the sake of securing a functioning minyan, members from both communities congregate in the one smaller hall, allowing for ongoing bickering and elaborate internecine rivalries to play out, only to be briefly interrupted by moments of communal prayer, before resuming in earnest.

Not only that, but there's actually a third *shul* upstairs, which *neither* group goes to – because both downstairs communities are in the Eastern European tradition known as Ashkenazi, and the small *shul* upstairs is in the Sephardi tradition, which incorporates Spanish, Portuguese, French, Yemenite, Iraqi, Middle Eastern and Egyptian Jews. Because this community is smaller still, their quest for a tenth man frequently involves poking their heads through the door of our hall, working out how many people are in our group, and then attempting to poach a spare to help make up the numbers. Frequently, that's my neighbour: 'Oop – I'm up,' he'll smile, 'Just like that. Ta-ra.' And he'll stroll off upstairs.

There are issues, of course, when the tenth man in the room is me. With polite, tight smiles, and sympathetic apologies, necks crane, heads turn, small talk is made, and the service stalls, until a real Jew can be found. Sometimes, I have to explain my presence to a newcomer who I can see silently totting up the faces in the room, confused as to why we haven't begun.

It isn't a surprise. I knew that this would be the case, and hardly expected rules to be waived on my account, no matter how winning my smile or breezy my morning hello. But the feeling of exclusion, of lingering on the periphery of acceptance . . . of not being who I know myself to be . . .

'I'm hoping to begin the Orthodox conversion process, you see,' I will quietly explain, and the newcomer will nod and smile politely. And we will wait.

Often Dayan Horowitz, the all-powerful headmaster, will be nearby, and if he hears me, and if he processes anything I have said, his expression gives nothing away.

The addition of daily synagogue attendance to my life does not transform me into an enlightened being. It just makes me more tired and more irritable. The sheen of the beginning of the adventure has worn off. Now, I'm just a man who feels out of his depth.

Eliana and I drift further apart. We – naturally – spend less time together, and the time we do spend together is often strained. Much of it is across Shabbat. Friday night dinners are still with Eliana's family, and on Saturdays Eliana and I now dutifully attend Regency Square *shul*, waiting around after the service, hovering nervously around the *kiddush* table at a respectful distance from one another, wilting under the gaze of the relevant authorities. It feels immensely stress-inducing to be seen by Dayan Horowitz, and yet extremely unwise not to be. On those occasions he briefly addresses us, my conversation is stilted and nervous, my eyes darting and panicky. One week he simply walks past me and briskly says, 'Hello, Sam', a two-word interaction which I turn over, despairingly, in my head for several days.

So our walk to, or from, the *shul* will frequently devolve into a fierce argument. I will feel waterlogged with a week's worth of early-morning Judaism, and yet here will be another double portion of it.

I'll make some bitter, sulky comment about Orthodoxy, Eliana will furiously defend the thing she loves above all else, and suddenly we'll be in the midst of a full-blown row.

'Of course I don't think it's OK to have slaves!'

'I'm not saying *you* do, but this week's Torah portion had all these passages—'

'Yep, and at the time they were amongst the most progressive things written on the subject!'

'Sure, but—'

'Also it's sort of a mistranslation – they were more like servants, there was a strict moral code. Plus, it was thousands of years ago, and no Jews today are saying it should still be practised!'

'I'm not suggesting anyone's actually in favour of it, but why not just *not* read out the verse that suggests slavery's a thing and these are the instructions for how to do it well?!'

Eliana and I will stubbornly argue to the point of exhaustion, through Shabbat afternoon and long into the night, eventually reconciling not because we've resolved anything particularly, but because neither of us can take it any longer, and we've reached a point where there's nothing more to be said other than an emotionally drained 'I love you'.

The weekday mornings come back around, and, as I make my way to synagogue, Eliana will sometimes send affectionate, encouraging messages.

I feel like they've been sent out of guilt. The knowledge that these wheels have been set in motion due to her needs.

I will muster a half-hearted response. And I'll feel that in doing so I'm being petulant, frustrated that I'm failing to respond to these challenges – challenges I rigorously researched and prepared for – with any real degree of stoicism.

At nights, my sleep is fractious and poor. And if I ever arrive at the synagogue even a few seconds later than Dayan Horowitz, I feel a stab of stress that bleeds into my entire week.

One Saturday morning I am sitting reading a book, awaiting the knock on the front door from Eliana, collecting me on our inevitable journey to the synagogue, and I discover something which stops me in my tracks.

It is a book about the conversion process, written by an Orthodox Jewish lawyer and academic.* And it says this:

> As a matter of Jewish law, upon conversion a person acquired an entirely new identity, as a result of which he or she ceases technically to be related to their former family.

I feel sick.

> A convert is given a Hebrew name, for which purpose they can choose any first name they like, and in place of the normal patronymic by reference to their natural father they are referred to as 'son of Abraham our Father'.

So as for the question that I urgently sought the answer to before I committed to the process – 'Can I keep my Hebrew name?' – the answer is – how terribly, terribly Jewish – both yes and no. Because whilst I can keep my first name, Jacov, the conversion process deems it fit to sever me from my parents – even, for pity's sake, from my father, my *halachically* Jewish, 110 per cent Ashkenazi father, the man who sat and taught me Hebrew, and led our family's hugely theatrical Passover meals, and played me the Jewish music – jazz-like *klezmer* standards and soulful Ladino melodies – that I grew up feeling I had always known.

* Greenberg, D., *How to Become Jewish (and Why Not To)* (Self-published, 2009)

I can only conceive of two very different ways to rationalise this knowledge – and both of them feel wrong. If I attempt to simply shrug it off, and force myself not to care, then I am dismissing the entire process as hollow, an exercise in rote box-ticking; it's all meaningless, right? Some made-up name you're barely ever called gets changed slightly. Who's going to know; who's going to care? If I tell myself that this bit doesn't matter at all, then why does *any* of this process matter?

And yet if I *am* to find value in the conversion, and if it does matter, then how can I be anything other than revolted by this needless act of cruelty – a refusal to acknowledge my connection to my own parents.

Either way, my thoughts on the subject can be reduced down to the following: how fucking dare you.

Weeks tick by. Each morning, I journey to the minyan – fruitlessly checking my inbox and the doormat for any response from the Beth Din, in a pointless ritual that becomes as much a part of my routine as the coffee I shakily pump out of the machine if I can spare the thirty-five seconds it takes from button press to final drip (I have, by necessity, honed the journey from bed to *shul* into an exact science).

I am still mostly unable to keep up with the recitals of the various blessings, but I do manage to at least learn their order. And, as the winter mornings begin to thaw, so too does my grasp of Hebrew, to the extent that I can, at times, work out where we are in the *siddur* by picking out words I hear, and finding them in the text.

By now, I am a regular. I see people complete their year of mourning and depart, and I see new mourners arrive. In one instance of black *shul* humour, a man is slow-clapped back into the room as he returns, having just lost another parent only a few months after his previous year of mourning ended.

'Heard from 'em yet?' my neighbour will ask, and I'll shake my head quietly – nervous to even address the subject aloud, lest doing so be overheard by the man judging me in the corner, and somehow taken as insolence. 'Well, just you keep on. It'll be worth it. You know, I wasn't so much for all this synagogue business when I was younger, but when I met my wife she said I'd better start taking it all seriously if I wanted to marry her, and now here I am.' And he gives a friendly chuckle. He seems delighted by the way life has turned out. 'Just like that.'

CHAPTER 13

We'll Be in Touch

I do keep on keeping on. Contributing, impotently, to the minyan each morning. Smiling, brightly and hopefully – yet meekly and unproblematically – at my indifferent assessor. Certain only of the total uncertainty which is now shaping my life, as I stumble and mumble my way through my morning blessings.

The total lack of any formal acknowledgement from the relevant authority adds what feels like a glint of madness to these daily rituals. I am, in so many ways, engaged in what feels like a very one-sided correspondence.

I hold out little hope for a response from Hashem, who I presume has a fairly big backlog to work through before reaching my tentatively delivered, poorly pronounced offerings.* But when it comes to my engagement with the Beth Din, I swiftly develop a rich, vivid fantasy life in which my every movement is being monitored by an advanced network of hidden CCTV cameras, well-placed spies, and state-of-the-art tracking devices which I have somehow unknowingly ingested (palmed subtly into the scrambled eggs, no doubt). They are remaining in the shadows by choice, I reassure myself, but they have a radar – and I am on it. My abundance of devotion is being logged.

---

* I also take solace in the pragmatism of Judaism even at its most religious, in which the general school of thought seems to be: whilst talking to G-d is to be encouraged, if you hear G-d talking back, seek immediate help.

When panic swells, or frustration builds, or *ennui* threatens to set in (any combination of the above proving more than capable of tackling me to the floor at any given moment), I take pains to remind myself that, although I might feel adrift right now, the process is not, technically, impossible. Obviously I know this. For one thing, I spoke to a host of people during my careful, (over) elongated period of decision-making, many of whom had navigated this exact journey. This isn't forever. There is an 'other side'. And what might that other side be like? Well . . .

'Come on in, guys!'
'So good to see you!'
Eliana's university friend, Jake, and his partner Rachel – his wife, no less – warmly usher us into their stunning flat, full of just the right number of books and a plurality of wine decanters ('Honestly, when you get married, everyone gives you decanters!').

For reasons not at all dissimilar to Eliana and me (a *halachic* hiccup in his past), the pair embarked – successfully – on the conversion. Now, in the diffused light of their unfeasibly stylish home – the type of place that couples live in in TV dramas, that make you roll your eyes and go 'well, obviously *that* isn't realistic' – over glasses of decanted kosher wine, they're going to tell us how they made it to the promised land.

It started badly, for one thing. An initial meeting so blundersome that it set them back a full six months.

'When I turned up to the first meeting with the Beth Din I wasn't wearing a *kippah*,' says Jake. This was a sartorial choice they didn't care for. 'That was definitely on me. But then other stuff they just don't tell you.'

Go on?

'Well, I came alone. Because it was only me who was invited

to the meeting. But, actually, they want you to be there with your partner – they want to see you're both an equal part of the process.'

In the full knowledge that I too would have fallen at this hurdle, lacking as I do the requisite skills in mind-reading, I inwardly wince in relief.

Jake and Rachel explain that, following this unpromising start, they doubled-down on their efforts and took pains to ensure that they were never again unprepared for a meeting.

As such, they seem to now know it . . . all. And as they generously communicate the whirlwind of their experiences, I hurriedly write down the facts, timings and variables that spill out of them.

The Beth Din will meet with us approximately every six months, and they meet on Tuesdays and tend to email on Wednesdays, except when they email at other times, or post you things, and there's never anything as clear as a 'Yes, you're on the course' – in fact there isn't a course, except there is, and I'll know I'm on it once you've been allocated a tutor, except they'll almost certainly want Eliana to have a tutor first, and once I've got a tutor I'll then want to be given the green light to move in with a family, in fact I might want move into that area of town beforehand anyway to start finding my feet, and either way, once I'm in that area, these are the *shuls* that are most accessible, the rabbis who speak most compellingly, the communities who are most inviting . . .

It is a dizzying bombardment of information.

Eliana takes it in her stride – she's far better than I am at absorbing the new. But then, also, less of this is entirely new to her – whilst she too is out of her comfort zone, she's closer than I am to the strangeness of it all.

We naturally peel off into pairs – Eliana with Rachel and me with Jake – and fall into hushed conversations on opposite sides of the flat. How . . . how did you do it? What was it like, moving into a stranger's spare room? And, Jake, forgive me for asking, but did you have to have . . .?

He didn't. Having experienced a more conventional Jewish childhood than I, Jake was spared the full gore of late-in-life surgery, and instead experienced the out-and-out weirdness of the ritual bloodletting of the tip of his penis. 'I was not prepared for how casual the whole thing was,' says Jake. 'It happened in his drawing room. He called in two blokes from across the road to come and be the witnesses. One was washing his car.'

Eventually, the evening descends, and it's time for us to leave Rachel and Jake to reorganise their decanters, or whatever married couples do.

'Honestly, if you have any further questions, just ask,' they say as we depart their dream home. I am laden with books and panic. I have nothing but further questions.

But, as Eliana and I discuss on the drive back, Jake and Rachel have offered – as well as huge quantities of completely invaluable advice – a tantalising taste of what is possible. A window into post-conversion life.

They exist in a world in which a couple can be a couple, serene and relaxed and bonded, living happily together in their own home, and the conversion is a memory – a fraught and challenging one, clearly, but a memory nonetheless.

'Ugh, it all just seems so *nice*,' says Eliana. 'Can we just have their lives, please?'

I project myself into our future. The conversion has been completed without a hitch. We have navigated our various meetings with calmness and poise. Shortly before the end of the process, an ancient piece of Aramaic was decoded by theologians which revealed that the word for 'circumcision' had long been mistranslated, and what the Torah was actually advocating for was just 'a nice warm bath followed by a deep-tissue massage', so I have that ceremonially done to me instead. Eliana and I are now married, and we contentedly welcome people into our home – an airy and spacious mid-century modern paradise, containing a plurality of SMEG products ('Honestly, when you get married, everyone gives you beautiful but overpriced Italian kitchen appliances!').

Right now, it's a distant, flickering mirage. But, as I know, as I've *seen*, it can be done.

For now, I turn my mind back to the business at hand – separating from Eliana once more, and pouring myself into bed in anticipation of the morning minyan. A despondent beigeness sets in.

As I close my eyes that night, the one thing that sticks in my mind is Jake's advice.

'Just when you're on the verge of giving up – that's when they'll get in touch.'

And, just when I'm on the verge of giving up, they do.

The words 'Beth Din' appear as a push notification on my phone. Immediately, the rest of reality fades into the background – all that exists is the slow-loading email app on my screen.

It is six weeks since my journey may or may not have begun – which is to say, something has clearly begun, but it feels impossible at this stage to perceive whether I'm travelling towards my intended destination, or indeed any destination at all, other than possibly a state of emotional collapse. I had been warned to expect some delay prior to any acknowledgement, but the subsequent silence had been so profound that my sponsoring rabbi eventually suggested I try another email address, one different to the point of contact listed on the Beth Din's website. It is from this address, I realise, as my phone loads the message with almost insolent slothfulness, that I have received my first actual response of any sort from the Beth Din.

My letter... I hold my breath, my soul ready to be slingshotted off towards its new destiny...

My letter... I close and restart my email app, and curse whatever signal blackspot I'm trundling through...

My letter...

...

My letter... wasn't received.

Right.

No, for some reason they had no record of my previous message. Yes, they have received it now. An official response will emerge in due course.

On one level, this is a body blow. However, I am nothing if not optimistic. And, just as it is entirely possible for someone to receive a brief two-sentence rejection from the *New Yorker* magazine and clutch it dear to their heart, thrilled that they are now officially 'in correspondence with the *New Yorker* regarding a feature!', so too could this missive from some anonymous bureaucratic outer promontory of the Beth Din be viewed in a positive light.

They know who I am. Or, well, they clearly don't know who I am, but at least now they're *aware* that they don't know who I am – which, in and of itself, is a step towards a world in which they do! So that's great!

You see? Everything can be positive ~~when you're borderline delusional~~ with the right mindset.

Two relaxing months later, I receive formal acknowledgement of my application. It comes from a more senior figure within the organisation, and is a message of some length and care, taking pains to remind me of the difficulties one might face, both during the period of conversion and afterwards and explaining that if I am truly interested in pursuing this further I should write back to that effect. The heading of the letter reads 'CONVERTING TO JUDAISM (REGULARISATION OF JEWISH STATUS)'. It appears that I am, as it stands, an Irregular Jew. Which feels about right.

Both Eliana and I spend sleepless nights composing lengthy, effusive letters in response. I discuss my career as a comedian and writer – acknowledging that it's an eccentric career by any measure, and outlining the lengths I've taken to ensure that my work might be compliant with an observant Jewish lifestyle. A swift edit, and re-edit, and reread, and barely suppressed panic attack later, and it is sent off into the ether. A brief sense of accomplishment and occasion, before the doubt and worry begins to build up once again.

The three subsequent messages I receive from the Beth Din, delivered at intervals as irregular as my Jewish status, become exercises in deep breathing and expectation management.

The first is a month later.

My phone buzzes with the notification I have been waiting for – a response to my response.

It loads . . .

. . .

. .

.

'Thank you, Max. I'm looking into why you have not heard back from us. We have had some IT problems and I suspect that is the problem.'

And so life goes on.

The second message inches things forward, slightly – it's an *actual* response to my response to their response, confirming that they are willing to send me a formal Conversion Application form! Which, naturally, they will deliver by post – ('As we do not favour distributing these electronically, you can expect to receive this by Royal Mail in due course . . .') – at which point I should respond and await their response.

And the third message sends me careening down an emotional cul-de-sac. It is an email informing me of two surprising but wonderful developments; the Beth Din are proceeding directly to assigning me a tutor! And what's more, they seem to have come to the conclusion that they accept me as Jewish! My eyes dart across the words repeatedly, my heart leaping in bewildered excitement – 'in the first instance I have appointed a tutor with whom for Max to study'. . . 'his Jewish status is not in question' – surely it's all too good to be true?

Ah. Yes. It is.

The email was meant for a separate couple, one featuring a different Max – a *halachically* Jewish Max – and his non-Jewish (or Irregularly Jewish?) partner Michelle. Who I have been cc'd in with. Hello, Michelle. Best of luck with everything.

Admittedly, viewed from a certain angle, this series of communiqués perhaps blows a hole in my theory that the Beth Din is an all-knowing organisation keeping meticulous track of my every movement – painting a picture instead of a small, haphazard, overworked administrative body with a slightly *laissez-faire* approach to GDPR.

But what if that's all careful psychological manipulation? What if the other Max's girlfriend is actually a sock-puppet account run by the Beth Din, designed to log my responses to pressurised situations such as this one? What if I'm actually at the centre of some grand and intricate plan, and not merely an afterthought, tumbling backwards through the cracks of reality and desperately seeking order amidst chaos? I shall simply never know.

Finally, in June, a letter arrives on my doormat. I open the envelope.

The logo on the top of the page reads: **London Beth Din**, and then, in smaller text, 'Court of the Chief Rabbi'. I feel my heart begin to pound. It's here: *'Application Form for Candidacy for Conversion to the Jewish Faith'*

The pages themselves say nothing about faith. Instead, there are a series of dry requests; for copies of personal documents – hastily found – and for a £50 processing fee made out to the United Synagogue. I hurriedly fill in the form with a nervous, shaky hand – my dubious-at-best left-handed scrawl becoming even more illegible than usual.

And I walk to the postbox at the entrance of Primrose Hill, and send off the letter. A mere six months after the conversion process began, the conversion process . . . has begun. I am travelling, at least, in the right direction.

CHAPTER 14

The Diagnosis

It is the very next day. A warm afternoon in mid-June. I am still on a high from the 'win' of having been acknowledged, when my mum asks me to phone her.

'Your father has been diagnosed with dementia.'

The words seem heavy and unreal.

I am cycling through a sun-dappled Regent's Park. It is a picturesque, beautiful day.

'The consultant seemed very sure. Your father is calm, relaxed.'

I pull over to the side of the road. I say very little, and listen to my mum.

She tells me that, when asked by the consultant how he felt about the diagnosis, he responded, 'It feels bad on my ego.'

Sharp, silly, self-deprecating, whimsical. All Dad. But seemingly nothing that this stressed, irritable, analytical-minded doctor understood. It was a use of language and a way of thinking that didn't sit within the parameters of his tick-box form. To the consultant, it was just further indication of a state of decline.

'Oh, Ma. I'm so sorry.'

'So am I, darling.'

Eliana and I are, technically, still in the middle of a completely pointless argument about whether or not bowing to a statue of

Buddha whilst on holiday would be a sacrilegious violation of Jewish laws against idol worship, or perfectly permissible because Buddha wasn't technically deemed to be a god. But, when I walk into the room, she looks at my expression and it's instantly forgotten.

'Max, what's wrong?'

As I start to try and talk, my words collapse in on themselves and I am sobbing furious tears.

And perhaps at this moment it would have been wrong of her to wrap her arms around me and console me. Or perhaps it would not.

We travel down to Portsmouth the next day. My brothers and their partners, too.

It's always a little warmer down on the coast, and today is particularly sunny, summery.

And here's Dad. Happy and contented and bearded, with a colourful jumper and an inexhaustible appetite. I hug him tightly, and kiss him on his bald head, and we chat, and drink tea together.

I play the piano badly, and Dad sings along, throwing out suggestions for obscure songs which I attempt to improvise along to. It is the thing we have always done – combine my dad's inexhaustible supply of old songs with my ever-optimistic attempts to will a tune from my rudimentary piano playing. My brothers join in, singing and playing, and my parents dance together.

We sit and we eat together as a family.

Dad seems to be himself. Charming, happy.

And, in the evening, I sit with Dad and we talk about it. He speaks calmly, reflectively, wittily, mischievously and candidly. He confesses to lapses in memory over the last year or so. Of sometimes having to search for words, in ways he hadn't before. I think, too, about moments of confusion Dad has experienced over the last few years – incidents that, up until now, we've explained away as a family, writing them off as part of Dad's happily-disorganised way of engaging with the world.

He is such a gentle person.

I will it into not existing. I demand that it isn't true.

I come back to London. I go through the motions of various work projects.

As is the inexplicable way of things, life continues.

But how can it?

How can the Upper Crust concession at Waterloo continue to blithely pump out undrinkable gritty coffee, as though entirely unmoved by my situation?

How can the No. 25 bus continue to slowly work its way down Whitechapel High Street – past every address I ever lived at in east London until I landed in the Docklands, and was then teleported to northwest London – feigning ignorance of the seismic changes playing out in my family home?

How dare the world continue existing with the same bustling indifference when there has been a fundamental pitch shift in the way I experience reality?

Don't people realise?

Each morning, at synagogue, there is a blessing in which one can pray for the health of a loved one. Each morning, I mouth my father's Hebrew name and I pray harder than anyone has ever prayed since prayer began.

And at the end of each service, Dayan Horowitz makes another blessing, on behalf of the minyan, wishing a speedy recovery to those who require it.

So, each morning, I queue up and I quietly recite the Hebrew name of my father to the man who, if all goes 'well', will be instrumental in forever separating us from one another.

'Shmuel ben Hannah,' says Dayan Horowitz, each morning. One anonymous name in a list of many.

And despite my outrage and fury at the wrongness of it all, I clutch the blessing tightly to my chest as I cycle out into the world.

Over the next days and weeks, as I attempt to come to terms with the dull horror of this new reality, another realisation starts to take shape. At first, the thought remains unformed and unvoiced – a distant, stressful combination of the unknowable and the unthinkable – and for want of any practical means of dealing with it, it's something that I suppress. Until, one afternoon, my mum mentions it on the phone anyway.

'Obviously, the idea is that you and Eliana would get married at the end of all this . . . so maybe it might be good to communicate to the Beth Din that it is important to you that your father is able to participate meaningfully in your wedding.'

My general approach has been one of, whilst not outright denial, certainly addressing the existence of the condition as little as possible, on the sound medical basis that if we discuss it, it might overhear us and feel encouraged. So when we talk about Dad, we often do so in terms of his accomplishments – things that disprove the notion that he may be growing less capable; a poem he has written that day, or an afternoon spent happily strolling around Southsea, unattended, eating lunch and acquiring some crucial second-hand books and genially chatting to passers-by and eating another lunch and ambling home (sometimes, heroically, to eat lunch). The notion of a decline of any sort is not something I wish to entertain. But Mum, who, despite being an artist, has always melded the creative with the practical – one does not deliver '800 lanterns handmade by mad Portsmouth schoolchildren' on time by accident – is prepared to be clear-sighted. And, as ever, hearing it said out loud makes it more real.

And later, when I sit with Eliana, I force myself to raise it.

'I know, I know,' she says. 'Please don't think I haven't been thinking it too, my love.'

And, as Eliana gently reminds me, it's not just my dad that we must think of.

CHAPTER 15

Lion

Eighty-nine years old, with a wasp-thin waist and an endless wardrobe of designer clothes, Lion is the most glamorous grandmother I have ever met.

Our first face-to-face encounter, after the Zoom meetings of deep lockdown, took place when restrictions were eased slightly; Eliana and I came to the front door of her flat and sat in the art deco foyer on chairs metres away from her, and chatted for hours.

When the lockdown begins to subside, and vaccines are distributed, we are able to go and visit her properly, and it becomes a weekly ritual, Lion welcoming us into her exquisite flat – Eliana hugging her tightly, me greeting her with sweetie-darling air-kisses on each cheek, 'mwah, mwah' (our delivery gradually becoming more theatrical each time we meet) – and the three of us proceeding to her living room, where Lion holds court.

She has lived one of those grand lives that seem to bestride the twentieth century: evacuated from London during the war, sent off to complete her education in Switzerland ('Where I was finished,' she says, with a twinkle), then returning from finishing school to become a house model for couturiers, where she dressed in the finest gowns, and was once dispatched into a changing room to help Hollywood bombshell Jayne Mansfield out of her dress, to the awestruck envy of her male colleagues. When she met Charles, the man who would become her husband, at a Jewish charity event, there was pushback from her parents, and their circle, proud, assimilated Jews, because he was 'a refugee'. But Lion didn't care, and they married, soon moving from suburban Stanmore to Primrose Hill because, incredibly, 'Large houses in Primrose Hill weren't in fashion then, so we got it for a steal . . .'

Here, in their allegedly unfashionable gorgeous house, with Charles's business career thriving, the pair became patrons of the arts; their home effectively a cultural salon where Lion would play host to an ever-changing assortment of theatrical and artistic waifs and strays – leading opera singers, actors and directors, as well as whichever stragglers Charles had rounded up after *shul* and brought back for lunch on a Saturday afternoon. Arias were performed over the chicken soup, and theatrical gossip exchanged as the roast potatoes were passed around the table.

'The lead male opera singer that season was in love with me,' says Lion, in a typical aside, 'though of course he was quite, quite gay.'

And then there were the artists. Lion felt a deep affinity for modern art – again, before it was in vogue – and began to collect not just paintings but friendships. She was drawn to the work that delighted her, gradually amassing a world-class collection, and many of those artists – Man Ray, Christo, Wifredo Lam – became her confidants and part of her social circle. David Hockney was amongst them – one of his photo collages sits on the wall of Lion's flat, and near the entrance there is a line drawing of Hockney's, depicting a smiling Charles, his mutton chops gloriously fat, rendered in brown pencil.

Before long, news of Lion's affinity for art got out. When Charles was entertaining business associates at home, they would ask, wide-eyed, where Lion had sourced such a work – 'Oh, from the artist, of course!' she would respond – and then, inevitably, they would ask whether she could acquire a piece for them.

She could, and so she fell into art dealing – though she was often horrified by the nature of the requests she received. 'It all went wrong when art became a *commodity*,' she says, her lips curling in distaste. 'They would say, "Can you get me a Dubuffet from such and such a year", because they'd heard that was the fashionable year, and I would say, "Well, no, but I could get you one from another year, and it happens to be extremely beautiful, and shouldn't the point be that you find it beautiful?"'

Far more appealing was the chance to support new artists, which she did at small galleries she opened specifically to showcase young and emerging talents. And then there was the theatre, and the opera at Glyndebourne (where she has been a member since the 1960s, and occupies seats so well-located they are more or less onstage), and dinners at Le Caprice – 'Oh, we went to the original one, darling, "the red hell", we called it, because of that fabulous red bar. We were there more or less every week . . .'

It was only when Charles became ill that the big house was sold, along with some of Lion's beloved paintings; they moved one road away, to the immaculate flat where Lion receives us, and where – until very shortly before I stepped into Eliana's world – Charles had been cared for by Lion and a group of nurses during the years in which he suffered with dementia, until eventually his suffering stopped.

On the first Sunday following my time in the wilderness, Eliana and I return to Lion's flat together once more. I am glad to see the diminutive, impish figure welcoming us again at her doorway. I have missed her.

'Oh, darling, I'm so happy,' says Lion, of the strange new chapter we're pursuing, 'although it's ridiculous, all these things you have to do – you're Jewish anyway.'

It's a throwaway comment that quietly delights me – and in my periphery I feel Eliana wince at its disruptive tremors.

'It will all be very strange, you know. Will you have to grow the curly-wurlies?' asks Lion, waggling her fingers by her cheekbones, imitating the sidelocks of the ultra-Orthodox.

Lion is religiously irreligious, a full-time synagogue avoider – her indifference making up the balance to Charles's fervour, perhaps. She keeps a kosher home, of course, and has hosted innumerable Friday nights, and Shabbat lunches, and grand Rosh Hashanah dinners over the years, but hers is a brand of Judaism that has never been contingent on the approval of a rabbi.

Back when she and Charles lived in their large house on the corner, as she delights in telling me, whenever rabbis needed to come to the house and speak to Charles for some reason, she would invite them into the dining room and sit them down at the table. There, directly in their eyeline, there happened to be an eye-catching painting; a Great American Nude, by Tom Wesselmann. Lion would delight in her private game of noting which of their guests afforded themselves a discreet glance, and which of them made a studied point of looking away.

She has even less time for the Beth Din, about whom she speaks freely and naughtily, delivering heroically unsubstantiated tales – 'Oh, they can be terribly wicked . . .' – that cause Eliana to blanch with panic and try to urgently intervene, vainly attempting to close the floodgates as Lion launches into some colourful, highly unsourced story about the various evils the court has apparently perpetrated over the years: conversions they have sabotaged, scandals they have suppressed, outrages they have been front-and-centre of.

As Lion throws around these cavalier allegations I feel the tension rising in Eliana, who is caught between an instinctive state of deference to her matriarch and a growing exasperation at how spectacularly unhelpful she is being. Lion, heedless, stirs the pot gleefully.

Despite Lion's vitality – she still drives, I learn, to my amazement and mild terror – the fact that she has lived to such a grand age is remarkable, given that throughout her life, it seems, she has been on the brink of death. She was born with a congenital (and, when she was born, little-understood) condition that makes it almost impossible for her to swallow.

She has overcome cancer, twice.

In 1972, she survived a flash explosion in which her face was severely burnt – she wore a veil for years, as she recovered. In 1996, she survived a car crash.

Nowadays, to combat the constant pain, she wears a morphine patch on her arm ('Oh, didn't you know, darling – I'm a junkie,' she says, as she adjusts it).

When I first meet her, despite being a little stooped ('I'm bent, you see!' she says, irritated, when her posture is giving her trouble), she moves quickly and appears in full flight, physically and mentally.

Her daily routine is magnificent; it begins with breakfast in bed, delivered by her housekeeper, before she rises at midday.

At some point before we arrive, she has inevitably read the day's global news headlines and developed iron-clad opinions on all of them, which she delivers with the weary authority of someone who was personally briefed by the relevant ambassador that morning (and, good grief, it seems entirely possible that she might have been).

In fact, she has read or watched everything – the latest TV show, the entire Booker longlist. Until Covid struck, she would be at the theatre on a weekly basis and could be found in the stalls of every well-reviewed play in town (a good few days before the reviews came out, naturally). Now, in this time of airborne confusion, she eschews live entertainment at the behest of her grateful and worried children and grandchildren, and instead takes pains to whirr through any and all of the must-watch TV series.

She is entirely adept at using her iPhone and iPad, is a formidable bridge player (she is very unimpressed with her longtime bridge partner, who has selfishly died), and retains up-to-the-second intelligence on the actions of every member of her extended family.

Her lunch and dinner are both served at fixed times, and she sits to eat a formal meal at her table, her housekeeper answering a bell(!) and emerging from the kitchen to serve each course.

It is an astonishing lifestyle from a different era.

Although she is close to ninety, and physically frail, it seems rather impossible to think of Lion as 'old' – it's just that she's been an adult for an immense amount of time.

As such, she is unflappable, and unshakeable. There is, seemingly, absolutely nothing she hasn't done, and she has what appears to be perfect recall (or, at least, the unwavering confidence of someone who firmly believes themselves to have perfect recall).

On one occasion, in an attempt to finally brush up against the outer perimeter of her life experience, I mentioned that I'd heard that someone in a grand townhouse a few roads along from Lion had a button they pushed, which caused the floor of their house to open up and a swimming pool to appear. Her response? 'Oh, darling, of course, there was a gentleman we knew in the seventies, and he had a ballroom which had that very thing...'

One Sunday afternoon when we arrive at Lion's flat she is re-archiving her enormous collection of photographs of previous generations of her family – black-and-white and sepia images stretching back to the very start of the twentieth century. She sorts the images into various piles – some, we notice, are being thrown away. Eventually, Eliana notices a pattern.

'Lion, are you . . . getting rid of anyone who isn't attractive?'

'Of course not, darling.'

She definitely is.

We sit and talk, and listen to the eye-popping stories Lion casually mentions about her ancestors ('The surgeon marked my grandfather's left leg instead of the right by accident, you see, and so they cut the wrong one off!') as she either immortalises them in her folder or consigns them forever to the Dustbin of Insufficient Beauty.

This meeting is slightly more hurried than our usual meandering chat, and for a good reason – I have, finally, received the email that I have been both yearning for and dreading: Eliana and I have been invited for our first meeting with the Beth Din.

This meeting, as the email makes clear, is to decide whether the starting pistol might actually be fired. Everything that has transpired so far – my initial letter, the back-and-forth of subsequent correspondence, my daily synagogue attendance – has merely been an eight-month-long journey to the starting line. 'Please note that such an appointment would be for purposes of an initial evaluation only,' reads the email, 'and does not by itself guarantee Max's acceptance as a conversion candidate.'

It is to be on a Tuesday (just as Jake and Rachel predicted), and so Eliana and I have forty-eight hours in which to ready ourselves for the encounter.

'You must tell me how it goes,' says Lion, as she walks us to the front door. 'Mwah, mwah!'

And we leave her – to the hairdresser coming round to titivate her scarlet hair, to another relative coming round to visit, to her latest PT session (she has, within the last year, decided to take up weightlifting), to whatever is next in her schedule – and she waves us farewell from the doorway.

She is, by any standards, a remarkable woman. And she gives off every indication that she will live forever.

But there is always that tiny, whispering worry. How long will it take us to finish a process that we don't know if we'll even be allowed to begin?

CHAPTER 16

Meeting the Beth Din

The exterior of the building on Barnwood Drive is a study in dull anonymity. It speaks of serviced offices, perhaps refurbished in the mid-nineties. There are few defining features. It might house a mid-sized accountancy firm, or the administrative hub of a moderately successful carpet dealership, or a local radio station that mainly plays 'hits from the fifties through to the eighties' and adverts for the sofa emporium.

There is no sign. No hint of the crucible of power that is behind the doors. Only the elderly Jewish couple walking out of the front door suggests that this is the location.

'Good luck!' they say, as Eliana and I tentatively approach the entrance. They don't know exactly why we're here, but, regardless, it's an appropriate sentiment. Today is the day of our first appointment with the Beth Din.

The morning has been a flurry of nervous activity. Meticulously getting dressed, desperately overthinking every item of clothing, attempting to second-guess how I might come across. I opt for my smartest, most formal double-breasted navy-blue suit, and then agonise over whether or not to stuff in a pocket square like I usually would – as though that decision might hold the key to my fate. I do, eventually, opt for a pocket square, but one that's slightly less flamboyant than normal. A solemn pocket square, I tell myself, as it flounces in the breeze. Eliana knocks on the door, in a formal dress.

Given that, in a dazzling demonstration of my adult independence, I remain unable to drive (I had always meant to get round to learning how, but invariably found myself without the time, or money, or both – though it seems increasingly ridiculous that it's a skill I lack as I get older), it is Eliana who drives us from Primrose Hill to Finchley. Even the journey to our destination has taken on new religious significance – our unchaperoned proximity to one another deemed permissible by the laws of *halacha* due to the transparency of the car windows, through which the public at large can attest to the modesty of our behaviour.

As we sit in traffic, we are both on edge. Breathing deeply. Long silences. Fidgeting. Knowing that there is no way to predict how this encounter will play out, or what our lives will look like on the other side. As we arrive, and walk towards the entrance, and nod and smile distractedly at the old couple wishing us luck, I feel gravity exerting ever more force on me – a pressure pushing me relentlessly into the floor.

'Whatever happens,' says Eliana, 'we'll be OK.' And I nod and smile a watery smile. It strikes me that there are a host of things that could happen that might mean we're not OK, actually – but now doesn't feel like the time.

At the front desk, it begins. An unsmiling security guard behind a screen demands our photo ID. It is taken, scanned, returned. We are let in, and stand inside an airlocked hatch.

The doors open, and we move forwards into a waiting room.

And there we wait.

Time slows to sludge.

When one meets with the Beth Din, one is not informed which of the Dayanim will be interviewing you. So one's imagination is free to spiral off in a million and one directions, and generate a billion hypothetical conversations with an infinite array of stern-faced gatekeepers. Who will it be?

Hurried, hushed men and women cross the corridors.

Eliana and I make furtive eye contact – our primary form of contact, at this point – attempting to work out if any of the passers-by might be for us. But no – it's not him . . . or him . . .

The waiting, I realise, is all part of it. From the very start. From firing off your first letter, to awaiting a response via email, to sitting in a waiting room. Their inefficiency is a supremely efficient means of reminding you where you stand. Or sit. Or pace.

And eventually, after lifetimes upon lifetimes, the head of the Beth Din, Dayan Landau, emerges at the top of the stairwell, and we are summoned.

'Hello, friends! This way!'

There is a cheeriness, bordering on jauntiness, to his manner – something that certainly hadn't featured in any of the fractured kaleidoscopic versions of this scenario that had played out in my head during the time that Eliana and I were waiting.

But no, the head of the Beth Din is, there's no way around it, somewhat bouncy. He leads us through an office space which could be a part of any generic council building in the country – and then into a room which could not.

There is a throne – an actual throne – in the room. The walls are lined with Hebrew books – many of them vast. And, again, there is – I fight the impulse, but my eyes keep darting back to it, unavoidably – a throne in the room.

We sit down in the room with the throne in it, and Dayan Landau sits opposite us, where he is joined by another Dayan. Neither of them sit on the throne. That's simply very much in the room.

Dayan Landau begins to speak. He opens a file, examines

my paperwork, and he talks about my case. He is thoughtful, studious.

He acknowledges that the term used on the initial letter I received is 'Regularisation' – but this, he makes clear, is simply a nod to the existing identity that would-be converts in my position might perceive themselves to have. Beyond that one-word acknowledgement, the Beth Din makes no further accommodations; what we are here to discuss is, in every way, a full conversion. The process is not an easy one, and not likely to be particularly quick – and then Dayan Landau looks up at me, a man straining to change the trajectory of his life via the power of a conversation. 'I can see you are desperate to speak. So. What would you like to say?'

And I begin.

I pour out my heart. I explain my childhood, and my background, and my parents' move to connect us to the most vibrant Jewish traditions we might be able to experience, and my decision to become *bar mitzvah*, and my life as a writer and performer, and how that led me to meet Eliana in the midst of an arts festival, and how a connection to Judaism first drew us together, and then pushed us apart, and how now, after a great deal of meticulous soul-searching, we hope that it might provide the basis for a life together, and as I talk I can feel the formation of a glistening bead of sweat on my left temple, just above my eyebrow, and I feel certain that if I were to wipe it away, or acknowledge it, or do anything at all other than look into the eyes of these men across the table and try to communicate my story – the ending of which they currently hold in the palms of their hands – everything would come crashing down around me. I aim to be, all at once, humble but confident, reverential yet relaxed, entirely myself and everything they want me to be. As I speak, in the corner of my eye

I see Eliana, her blue eyes glistening in silent support. And also the massive throne.

I finish speaking.

My monologue is . . . acknowledged. They have listened. We move on.

They turn to my notes.

'It says here you're a writer . . . for magazines . . .?'

I explain that I write about all sorts of things – that I'm fascinated by the world.

Fair enough.

'And . . . comedy?'

Here we go.

'And what kind of a job is that? D'you get paid enough?'

To be fair, they've got me on that one.

But also – the interrogation seems avuncular. They appear concerned for my welfare – more bemused by my life choices than disapproving of them.

I explain that I realise that my vocation isn't the usual path. But I know that one needn't be incompatible with the other.

They nod. Fair enough.

And then Dayan Landau returns to his earlier theme: the challenges ahead.

'You know, to become Jewish – there are many rules. Some of them might even come across as strange to the outsider. In fact – you know, you could even include them in one of your comedy shows, haha!'

'Haha!'

To my astonishment, we're all good-naturedly laughing together – and then, incredibly, he cuts himself off mid-laugh.

'Hahah— No, G-d forbid!' It's a spectacular volte-face; suddenly he is entirely serious once more.

Dayan Landau emphasises the ordeal of it all. The living apart. The refraining from contact. The need for learning with a tutor. The likelihood I will need to move in with a family. And the procedure at the end of it all, which might just be a pinprick or a – no, in my case, the full works. At this, the other Dayan leans in, curious.

'You're . . . prepared to do that?'

I nod. 'I am. I can't pretend that it's something I relish the prospect of. But I understand that it's a key part of the process.'

They nod.

And you, young lady?

The laser beam is turned to Eliana, and now she speaks. About her lifelong love for her identity – her family, her grandparents' survival, growing up as part of Beit Shalom, her deep affection for her community.

Her words, like mine, are absorbed into the silence.

So how long does the process take? Ehhh . . . it depends! There is no set length of time. It's entirely impossible to say. But also . . . eighteen months. If all goes well.

I write down the figure, enthusiastically. Too enthusiastically. I am told to cross it out – they won't be held to that length of time. I dutifully cross it out.

After ninety minutes, we are stood back outside in anonymous, suburban north London. Exhausted. Drained. But we have survived our first meeting.

I said everything I wanted to say – except one thing. We have been advised by our circle of Supportive Rabbis that, in this first meeting, I should refrain from telling the Beth Din about my father's condition. They will feel a sense of pressure, and they won't like it. And so, acting against my every instinct, I refrained from discussing the changes in my father's life – the ticking clock that I simultaneously cannot bear to acknowledge, yet cannot stop thinking about. My silence was an act of extreme willpower. The sentences crowded my mouth, but I locked my jaw shut and swallowed them down.

There will be next steps. We will hear from them in due course. Not immediately. These things take time, they said.

Eight weeks later, we receive acknowledgement that, following our meeting, Eliana is to be assigned a tutor. Once she has completed ten hours of lessons, we may write to the secretary once more, requesting that the conversion coordinator communicate to the Beth Din our desire for another meeting.

Although there has been nothing so straightforward as a formal acceptance, it is here and now that, officially, exhaustedly, I have left the starting line.

And so that, too, represents another landmark. Ten months after beginning the process, we have . . . begun the process.

CHAPTER 17

Ohhh, You've Got the Wrong Soul Too?

'As soon as I found out, I just burst into tears. I had this total identity crisis – a meltdown, really. And then Russ and I split up for a bit, because it all seemed too much . . .'

I am having one of the most intense conversations I've ever had with a woman I met two minutes ago – and am surrounded by small groups of young professionals, all having variations of this same discussion.

It is a gathering that has been convened by another of Eliana's lifelong friends – her neighbour, Arielle, who, after eight years of dating her non-Jewish boyfriend, Baz, has recently found herself in a similar boat to us; on a joint quest for an Orthodox marriage, and navigating the subsequent life-upheaval that this brings about.

There are differences in their mission – firstly because they are their own people, replete with their own entirely unique family backgrounds, values, hopes, dreams and complications, and secondly because the conversion they are embarking on is Sephardi.

Those of you who have been taking notes in preparation for the test at the end of the book (only joking, the test will occur in person, in six months' time, on a highly in convenient

Tuesday afternoon. Dress smart.) will recall that 'Sephardi' is a term referring to Jews originating from the Iberian Peninsula, the Middle East, and so on – an ethnic grouping with its own traditions, tunes and rituals which differ from that of the Ashkenazi Jews of Eastern Europe. The American stand-up comic Modi Rosenfeld makes great play of the differences between these two cultures; the bolshy, alpha Sephardim versus the nebbish, angsty Ashkenazim.* So distinct are these two strands of Judaism that they each have their own distinct prayer books, orders of service, synagogues . . . and their own Beth Din.

There are actually multiple Batei Din (that's the plural of Beth Din, I'm afraid) out there – different courts attending to the varying needs of the Masorti, Reform and Liberal communities. But, because life is bewildering, there are also two *Orthodox* Batei Din in London that oversee conversions – and it is to the other one, the institution run according to Sephardic principles, that Arielle and Baz are pleading their case.

The reason for this is quite simple: Arielle is Sephardi. She is Sephardi because her father, of Egyptian descent, is Sephardi – and because her mother, a highly glamorous Swedish model, converted via the Sephardi Beth Din some years ago. As a result, Arielle and her siblings – all of them tall, willowy and blonde – make unlikely and glitteringly exotic additions to the Jewish gene pool.

It's a natural fit for them, then – they already have a clear connection to the Sephardi way of life. 'But frankly,' says Arielle, 'I'd have gone to them anyway if I had any choice. They're so much more sane.'

---

* It's somewhat reminiscent of a classic *Simpsons* episode in which Groundskeeper Willie delivers a piece of stand-up about the differences in putting technique between North Edinburgh golfers and South Edinburgh golfers – only instead of the indifferent silence Willie is greeted with, Modi's (almost entirely Jewish) audiences invariably respond with gales of laughter and recognition.

They've heard nightmarish things about couples attempting to convert via the Ashkenazi Beth Din. Couples whose conversion has taken seven years. People who simply haven't been permitted to complete their conversion. People who haven't even been allowed to start.

The Sephardi conversion programme is no walk in the park – it's rigorous, time-consuming, emotionally draining – but it appears to be underpinned by a certain layer of pragmatism.

One simple example of this is exemplified in the manner they run their conversions. As soon as someone is accepted on the course, they are introduced to other individuals, and couples, who are going through the same thing.

This idea, eminently sensible, immediately creates a state of conviviality and communality; a support network, a friendship group, a series of shoulders to cry on and study notes to crib from and lunches to be invited to.

The Ashkenazi conversion process, by contrast, is something that one embarks upon (eventually) entirely in a vacuum. There's not a single suggestion that it might be beneficial to spend time with people experiencing the same disorienting series of events as you – nothing so vulgar as 'pastoral support'.

As a result, Eliana and I find ourselves falling in with Arielle and Baz's crew of fellow aspiring-converts-and-their-partners – who, on this occasion, are convening for a casual late-afternoon Shabbat meal which, incredibly swiftly, transforms into a group-therapy session.

It is only once we all start talking – at a thousand miles per hour, nodding and empathising, excited and frustrated, tearful and relieved, hearing our experiences reflected in those of another – that I realise just how badly needed this has been.

*

Astonishingly, despite all of the afternoon coffees and long lunches and pub catch-ups that have been derailed by my endless, torturous soul-searching, I have managed to retain a circle of friends. They are drawn from the various eclectic chapters of my working life – comedy, magazines, wrestling – from university, from college, from all the way back to nursery school in some cases.

And friendships – deep, proper friendships that gain in quality and flavour over the years, like a good wok – are some of the things that are most sustaining and important to me in the world. A good friendship adds context and commentary to the absurd endeavour of being alive – it is a safe haven of collective memories and nonsensical in-jokes, an ongoing exercise in taking stock of the universe, and in creating the narrative by which to measure one's days.

The fact that I have this outlet means that, in many ways (as I remind myself when I'm feeling self-pitying), I'm incredibly fortunate.

But the problem is, as thoughtful and tolerant as my friends are, so convoluted are the conditions governing my life, and such is my state of emotional free fall, that none of our conversations can really touch the sides.

As the months go by, we'll make time to see one another, I'll ask them about their life, they'll bring me up to speed, and then, inevitably, they'll ask me for an update . . . at which point I'll vomit forth as much of the unwieldy story as I think they can stand. And they will gamely tolerate my incomprehensible rantings, and respond with concerned, well-meaning questions, and wish me luck with it all, and nod supportively (whilst, quite possibly, privately shaking their heads in concerned disbelief). It's a much-needed chance to vent. But it doesn't really get to the heart of things.

But talking to other people who are also in the midst of a conversion? Hook it to my veins.

'Before each meeting we'd just sit in the car together and scream. Get everything out.'

'Oh yeah, obviously I'm having nightmares about the Beth Din.'

'Have you started with a tutor yet? I've been writing up all my lessons on a Google doc, so you can use them as study notes if you want!'

'Honestly, everything you've just said? Exactly the same.'

'I had no idea how much I needed this.'

There's a slightly feral energy to this boozed-up exercise in mass-catharsis – everyone overcome with relief at the opportunity to have the hyper-specific conversations that simply can't be had elsewhere.

By the time we leave, a WhatsApp group has been formed, and we find ourselves invited to a dinner and informal tutoring session. Unbelievably, it is taking place at the Sephardic Beth Din.

Yes, in an arrangement that feels extraordinary to me, the Sephardic Beth Din not only encourages converts to mingle and socialise with one another, they also help facilitate the learning that is required of those on the programme.

The notion that one might have a positive relationship – or, in fact, *any* relationship – with the Dayanim, is, based on my experiences to date, mind-blowing.

But it is, indeed, the case; sat around some folding tables in a sparse meeting room at the Sephardic Beth Din's HQ, Arielle and Baz and their cohort spend occasional evenings actively learning about the intricacies of Jewish law with a Dayan, who sits and eats and chats with them, assuming the role of mentor and teacher, as opposed to simply presenting as a distant figure of fear. I don't spot a room containing a massive throne, but who's to say it isn't there somewhere.

'Honestly,' says Arielle, 'just jump ship. They're so much more reasonable.'

The prospect of a conversion process that might leave me more intact (emotionally, at least) is immensely tempting. But it's not actually a possibility. Not really. Because the thing is, Eliana is Ashkenazi to the core, and – even by our Beth Din's own judgement – so am I. In Orthodoxy, whilst Jewish status is famously conferred by the mother, one's cultural and liturgical traditions are passed down by the father. The Jewish hinterland I have inherited from my dad – with its Yiddishisms and its melodies – is entirely Ashkenazi. So whilst there might be a clear argument for my pursuing a conversion that appears more attuned to the realities of actual human beings, to do so would be to sever the delicate thread of connectedness to my own heritage that I have sought to strengthen.*

Arielle and Baz have started the process after us, so we're not quite 'in sync' – but I am hugely grateful that people we know are on parallel tracks. Just as it is a relief to have the guidance of Rachel and Jake, friends who have successfully traversed this path ahead of us and made it over the finish line – to be with people going through approximately the same thing, at approximately the same time, feels like a hugely potent source of support.

Anything that might make us feel less isolated is a much-needed development, as the conversion seeps further into the cracks of our lives. Eliana is now studying with her Beth Din-assigned tutor once if not twice a week (she is taking on as many

---

* Also, given my Ashki leanings, it's highly likely the Sephardic Beth Din would have passed us over to their counterparts anyway, even if we'd gone to them first, so it's all moot.

lessons as she is allowed, in a bid to progress us to the next phase of the process) and so is immersed in a whistlestop tour of the vastness of Jewish knowledge.

I, for my part, have been learning too – meeting for independent lessons with one of the Supportive Rabbis, taking care, as ever, to walk the tightrope between 'appropriate enthusiasm' and 'suspicious over-eagerness' by making it clear to the Beth Din that these sessions are entirely *informal*, strictly a precursor to any official tutoring I may or may not be lucky enough to have, and not an attempt at pre-empting or jump-starting any official processes.

And whilst Eliana's sessions are primarily on Zoom, mine are invariably in person. I am now regularly venturing, for the first time, to Golders Green – cycling past fast-walking teenaged boys in suits and wide-brimmed black hats, and elderly bearded men stood chatting on street corners, into the heart of the quadrant of London that is referred to by its Orthodox denizens as, simply, 'The Area'. Here, in a Supportive Rabbi's front room (book-lined, naturally – floor to ceiling), we sit and discuss, well . . . anything. He is intellectually omnivorous, and gives his prognostications on the subjects we discuss – which range from the beginnings of the laws of kosher to the nature of Jewish philosophy – with a delivery that is wry and knowing. The lessons themselves are stimulating – exciting, even. They feel vaguely like how I imagine it might be to have a tutorial with an Oxbridge don, someone with total mastery of a subject at their fingertips, hard-won from a lifetime of deep study.

But the encounters are also representative of the growing strangeness in my and Eliana's lives – our days increasingly given over to studying strange new concepts, and our time spent together increasingly unrepresentative of the way we would, under ordinary circumstances, have chosen to live.

As Eliana comes to finish the allotted series of classes she has been prescribed, she writes to the Beth Din to that effect, asking if it might be possible for my own learning to begin.

Her email goes unanswered.

What is one to do, in a situation such as this? When one exists in a state of total powerlessness?

We do the only thing we can possibly do; we wait, we keep our heads down, and we keep on keeping on. Studying. Minyan-ing. Hoping. Waiting.

Another month passes. I look at my calendar with disbelief, and write an email. It is, as ever, written with atomically measured courteousness, taking the greatest of pains to ensure that there is no suggestion of pressure, or entitlement. But, buried in the fifth and final paragraph, I reach the observation I have made. 'Today is, by chance, one year to the day since I first wrote to the Beth Din . . .'

A full calendar year has passed. My 'journey', thus far, appears close to static. If progress of any sort has been made, it feels as though I am millimetres into an ultra-marathon. Another week later, feeling close to hopeless, I email my sponsoring rabbi, seeking any additional help whatsoever.

Finally, a few days later, a response emerges. Our second appointment with the Beth Din, confirmed for the new year.

It is a blustery winter in London, and as the year comes to an end Eliana and I both dress in our smartest clothes – but not, this time, for a close study of the progress of my soul. No, today there is to be a wedding. As is fitting, I wear my *most* flamboyant pocket square.

Eliana's brother Michael and his partner, Talia, are getting married. It is a gorgeous affair – a ceremony in the historic New West End Synagogue, followed by an indulgent reception, with celebrations extending late into the night.

As Michael and Talia recite their vows to one another, I sit in the middle of the crowded pews on the male side of the room, and look across to the banks of women shimmering in their finery, where Eliana, an impossibly glamorous bridesmaid, sits out of reach.

And later that night, as the music of the band foments the partygoers into a pulsating, Dionysian frenzy, Eliana and I dance, inches apart from one another, unable to touch, lest the world come crashing down around us.

CHAPTER 18

Round Two...

The new year rolls around. In the bleary mists of January, Eliana and I begin readying ourselves for our second meeting.

This time, our preparation feels different in nature – Eliana now needs to ensure that she has retained every bit of information she has learned thus far with her tutor, who will have sent a progress report to the Beth Din, for their eyes only, which she must be sure to live up to. And I will need to be prepared to demonstrate, if called upon, those things which I have learned informally, in order to ensure that I am deemed worthy of learning those same things again, formally – along with everything else the official syllabus might require of me.

I now begin to realise that each of our subsequent meetings will be exponentially more stressful than the last; that in every encounter we will be called upon to present the fruits of the preceding six months of study, as well as demonstrating that we have continued to hold on to all that we learned before.

And it's not just about what we're learning – it's about what we're *doing*.

The laws – the *mitzvot* – that govern Judaism are manifold. According to religious tradition, there are 613 of them – and, according to cultural tradition, there are a billion dissenting arguments from rabbis across the centuries about whether that number is accurate, and what the actual figure should be. Each *mitzvah,* to use the singular form, represents either a positive deed that must be adhered to – such as paying wages on time, or giving 10 per cent of your income to charity – or else a negative action that must be avoided – such as cursing your parents, or having sex with an animal (both of which feel like fairly solid rules to live by).

It is commonly agreed that, however many *mitzvot* there are, it definitely isn't even possible to keep them all – a significant proportion of them being directly related to one's day-to-day interactions with a temple in Jerusalem that was destroyed by the Romans approximately two thousand years ago. But, at the forefront of those *mitzvot* which are still in play, there is one which shapes Orthodox life in the twenty-first century perhaps more than any other: the keeping of Shabbat.

Keeping Shabbat is something Jews of various denominations across the world do in a multitude of ways but, with the commencement of the conversion, I have now entered the phone-off-at-sundown, strictly-no-tech world of Orthodox Shabbat.

The timings, which can be found intricately mapped out in specialist diaries and websites and on 'HebCal', the invaluable addition to any good Jewish boy's iPhone, shift with the seasons in weekly fifteen-minute increments across the year, but they are clear and inviolable: forty-five minutes before sundown on a Friday, one's phone is turned off. Relevant house lights are left on, or placed on a timer. All work ceases, all commerce and handling of money stops, and the concerns of modern life recede into the distance. No cooking is allowed, yet food – prepared in advance – is entirely central to the day's events.

There is, without doubt, a wonderful quality to this new time spent free from technology – a window of unwinding and reconnecting with the self and with those around you, a period of deep thinking, relaxed and extended conversations, frequent napping, and uncommon amounts of reading. My whirring work anxieties, those of a freelancer navigating a preposterously uncertain industry, for once fade into the background. The counterintuitive feeling of stepping away from my phone, something to which I have for so long been hopelessly addicted, can, clearly, only be a positive, even though it is at first disheartening to experience the distinct lack of 'essential career-changing emails demanding an immediate response' which I am incorrectly convinced my phone will be flooded with when I turn it back on.

But it also does other things. It separates me from my family. Whilst living in different cities, and different bits of London, has long rendered regular Friday night dinners impossible, we instead developed a practice of a Friday night Zoom – a collective familial debriefing, a sharing of the week's inanities and profundities, and a chance to usher in the weekend by blessing the candles, the wine and the bread (or, admittedly, at times the malt loaf, or Jamaica cake, or corn cracker), in a moment of togetherness.

It is a small part of my life, but it is not insignificant. And, since the diagnosis, it has become more crucial still.

Whilst I speak to Dad throughout the week, instinctively phoning him when I'm dashing between meetings, or cycling from *shul* into town to meet Ivan and give the world all of our double-act comedy that it needs (if not considerably more), it is only on Friday evenings, when Mum has set up the iPad and distributed the Zoom link to her sons, that I can be sure that I will see Dad's face. And even then, thanks to my mother's experimental, ceiling-focused approach to the framing of the iPad camera, that's not a strict guarantee.

But in these gloomy winter months, with Shabbat descending in the mid-afternoon, my chance to join my family on these calls vanishes.

'Why don't you just do it on a different day?' says Eliana.

'Because... because this is when we do it. For the same reasons that I now *can't* be with them, ironically.'

WHY DON'T YOU JUST HAVE SHABBAT ON A DIFFERENT DAY!? I feel like yelling.

Eliana has always, always, kept Shabbat. She has never known any other way of being. She has navigated – somehow – school and college and even university life whilst keeping this *mitzvah*, meaning her Friday nights, even if they occasionally took her to some sticky-floored bar, remained entirely tech-free – no phones, no cars, no switching on and off of lights, no using a pen, even. Whilst she embraced modern student life, and various delighted fellow students, enthusiastically, this sense of what was important to her is something that never flickered. When it comes to using her phone over Shabbat, it's not that she never 'succumbed to the temptation' – succumbing to temptation being amongst Eliana's main hobbies – it's that the temptation has simply never been there. She is entirely modern yet entirely Orthodox – gleefully addicted to television, a curator and archivist of important memes, utterly plugged into modern life, and yet capable of switching modes, switching off, sliding happily into this other world, a place that she loves and draws strength from. She is captivating, and she is the most confusing woman I have ever met.

It is Friday, and it is dark outside. I sit by lamplight, reading and rereading the informal notes I have taken from my informal lessons. The clock ticks to 6pm.

I look over at my laptop in the full knowledge that, somewhere in Portsmouth, a Zoom link is being inexpertly emailed, and that soon a chaotic assemblage of parents and siblings and partners will be logging on, wherever they are in the world, and chatting over one another enthusiastically.

I close my eyes and push the thoughts away.

*

There is a principle, when dealing with the Beth Din for the purposes of conversion, that you will meet with a different Dayan each time, until you have met them all. It's a means of ensuring that you get a fair hearing – that you don't continually meet with the same person, thus either becoming the beneficiary of favouritism, if they like you, or doomed never to progress further, if they don't.

And so, whilst we're still not told *who* we'll be meeting ahead of time, we can at least tick Dayan Landau off the list, making the unavoidable game of generating infinite versions of the upcoming meeting in our heads at least marginally more focused.

In the end, to our surprise, we are told exactly who we will meet with. It is to be Dayan Horowitz, my daily acknowledger, and he has messaged to let me know that he has contracted Covid. As such, the meeting will still be going ahead, but it will be a Zoom call.

Despite there being no need for us to travel to deepest Barnwood Drive, past the airlock and the airless reception, and up into the Throne Zone, the time prior to our Zoom meeting feels exactly the same. In an atmosphere that feels hushed and tense, I once more overthink the task of getting dressed. And then, when the hour is nigh, we take our seats and wait.

Eliana and I have realised that we will need to log in from separate Zoom accounts – it being far too great a risk that, were we to sit next to one another and try to squeeze into the same frame, we might inadvertently make physical contact. So we are in separate rooms – separate buildings, to be on the safe side. I sit alone in front of my laptop, surrounded by my books and my notes, and I wait, silently, to be judged once more.

When met with a wall of total inscrutability, it is entirely impossible to tell if a meeting has gone 'well' or not. Questions are asked, and our answers – carefully prepared, and researched, and revised, and remembered – are given. In the main, we are quizzed on the things we have learned and the observances we have taken on. There are digressions, too, into our professional lives – further cautious queries about my work in comedy, and Eliana's writing, to which we give answers that do not appear to cause immediate, visible alarm. As far as can be discerned, the end of the meeting is approaching, and has been reached without major incident. And so I look down at the words I have prepared.

I wish to tell the Beth Din about my father's diagnosis. In the lead-up to this encounter, I consulted the Supportive Rabbis, who advised me that, again, the Beth Din were unlikely to be receptive to the news. That they won't care to feel any sense of being pressured.

But I can't remain silent. Not for another six months.

It is deeply important to me that they know. No, more than that. It was important to me before, but I held my tongue – now, it is essential.

Very well, comes the response. There are ways you can broach the subject. Carefully.

So, carefully, I do. I read from the message I have written out in the back of my notebook, taking pains to speak in the same forensically modulated tone – contrite, sombre, quasi-apologetic, yet somehow firm, but also in no way demanding. And with no suggestion of an ask. Just the facts. The diagnosis. A reassurance, even, that I'm not seeking to use this as any sort of emotional leverage. I had written to the Beth Din before my father's diagnosis. Long before, actually – but not too long! Don't let them feel you are in any way displeased by the wait. But this is what has happened. This is the knowledge I live with.

I finish speaking.

'Your message is well received', comes the response, with a glassy, unreadable smile.

Is it now? Well. That's good.

Further down the rabbit hole we tumble. Three weeks after our meeting, an email appears; I have been granted a tutor, and in the same breath we have been given an appointment for our next meeting, in the summer.

'We are also pleased to hear that you have been able to find a way to ensure your acting commitments are Shabbos compliant,' reads the message, which continues with a curious passage: 'and are encouraged by the fact that you have both committed, going forward, to ensure that you do not participate in non-kosher social gatherings.'

It's unusual for two reasons. One, neither of us have any idea what 'non-kosher social gatherings' are, and two, we never made any such agreement. It was never discussed in the meeting.

I now regularly return to The Area, a few roads along from the house in which I conducted my informal learning, to begin my formal learning. Here, I meet my tutor, Rav Dov – an affable, smiling Gibraltarian rabbi – and, over endless coffees in his living room, we dive into the syllabus proper.

Twice a week, initially in person and then, once we find a rhythm, over Zoom as well, I learn dense acres of Jewish law.

I learn far more than I have ever known previously about the Jewish festivals. Some of them immediately speak to me – the cleansing, purifying nature of Rosh Hashanah and Yom Kippur; a chance for renewal, for making amends, for taking solemn and sincere steps to right any wrongs you have committed, an opportunity to try and truly become a better person as a new year begins. Some of them do not – Sukkot, which takes place a few weeks later, mainly involves waving what is essentially a massive lemon and eating your meals in a temporary hut in your garden.

'There is an old saying,' my tutor tells me. 'He who eats in the sukkah when it is raining . . .' I furiously scribble down his words as he continues, 'is an idiot.'

I learn an endless stream of statutes and prohibitions and concepts, some that seem wise, others confusing, and others unthinkably bizarre.

I learn about the ritual of Kapparot – a blessing once made on a live bird but now generally made on money, but which nonetheless historically involved, yes, swinging a chicken around one's head, and thereby transferring one's sins into it.

I learn about the red heifer – an unblemished red cow, near-mythical due to its rarity, used in specific sacrifices in the days of the Temple.

I learn about the superstition that a woman should not drink the wine used during the weekly post-Shabbat ritual of *havdallah*, or she will grow a beard.

I learn about the rule demanding that Jews do not practise sorcery of the *ov* – which apparently involves burning a type of incense and hearing voices emanating from one's armpit. It's a relief to know that there's a *mitzvah* I can tick off my list, at least most days of the week.

Religions, which, by their very definition, are reliant on faith, defy rationality. As such, it is sensationally easy to find seeds of madness in the beliefs of any and all of them. Picking holes in a religion is the easiest thing in the world, and I haven't the slightest interest in doing so.

There are infinite ways to live one's life, and the ones that feel least interesting to me involve proscribing or deriding the choices others make. The behaviour of the self-congratulatory atheist is entirely as irritating as that of the devout believer who pities those who aren't yet saved. In both cases, the abrasive texture of their smugness comes not from a sense that other people's values are wrong – disagree with whomsoever you choose – but rather that their specific values are right. Comparatively, Judaism's total disinterest in declaring itself the correct religion for the entire human race, and its active aversion to seeking converts, is something I always found rather appealing – although admittedly this is a charm that has somewhat faded for me, now that I find myself locked in the antechamber of what I had been certain was my own identity.

Anything can be deconstructed, really.

What do *you* find meaningful? Music? What, 'nice sounds'? Grow up, mate. Reading novels? 'Decoding some shapes in order to hear a voice in your head tell you about a thing that never happened?' Pffft, embarrassing.

Or, if you prefer, you could zoom out further until it becomes apparent that meaning is, in and of itself, illusory – it merely being the by-product of a combination of sloshing chemicals in the underpowered computer we choose to call a brain. Pull back the aperture of your understanding until you perceive that we are but briefly animated sacks of meat powered by misfiring electrons, and that nothing matters at all.

This realisation frees you up to eliminate all ritual from your existence. Celebrate no birthdays or anniversaries, attend no funerals or weddings. Mark nothing. Do nothing.

The alternative, of course, is to enjoy yourself, to build a life that contains meaning, wherever you find it. And, in doing so, acknowledge that huge amounts of what one does won't be born simply of logic. Decisions will be made as a result of instinct, or passion, or hope, or love, or, occasionally, faith.

Basically, what I'm saying is: Ricky Gervais, it's all well and good crowing triumphantly about being an atheist, but if you're then going to go on record as calling your girlfriend your 'soulmate', then the least you could do is point to the so-called soul on a scientific chart, you long-haired hippy freak.

My notebooks fill with the wisdom of the sages, and my own wide-eyed queries. Frequently, Rav Dov opens one of his many huge, thin-paged tomes containing reams of Jewish law. The main, dense Hebrew text is surrounded by even smaller writing – which, I am delighted and unsurprised to learn, are a series of different explanatory commentaries, which, in spectacularly Jewish fashion, all seem to completely disagree with one another. On any given page, Maimonides might be being heckled mercilessly by Raavad. At times, Judaism seems less like a religion than a centuries-long argument.

Our sessions are long, and often late. The morning minyan is never less than early. I am, in the midst of this, attempting to finally learn to drive. And Ivan and I are, doggedly, clinging to the sitcom commission we received pre-Covid, and which we have managed to keep on life-support since then by dint of rewriting the entire series approximately once a week according to the whims of ever-changing safety regulations, production budgets and TV commissioners.

I am exhausted. But I am, it feels, slowly getting somewhere. I get home late, prepare my morning coffee, set my alarm, refrain from conducting any sorcery of the *ov*, and collapse into bed.

CHAPTER 19

Stairway to Hendon

It is midway through conga-dancing around a garden with seventy black-hat-wearing religious Jewish men, a quarter of them (the teenagers) blind drunk, that I feel that sense of a record-scratch moment.

Hi – you're probably wondering how I found myself in this situation . . .

Jake, who is conga-ing just behind me, leans in with a smile. 'Yep. This is when it starts to get . . . lively,' he murmurs.

We have come to Hendon, to the heart of it all. We have been invited by Eliana's tutor to a Shabbat evening meal – before which evening prayers take place.

As I am starting to discern, in The Area there is a multiplicity of locations in which one can *daven*.* Forget multiple *shuls* in the neighbourhood, think multiple options in a single street: grand *shuls*, humble *shuls*, even surprise *shuls* without any indicative signage. The place we find ourselves, for example, simply appears to be someone's house, but, as we are welcomed expansively at the front door and ushered through the building by the unfathomably relaxed hostess – Eliana and Rachel peeling off to join her in a roomful of women, as Jake and I tumble into the garden to join the rapidly gathering throng of men – what breaks

---

* That is, pray.

out is a rollicking, spontaneous, chaotic flashmob of a full-blown Friday night service.

There are tunes for *everything*. The singing is full-throated and imbued with a sense of unfettered delight. Still more people accumulate in the garden. Elderly men chat boyishly, and younger teens shake hands with one another, in a performative display of adulthood. Everyone knows everyone. Whisky is . . . everywhere. This is *shabbos*, baby, Hendon style – and it's a mesmeric thing to become absorbed into.

I am helpfully handed a small pamphlet containing the evening's prayers, which I am utterly incapable of following; it is full of densely packed Hebrew text, with not a hint of English anywhere (the *siddur* that I am becoming – shakily – familiar with offers English translations of the Hebrew prayers). It doesn't matter – a grinning teen, almost levitating with drunkenness but still flawlessly polite, happily shows me the relevant page, whilst offering me another whisky. Before long, the conga-ing breaks out.

At the eventual end of the service, the congregants, surely numbering in their hundreds by now, exit, clown-car-like, through the front door of this small suburban house, and disperse their separate ways, off to commence their various Friday night dinners. As Eliana, Rachel, Jake and I all wander down the road together, we hear the clattering of rushing feet behind us; we turn, to find the hostess of the house we have just left.

'I just wanted to say,' she says with a beatific smile, 'it was so lovely to meet you! Please, honestly, come back any time.'

Hendon, I am realising, is a different world.

This understanding is cemented further when, shortly after, I consume the largest meal that has ever been served to anyone in the known history of humanity.

Eliana's tutor, it swiftly becomes apparent, is superhuman.

She has ten children. She works constantly. She volunteers. And, amongst all this, somehow, she has prepared . . . well . . .

It begins shortly after we are welcomed into the house – one of our fellow conga dancers, I realise, is her husband, and we fall into step with him as he walks us round the corner to our dinner destination. As we are led into the long dining room and take our seats, I spot three expansive bowls of salad. 'Ah, a light dinner!' I think. 'I think a little of each of those should absolutely hit the spot.' And, once the ceremonial blessings have been made and the meal has begun, I help myself to three fairly indulgent portions of salad, as befits a satisfying, if not slightly overfilling dinner. Then the meal *really* begins.

Soups emerge. Roast chicken appears. Still more salads spontaneously generate. Roast beef manifests. Potatoes assert themselves. As do other types of potatoes. Yet more varieties of meat are suddenly in existence. As are dishes laden with vegetables, and pies, and chips, and of course there's the *challah* which you could always dip in the horseradish *chrain* or else the beetroot mayonnaise which is somehow handmade, in fact everything seems to be handmade and surely not but now unthinkably *dessert* is on the horizon and here are the crumbles and whips and sorbets and dark chocolate and mints and cakes and *babka* and other cakes and other *other* cakes . . .

There were at least twenty of us dining that night. All of us ate until we could eat no more – and still the courses kept flowing. Had I taken just one bite of each dish that passed me, I would have been overly full. And, G-d help me, I did not just take one bite.

To this day, I could not explain how anything other than a large professional catering company, toiling through the week, could produce the quantities of food which were distributed that night. But, no, they were inexplicably the product of one woman – a woman already so busy that, were I to attempt to tackle the other responsibilities of a single day in her life *aside* from the culinary preparation, I would immediately crumble to nothing. Had I attempted the handmade beetroot mayonnaise alone, I'm sure I would have somehow started a small house fire.

The meal runs late into the night. This is not purely due to my alarming, ill-judged gorging, which isn't a feat being replicated by everyone; our host and hostess, for instance, and their many children – all of them remarkably polite, well-mannered mini-adults – navigate the meal via the innovative method of 'only eating a reasonable amount of food'. Instead it is due to the way the conversation flows – which, I realise, is all part of the underlying structure of the dinner itself. We loop between introducing ourselves and getting to know one another, and discussing the week's events, and then, suddenly, breaking out into song; ornately printed pamphlets are distributed containing the Hebrew text, although at least half the table seems to instinctively know the words and the tune already. These, I learn, are *zemirot*, 'table hymns', and are liable to break out midway through any Shabbat meal. I keep up as best I can, humming and swaying, and allowing myself to become swept up in the melodies. And then the music subsides and, after more chatting, our host segues into a sort of casual mini-lecture; a short disquisition based on that week's Torah portion, and the practical extrapolations one might use in one's day-to-day life. And then more singing, more chatting, more food, more singing . . .

The meal is entirely unhurried, and our host family appear as vibrant and awake at well after midnight, when we eventually leave, as they did at the start of the evening – it is a bravura, unrepeatable, once-in-a-lifetime display of hosting. Which, somehow, is something they do every single week.

Out in front of the house, in the bracing night air, Eliana and I say our goodbyes to our fellow diners. During the meal, across the table, I had noticed recognisable faces: a couple who are taking the Sephardi conversion, who we had previously met in Arielle's basement at her afternoon of cocktails and intense emotional support and peanuts.

We exchange pleasantries. And then we say our goodbyes, at which point...

Ah yes, another difference in the two approaches to conversion.

Whilst Ashkenazi couples are expected to live apart throughout the process, Sephardi couples... are not.

It is difficult to overstate how vast a difference that is.

Perhaps it comes from a differing interpretation of Jewish law: the aspiring convert is not yet Jewish, therefore they need not be held to Jewish law? Perhaps it is another dash of straightforward Sephardi pragmatism: why render a difficult process more unnecessarily difficult?

Regardless. It is a mind-rattling realisation.

There is a deeply felt unspoken parting of the ways as we peel off in our various directions.

The Sephardi couple return to their home, together.

Needless to say, Eliana and I do not.

Tech-free, we walk from Hendon back towards our respective homes in Primrose Hill, a ninety-minute journey which, at this point, due to my monstrous over-indulgence, I am hugely grateful for, this walk presumably being the only thing standing between me and some hitherto unknown-to-medical-science variant of Super Gout.

And as we walk, we do what we do with increasing frequency on Shabbat: we fall into an argument.

This time, the sharp injustice of our enforced separation has risen to the back of my throat once more, and I cannot hold it in.

'It's barbaric,' I say.

'Barbaric? How can you possibly use that word?' responds Eliana, incensed. '*War crimes* are barbaric.'

When we end up in these furious rows, Eliana invariably falls into the position of defending Orthodoxy – even if she doesn't agree with the logic that has been employed to reach a conclusion, she appreciates that there is some. She defers to the law – to the *halacha* – and to the rabbis' interpretation of it. She finds the force of my dissent undeferential and alarming, and I find her toeing of the party line maddeningly frustrating.

It's not just on Shabbat that we argue, although during these long Saturday afternoons – with our phone-free proximity to one another, with the loudness of Judaism around us – it proves more likely that we will. But, increasingly, my temper is fraying throughout the week, too.

'How was *shul*?' she will say, most mornings. Generally, I will mumble 'fine'. Until, eventually, forlornly, one morning, I don't. 'It was pretty much the same as it always is,' I splutter, miserably. 'Basically the same people, basically the same words. That's almost the entire point.'

And so she stops asking.

But even as I feel overwhelmed, crushed beneath the pressure of it all, I feel wretched at moaning at Eliana.

How's *that* any good? Me snapping back, tarnishing a thing she loves. A thing I am *trying* to embrace – whilst painfully aware of its seeming refusal to embrace me.

So the arguments continue.

We fall into a cycle – I will air a grievance, give voice to the pain that this nullifying of my identity is causing me, and Eliana will then push back with an exasperated explanation of *halacha* – recounting yet again why, by definition, I can't be Jewish.

'I wish these weren't the rules, but they are; someone is considered Jewish if they have a Jewish mother!'

My voice is ice. 'I have a Jewish mother.'

It is an argument that infuriates and agonises me, and makes me feel entirely distant from her.

'Your nearly ninety-year-old grandmother can accept me!' I say, remembering Lion's flippant assessment of me – 'You're Jewish anyway'.

'So?' says Eliana. 'She's a different person to me! We have totally different views! Different relationships to religion!'

In one particular low point of an endless row, we both eventually fall asleep, not just still in the grip of an argument, but still on the phone to one another, furiously silent.

I wake up the next morning – the call is ongoing – and I go to synagogue. The phone in my pocket. Eliana is woken by the hum of morning prayer. I cycle into work afterwards, our ludicrous cold war continuing, until I get to my office and neither of us can quite take the whole thing seriously any more.

At the end of yet one more pointless, poisonous row, Eliana finally relents, and says something I had longed for but never expected.

'I thought that if I said this, you'd throw it back at me – use it to question why the conversion is important to me,' she says. 'But I do believe you're Jewish. I do.'

It's all I need to hear.

It is a lifeline amidst the deluge. It is the sense that the person I am drawn to is, despite everything, on my side.

CHAPTER 20

A Series of Plot Twists

Against all known odds and to my utter disbelief, the sitcom that Ivan and I have been writing – greenlit pre-lockdown and then constantly, eternally, pushed back, with the goalposts moved and the playing field reshaped – actually goes into production.

It's been a gruelling, protracted period of waiting on the inscrutable, delayed, often seemingly arbitrary decisions of various distant authority figures. Luckily, this is a technique I have been honing. And, in this instance at least, my optimistic waiting has proved fruitful. We're making a TV show!

It is a tale loosely inspired by my years as a teenage professional wrestler, and the dingier companies I performed for during that time. Suddenly, Ivan and I are spending long hours on location – a strange, faded, hotel-and-darts mecca of the 1980s, with walls lined with sensational publicity photos of long-forgotten variety acts who played there back in the day.

The euphoria of being given the chance to shoot a project of our own is tempered by the total impracticality of attempting to do so. Covid is resurgent, and so large chunks of the budget – we are never told what the budget for the show actually is, only that, as a general rule, there 'isn't enough money' – are spent on the various necessary mitigations. There is an on-set 'Covid supervisor' who oversees people's lateral flow tests, and who can be found silently sidling up to crew members, tapping them on the shoulder, and beckoning them away, sometimes never to be seen again. He swiftly becomes known as the Angel of Death.

And then there is Shabbat. 'Yep, these are the times,' I explain to the frazzled production coordinator, gesturing at the helpful printout I have made. 'Yes,' I say, 'they change each week.' Battling, as we are, a dearth of resources and a surfeit of the coronavirus, my declaration that my shooting hours must be Shabbat compliant does without doubt add further tension to an already fraught set. But, across the history of film and TV, there has been *more* outrageous behaviour. Compared with, say, Marlon Brando's approach to making *Apocalypse Now* – refusing to learn the script in advance, turning up to the shoot spectacularly overweight after being asked to look emaciated, demanding to change his character's name and then changing it back, and reading half of his lines off large cue cards and improvising the rest – my assertion that I must finish work before sundown on Fridays is fairly mild.

In those moments I'm not needed, I am in my trailer, revising furiously for my next Beth Din meeting (whilst absorbing with wonderment the fact that I, currently, have 'a trailer').

'So, these meetings . . .' says Ivan, when he pops his head in, attempting to get to grips with what I'm revising. 'Everything could fall apart if you don't successfully recite the magic spell you have to say before eating a banana?'

'It's not a magic spell, it's a blessing,' I say.

. . .

'But, broadly, yes,' I add.

And then we're called back to set.

There is absolutely never enough time to film anything. The shoot is intense and contracted. The days are long, the weather is bitingly cold, and I spend most of it dressed in skintight lycra. Schedules shift constantly as various crew and actors are whisked off to various states of quarantine. Scenes are rewritten, and crunched down, and omitted in their entirety. Ivan, newly a father, is sleep-deprived to the point of hallucination.

Around the country, every film-set we are aware of is being shut down for weeks on end. This simply isn't an option for us – our workaholic director is contractually bound to start shooting another (far bigger-budget) show the day after ours is currently scheduled to end. If we lose even a day, we're done for.

Is it right to try and keep pressing ahead with something, in the face of common sense, in the face of all available evidence? Should you always keep chipping away at something impossible-seeming, attempting to push through to the other side, just because the act of doing so speaks to something you desire? At what point does it become more prudent to just . . . stop?

Another dry-mouthed Tuesday morning of preparation. The now-familiar combination of suit and shirt and shoes (I'm foregoing the pocket square entirely at this point). An ever-growing array of papers and books spread out around me, which I am reading and rereading, neurotically. Eliana knocking on my door, her car outside. It can mean only one thing. Back to the Beth Din we go.

With another meeting, and another period of intense prepping, comes another goal. Now, due to my regular lessons, I am a semi-regular visitor to The Area. The hope, next, is to be able take the plunge: to be given permission to become a transplant, and to live amongst the people of Hendon or Golders Green. To move in with A Family.

Back through the airlock and into the waiting room and finally into a new meeting room – throne-free – where we sit with a new Dayan: Dayan Katz.

The meeting starts slowly. There is, if not a frostiness, then a cautiousness. Questions are asked, as he seeks to gain the measure of us.

But Eliana and I have been waiting for this moment. We are well trained. We're in the zone. We are thoroughbreds, loaded with knowledge – the facts we have been studying are at our fingertips.

We sight-read Hebrew and we answer questions about the laws of kosher and of Shabbat and festivals, and I successfully recite the blessing that one says before eating a banana, and Eliana leaps in with the blessing one recites *after* a banana.

And with each answered question, the Dayan seems to relax. There is a warming towards us. We are getting along. We are – sure, I'll say it – vibing!

I have, once more, prepared a statement for the end of the meeting, to be recited if all goes well. This time, it is an entreaty that I be allowed to progress to the next stage of the process, the aforementioned transplanting. To my dumbstruck surprise, I do not need it.

'I propose that you next move in with a family,' says Dayan Katz, halfway through the meeting, apropos of nothing.

My eyes light up. I can't believe it. I can feel Eliana's excitement rising within her, across the table from me.

The entire line of rhetoric I have been building to is completely derailed – instead, I splutter my grateful thanks.

The meeting really couldn't have gone better.

And then Dayan Katz looks up and throws in a final aside – a masterful, Steve Jobs-like 'one more thing'.

'Oh – and Eliana, you'll be wanting to move to The Area too?'

Eliana's face freezes.

'. . . Yep!'

'I'm sorry that was sprung on you,' says Eliana's tutor. 'For what it's worth, I don't think it's something you'd be obliged to do.'

It's certainly a plot twist. Whilst I have been spending so many months psychologically preparing for this upcoming change in my life, Eliana has not.

Whilst I have spent the last months unmoored, Eliana, on the contrary, has deep roots within her world – of Primrose Hill, of Beit Shalom. It's a world she is so sure of that it has reshaped the future I have envisioned for myself. She never imagined she would be required to move away. It wasn't in the small print on the website. It isn't anywhere in the Torah. It's just . . . something a man in a meeting has asked her to do.

She is in two minds. Obviously, there is a side of her that doesn't actively *want* to be airlifted into a strange family's house, to replace the comforts of her own family life with the total uncertainties of another.

But then, there is another side of things.

There have been times when, at the end of another of our long, relentless arguments, Eliana has said, of the conversion, of the circumcision, of all of it: 'If I could do it instead of you, I would.'

I have always believed her.

And she can't do it *instead* of me. But she has tumbled down the rabbit hole with me. Joined me in all there is to join. Sat with me in the meetings. Revised with me late into the night. And here, at a crucial juncture, as I am about to take a step from the uncertain into the unknown, is a chance for her to be with me.

'Will it make Max's conversion process easier if I do?'

'. . . Yes, it might.'

'Then it's not a question.'

And so it is to be. We are both, officially, moving to The Area. Now it's simply a case of finding two religious Beth Din-approved families who will let us live in their houses for an unspecified amount of time, and moving in.

It's lovely when life starts to feel simpler.

CHAPTER 21

Coffee with the Bernsteins

As with so much of this whole crusade, hidden beneath the various layers of mystique there is, actually, a straightforward answer.

There is a list, somewhere in the bowels of Barnwood Drive, containing the names of families who have been given the kosher stamp of approval by the Beth Din for the purposes of taking in prospective converts, and who are open to doing so.

In my dreams, more often than not, I now find myself tumbling into some new strange and unsettling home; I am led into an ancient castle where I lie on a straw-lined bed as a semicircle of serious-minded Rabbonim watch over me; I am beckoned into an elaborate treehouse in the depths of a forest, overseen by a Baba Yaga figure – the door to my cramped bedroom doesn't close, and when I look up I see her enormous bloodshot eyes peering at me through the crack; I am attempting to follow directions to an apartment within an endless Soviet block of flats – running up and down thousands of grimy concrete steps, crisscrossed above and below me, Escher-like, my footsteps echoing as I try to close in on the distant voice of my frustrated host, growing increasingly irate at my inability to find the correct address, as I keep running faster and faster, growing short of breath, my panic rising...

It is a nonsense, obviously. In the calm light of day, with a fair wind behind me, I am able to feel excited by the prospect of this next step, to default to my usual mode of bordering-on-reckless optimism. To remind myself that I am generally ever-delighted at the chance to meet new people. That a temporary leap to Hendon represents a unique chance to immerse myself in Jewish life more deeply than ever before and, thus, is part of exactly how I sought to derive meaning from this process. Of course it's all going to be all right. Why wouldn't it?

'Oh, you could get someone *awful,* couldn't you!'

My morning minyan mates are ever intrigued by my progress and, when they check in on me, they cheerfully inform me of previous instances in which this stage of the process has all gone horrendously wrong.

'I heard about a guy who was staying with this one old woman, she went through the receipts in his bin. She spotted he'd bought some non-kosher milk – and she reported him to the Beth Din!'

'Cor, don't you find the whole idea a bit terrifying? I know I would.'

'What if they're totally mad?'

It's helpful stuff.

As the weeks go by, the notion of who might be on The List grows ever more irrationally unsettling in my mind – an elderly widow who demands that I exclusively dress in the clothes of her late husband? A butcher whose bloodstained aprons dry on a hanger over my bed, dripping onto me as I sleep? A friendly couple who proudly discuss the many achievements of their beloved children, except when I meet the 'children' I realise they're all just hand-painted garden gnomes?

For my own sake, and my own sanity, I need to take my destiny in my own hands as much as I can. Which is to say, not very much.

But I do speak to my de facto mentor, Jake.

'If you could get the Bernsteins . . .' he says, 'then you'd have really hit the jackpot.'

The Bernsteins, Jake informs me, to my surprise, are not on The List.

This is not because they are not in good standing with the Beth Din. On the contrary – they are a family of unimpeachable reputation, well-respected pillars of the community.

They have simply chosen not to be on The List because they are not regularly in the practice of housing wayward pilgrims midway through an amorphous, open-ended spiritual quest.

During Jake's time in The Area, he'd stayed with a kindly older woman, who had sadly since died. But it was through her that he met – and clicked with – the Bernsteins, who, Jake discovered, occasionally took people in.

'They're the nicest people,' Jake assures me. 'You'd love them. I'm just not sure if they're in the market for another . . . person.'

How does one ask permission to move into a stranger's home for an unspecified period of time? 'Hello. We've never met. May I live with you until some men say I don't need to any more?' doesn't seem like the ideal opening salvo.

In this instance, the request takes the form of a pincer movement. On the one hand, an introduction and an enquiry from Jake. And, on the other, a trusted authoritative endorsement from a leading member of the Supportive Rabbis.

A meeting is secured.

Over the years, when seeking to move into various flats, houses and living arrangements, I have presented myself in all manner of ways.

I once locked-in my tenancy in a deranged house-share in Bow by bringing a bottle of vodka to the viewing, which then became an impromptu karaoke evening, resulting in a very happy three years living in what I was certain at the time was the finest address in London, but looking back I now realise to have been a slum dwelling.

And, when viewing the flat in the Docklands that was to become my home, I recall theatrically shaking my head disappointedly at various perceived flaws in the property, in a transparent bid to put off the other person being shown around – a man who was clearly immensely wealthy, and who gave every impression of having the cash needed to buy the place physically on his person.

And now, in a dramatically different chapter of life yet again, I find myself sat in the living room of Joel and Ronit Bernstein, Eliana next to me (but a respectful distance away), attempting to present myself as a plausible candidate for . . . moving into their family home.

It is, from what I can see, a beautiful house. Large, practical, not flashy, but immaculate and beautifully kept. There is a capaciousness to houses in The Area, I am coming to understand. They are designed to be *used*. These are homes constructed to withstand the impact of dozens of excitable children playing in the living room and charging through to the garden, for neighbours to appear at any given moment, perhaps bringing with them a cousin or two, or five, who happen to be down for the weekend, and for the ongoing holy endeavour of communal eating.

It's a big house. But does it have room for one more?

'So,' says Ronit, 'Jake messaged us and said you want to become Jewish.'

There is a directness to Joel and Ronit that is immediately endearing. No time for pussyfooting around a subject, wasting time on niceties. They're both so *busy*. They work long hours. They're both involved in innumerable community and charitable projects. And then there is the small matter of their seven children.

As we chat – I roll out my now-familiar origin story, Eliana chipping in with her side of things – the Bernsteins' various children come and go, introducing themselves (again – unfailingly politely! My dealings in The Area have thus far exposed me to the politest children on the planet) and then running off to finish some homework or do some additional Torah study or go for a run. The Bernstein boys are keen athletes – somehow squeezing in huge late-night and early-morning 10k runs or laps of Regent's Park's Outer Circle on their racing bikes – in amongst their education (both secular and religious) or their jobs.

'I'd be going too,' says Joel with a straight face, 'only I think I've pulled something in my foot. Or maybe broken it. Ronit, what if I've broken something?'

'Oh, what*ever*, Joel.' Ronit rolls her eyes with a power that could topple governments. 'My husband is something of a hypochondriac.'

The Bernsteins are dry and solicitous and welcoming, and our conversation flows warmly and easily.

They are intrigued by me. 'I'm fascinated,' says Ronit, listening to my story. 'You really thought you were Jewish?' I really did.

And I am intrigued by them. Their openness to taking in people like me; why on earth would they choose to add additional stress to such full lives?

Ronit explains: when they were first asked, some years ago, they had found themselves at a fortunate point in their lives. Joel had been promoted, they were happily raising their young children – things were going well. And so, when a young non-Jewish man who had found himself sat round their dinner table enjoying a meal at their house asked if he might stay on a little, to learn more about a way of life he felt drawn to, Ronit felt it right that they say yes. They had been very blessed in their lives, and it was important to her that they pay it forwards. 'Obviously Joel thought I was mad,' says Ronit.

In short, they have periodically taken people in over the years without ever accepting a penny in payment, and they have done so simply because it is a *mitzvah*, an inherently kind thing to do. And, midway through our conversation, it becomes apparent that they are prepared to take me in too.

'So, you'll let us know when you'd like to move in, and we'll go from there, yes?' says Ronit breezily.

Eliana and I beam with excitement.

My swamp of nightmares has been drained. The unknown is unknown no longer. I'm moving in with the Bernsteins.

A few days later Eliana receives word that a neighbour of the Bernsteins might be willing to take her in. By which I mean Eliana receives a voicenote from said neighbour, immediately welcoming her to stay at their house for as long as she'd like, without having met her.

It is a display of generosity so unconditional that it feels very much as though we're on the verge of being the victims of some sort of phishing scam.

The Bernsteins, at least, requested a short face-to-face meeting before flinging open their doors without any preconditions whatsoever.

Sarah Green, across the road, has dispensed with even that extremely low-level precautionary measure. The voicenote is long and forthcoming – she explains that she and her husband, Avi, are soon going away for a few weeks, but that Eliana is welcome to move in whenever she likes; if they're away, she can collect a key from the neighbour. This is the room she'd be staying in . . .

We listen to the voicenote again, mouths open in amazement.

When we visit the Greens a few days later, to introduce ourselves, the door is, appropriately, open.

Sarah has been hosting a large group, who she waves out, and she welcomes us in in the same breath. Her home embodies the bustling Hendon community hub – a space full of the comings and goings of friends and neighbours and loved ones.

As we attempt to express our awestruck thanks at her taking in Eliana, she won't hear anything of it. Sarah, too, has taken in people on this journey over the years – a natural inclination, given her work as a teacher of Jewish studies. Her children, now grown-up, have flown the nest (to nearby roads, naturally), and she claims to be enjoying the empty house. This feels like a somewhat dubious claim, given the hordes of visitors coming and going during our short time there, and the fact that she is putting up numerous additional guests over the coming weeks. Without the slightest sense that her behaviour is in any way remarkable, she tells an eye-popping story about having recently hosted an entire wedding party at her house for the entirety of their stay in London – a group of people she had absolutely no connection to, and a wedding she wasn't even invited to – simply because it became apparent that they needed somewhere.

'You'll stay for lunch?' she says, and we are powerless to resist.

Sarah's kitchen, it becomes clear, is industrial in scale – seemingly effortlessly, and certainly without ever having written anything down, she retains the logistics required to single-handedly run what is effectively a small restaurant – somehow casually throwing together food for twenty, instinctively knowing where everyone should sit, welcoming latecomers, and pulling up extra chairs for stragglers who find their way to the table.

We are fed and watered and gin and tonic'd and waved out

of the door and invited back and Eliana is urged to move in whenever she'd like.

So, eventually, it comes to pass that this morning minyan at Regency Square is to be my last – at least for the foreseeable future.

I tell my *shul*-neighbour that I've been given the go-ahead to move. 'Oh, very good, very good. Where you off to then? Redwood Road? Cor, that's heavy metal that is! Haha!'

CHAPTER 22

The Area

Day one at the Bernsteins. I wake up and, not yet acquainted with where I am, promptly roll the wrong way out of the single bed, smash my head on the eaves, then tumble backwards onto the floor. Conditions are perfect.

I have slept inexpertly. Usually, my ability to slide near-instantaneously into the deepest of REM cycles, wherever and whenever I happen to be, is more or less my primary skill, but on this night it lets me down. Instead I doze fitfully, floating in and out of a thin, restless sleep, feeling the unwanted flickering of my mind, and the pressure of first-night-of-term nerves.

Moving in the night before was both straightforward and strange. Having packed my large, beloved, pretentious Globetrotter suitcase, Eliana drove me from Primrose Hill to my new home.

There, Ronit welcomed us both at the door, and swiftly explained how I am to be seamlessly absorbed into their relentlessly efficient family unit. There is a supper on the table every night of the week – should I wish to partake I need simply let her know in advance. Likewise Shabbat dinners and lunches. Otherwise I am free to come and go as I please. Oh – and the open invitation to any and all meals applies to Eliana too, of course.

With that, Ronit left the two of us to say our goodbyes. It felt like a pointed gesture in the best possible sense; your lives are your own.

Eliana stood outside the front door, and we protractedly, helplessly waved one another goodbye, neither quite knowing how to address the overwhelming weirdness of it all. Eventually she left, and I quietly closed the front door. Alone, definitively, in this new space.

My brief endorphin rush of certainty – *I am moving in with the Bernsteins!* – was swiftly and comprehensively replaced with a whole new league of uncertainty, as I unpacked my things and clambered into bed. *What am I doing? What on earth does my life look like now!?*

In the first instance, in the grey depths of the next morning, it means finding a new minyan.

I stagger downstairs and meet Joel, who has kindly invited me to tag along with him to the *shul* that he attends each morning, at the end of his road.

It is an entirely new genre of *shul* to me, a *shtiebel* – that is, as much a place of study as it is a place of worship (though in Orthodoxy these two concepts co-mingle to the extent that they become almost one and the same). Throughout the day, the narrow tables are packed with men of all ages in black hats studying Talmud and Mishna. But, in the mornings, the narrow tables are instead packed with slightly different men of all ages in black hats *davening shacharit*. Admittedly, to the uninitiated this will present only the subtlest of visual differences. No issue here in assembling the necessary ten Jewish men – rather, the main logistical concern is whether one can squeeze into the heaving room at all.

Joel, well acquainted with the *shul*, has already nimbly made his way through to his regular place (as with school classrooms, *shuls* retain unwritten seating plans, with people returning to their favoured spot in the room via muscle memory and common agreement).

Spotting me already bewildered and lagging behind, Joel waves me towards him, and the dense rows of praying men shuffle slightly to allow me through.

I struggle to find space at a table. I struggle to find a *siddur* that offers any accompanying English text alongside the Hebrew. I struggle to find the right page. I struggle to keep track of the speed and the cadences of the man leading the service. I struggle not to lose my mind.

With the rabbi leading the service barrelling ahead, I flick through the pages of the *siddur* urgently and fruitlessly, feeling a low despairing panic as I swiftly grow ever more lost. This all feels like a bait and switch – no sooner had I begun, *just*, to comprehend the rhythms of Regency Square, then I have been teleported to a new, yet-more-confusing location.

Joel and a helpful neighbour at my other shoulder both kindly indicate where I should be whenever they happen to look up and spot me struggling.

But these men – and everyone here, in fact – are world-class *daveners*. They are busy men, their morning prayers honed over a lifetime of practice, and they are primarily heads-down, focused, getting it done. I struggle to the end of the service, grasping at phrases I half understand.

Once the prayers have concluded, people stream hurriedly out of the doors, rushing off to run businesses, do deals, litigate high-profile court cases or complex property disputes, and – in at least one instance – to record a short voiceover for Ariel washing powder.

Eliana moves in with the Greens, a seventeen-second walk away from me, and so the strangeness of us being Primrose Hill neighbours – together-yet-not-together – is both replicated and amplified by our new surroundings.

Up until the move, I've only had a fleeting sense of the neighbourhood – all of my time in Hendon has been spent either in, or else travelling to or from, specific homes. I have seen life whirr by as I have cycled, urgently and borderline-late, to appointments with Rav Dov, or a Supportive Rabbi. But those journeys have always been pointed, focused – Google Maps-powered in-and-out missions, taking me to where I need to be and then back home again, in time to get not quite enough sleep and then awaken to dance the dance once more. But now my horizons have shifted. I have a new address, and a door key, and now it's the rest of the world that is beginning to retreat into the distance, and becoming 'a place that I sometimes visit'. Hendon is now my home, and it's time to get my bearings.

There is a Jewish dish known as cholent.* It is a dark and foreboding stew consisting of beans and grain and potatoes and the occasional shred of mystery meat. It is, primarily, fuel; something first cobbled together by the Ashkenazim of medieval Europe, refined by Polish Jews as a means of surviving the unforgiving winter, and now served out of a combination of nostalgia and practicality – offering as it does some ancestral taste of the Old Country. Plus the bonus that it can be manufactured in huge volumes and at low cost, shovelled hastily onto paper plates at every *kiddush* going, and kept bubbling on a low heat throughout the entirety of a long Shabbat. It has the approximate density and texture of congealing concrete, the remarkable ability to taste of nothing at all, and a single serving will leave you uncomfortably full for a day and a half. (For the record: I love it.) The neighbourhood I have moved into, we discover, is known colloquially as The Cholent Pot. It is the area within The Area where Jewish life is at its most dense. The epicentre of *Yiddishkeit*. A place where I

---

* By the way – it's a lesser-spotted hard -ch- in cholent, not the plosive valar fricatives you've been employing for *challah* and *shacharis* and so on.

am, for the first time, surrounded almost entirely by Jewish life: kosher restaurants, kosher shops, Jewish schools, even a community-run Jewish ambulance service. To discover life in Hendon is akin to stepping into Diagon Alley – it is an environment overlapping with London, but somehow part of an entirely separate world. Something that has been there all along, if only you knew where to look.

There is a close-knit domestic quiet to the residential suburban streets – rows and rows of large, sturdy houses, some hyper-modern and manicured, some plain and unassuming, and a few seemingly untouched since the mid-seventies, with wild lawns and cracked, desiccating paintwork. There is a hushed, frenetic quality outside the many *shuls* – the men of the *minyanim* often hurriedly gathering outside to smoke or talk business, before or after their *davening* is done. And there is a raucous bustling chaos to the shops that line Golders Green Road, the busy arterial stretch that runs through the heart of the neighbourhood. Given the centrality of food to Jewish life, there are a plethora of caterers and grocers and delis and bakers and butchers (I swiftly discover that, as with *shuls*, everyone seemingly has a 'butcher they don't go to', as well as the one they frequent with fierce loyalty). And, at the centre of it all, the nexus point of The Area, exerting an unstoppable magnetic pull drawing all life towards it, there is Kosher Kingdom.

The leading kosher supermarket in London, if not the UK, if not Europe, Kosher Kingdom is a place of sensory overload, its shelves piled high with every sort of *hescher*-certified product anyone could possibly want or need, and more.

There are bagels, salads, fresh smoothies, individually wrapped vegetables (pre-washed and carefully checked for insects in accordance with kosher law), a handmade sushi concession, sandwiches made with apple juice instead of water (which means the blessing recited after consuming it is shorter than the elaborate '*bensching*' of a Friday night dinner), hot deli food, cold deli food, smoked salmon, dips, sauces, oils, condiments from brands you've heard of (Heinz ketchup!) and brands you haven't (Glicks ketchup!), kosher eggs (pre-checked to ensure they are free of blood spots), an immense pick-and-mix aisle full of towering plastic scoop bins loaded with gelatine-free sweets, an aisle dedicated to kosher booze in all its forms, a bakery aisle loaded with *challah* and sweet *rugolech* and honey cake and biscuits, and shelves laden with Shabbat-friendly toothbrushes and cleaning supplies, and crisps and chocolates and toys and cards . . .

It opens early and closes late, and its aisles are perpetually teeming with cackling schoolkids, and hyper-practical young pregnant women surrounded by toddlers, and confused husbands video-calling their wives to ensure that the jar of pickles they're holding is the right one, and tiny elderly women pushing shopping trolleys containing triple their weight in food, and teenage *yeshiva* boys charging past whilst arguing with one another furiously, and a smiling non-Jewish Indian shop assistant who proudly wears a huge *kippah* and seems as well versed in Jewish lore as anyone else in the neighbourhood . . .

It is bracingly expensive (as all kosher food is), it is total unmitigated chaos, and it sits at the very heart of the community.

Dazzled and dazed, I make it through the queues and the carnage and stagger out into the morning sunlight. I have bought some chewing gum.

I conclude that, on balance of probability, the heady, dense atmosphere of Joel's *shtiebel* is unlikely to be the minyan at which I will spend my mornings during my time in The Area.

But – tentatively adjusting as I am to my new surroundings – by the time my second Hendon morning is upon me, and my forehead makes contact with the eaves once more, I have not yet gathered the expertise or the confidence to decide upon an alternate destination.

So, marching out of the house in hot pursuit of one of Joel's super-athlete sons, whose walking pace exceeds that of my mid-level jog, back to the *shtiebel* I go.

The room is packed once more. It is still overwhelming, but fractionally less so than the day before. I begin to discern the outlines of the blessings I have been learning.

And then, through the slats of the *mechitza,* the divider which keeps men and women apart during prayer, I notice something different to yesterday; there are far more women present today. That's nice, I think, blithely, reading nothing more into it. Big mistake.

Within Orthodoxy, the convention is that women are not subject to 'positive time-bound *mitzvahs*', such as the obligation to pray at certain times, which falls to men.

This means that, should one spot a profusion of women over on the female side of a *shul* on a weekday morning, it might mean one of a few things.

Perhaps they all happened to wake up that morning, simultaneously filled with the desire to do some additional, non-mandated communing with the Creator. Or, alternatively . . . they're attending a circumcision.

It is as the baby is carried in on a pillow that I realise, belatedly, which of these options is the more likely.

I feel a rising panic.

Blocked in, shoulder to shoulder, with congregants on every side of me, I am, effectively, trapped in the room, with what is essentially a front-row view of the impending proceedings.

I have made as close to 'my peace' with the idea of this procedure as I can. I have gritted my teeth and committed to it, rendered it a theoretical certainty at some point in my future – I mean, I've sent a cartoon drawing of the style I want to the nice man who'll ultimately be tasked with *doing* it; how much more peace can a man make? Nonetheless, what I am not keen to do is watch an example of this procedure take place, live, less than five metres away from my face.

The baby is carried to the front of the room, and baby-and-pillow placed on the lap of a man sat on another large wooden throne. Or maybe it's the same throne as before – perhaps the Beth Din have tasked a group of strapping young Torah students with carrying it around to various events I attend, to add an additional level of gravitas.

On a nearby table, I suddenly notice a glinting, glistening toolkit. The *mohel*, a slight, bearded man, removes the baby's nappy, and salves its soon-to-be afflicted area with Vaseline . . .

A number of things can be true.

Circumcision is an ancient tradition common to multiple religions and numerous cultures around the world, a virtually risk-free procedure with a number of possible health benefits and little evidence that it diminishes an individual's experience of the world. And also, watching a baby have its foreskin cut off is a thoroughly unpleasant way to start one's day.

As the *mohel* leans in to begin his work, the incensed, relentless shriek of the baby rings out.

I grip my chair, fighting the urge to . . . what? To issue a scream myself? To charge forward, leap across the tables, and carry the baby away down the street? To punch myself in the face? I don't know.

As the *mohel* slices and cuts, the atmosphere is a strange combination of excitement and horror, joy and revulsion. Delight and pride in the ancient significance of the ceremony, and a ripple of unease at the bloody reality of it. I feel a sense of slight relief at the realisation that those surrounding me are, like I am, squeamish and skittish about being ringside for such a gory display, and not simply exultant, wide-eyed, caught in the grips of some religious euphoria.

'Even I always feel quite conflicted at these things,' mutters a nearby man to his wincing neighbour, 'and I'm a doctor.'

It is over in minutes. Suddenly I am being handed a plastic shot glass of whisky and a warm sticky pastry (a *rugolech*, in fact, from where else but Kosher Kingdom), and I walk out, shell-shocked, to begin another day in Hendon, vaguely wondering where they'll find a pillow big enough for me, when the time finally comes.

Having now gathered the confidence to explore my new neighbourhood – if not yet the presence of mind to get out of bed in the correct direction – I now spend my mornings '*shul*-shopping' – attending a different minyan each morning, in a quest to find the one which works best for me.

I visit *shuls* in modern office blocks and grand stone buildings, in gated courtyards and up pokey flights of stairs, well-attended *minyanim* which I must slip into at the back in order to find a space, and small gatherings of men who eagerly wave me in as a contribution to their hoped-for quorum of ten, before I have to break the bad news that I am unable to help them on that front, no matter how desperately I would like to.

Each *shul* has a different flavour and feel, its own quirks and traditions.

I stand out, a little. Firstly – and this varies, *shul* to *shul* – I am now in 'black hat' territory.

There is an extraordinary amount of information that can be conveyed by the headgear of a Jewish man.

A knitted or suede *kippah* might communicate that you are on the Modern side of Orthodoxy – a satin *kippah* could indicate that you are Masorti or Reform. Black velvet? Now you're getting serious – these *kippot* (and there are infinite subtle variations, particular to the traditions of different sects) are frequently indicative of ultra-Orthodoxy and, for many – particularly young men studying at *yeshiva* – are worn with an accompanying black fedora on top. And if your *kippah* is a lurid colour and features a cartoon smiley face? Well, you're either a local eccentric or, more likely, you're currently attending a *bar mitzvah*, and it's one of hundreds of identical ones designed as per the *bar mitzvah* boy's wishes for the attendees to take.

The head coverings of women, too, tell a story – in pursuit of modesty, married ultra-Orthodox women will almost certainly cover their hair, either with a headscarf or a wig known as a *sheitel*. The fact that this wig is made of, yes, human hair, does pose something of a contradiction in terms – meaning some ultra-Orthodox women will seek out *sheitels* which deliberately look slightly artificial or dowdy, whilst others will simply seize the opportunity to have a good hair day every day of the week, and buy something far more glamorous than their actual hair. The women of Modern Orthodoxy, meanwhile, having instigated something of a quiet rebellion, are more likely to simply wear a hat to *shul* (and over in the freewheeling world of Reform Judaism, that hat could even be a *kippah*).

The men who pass me by on the streets of Hendon and sit next to me in *shul* are, by and large, black-velvet *kippah*-wearers – and I, manifestly, am not. Having long been attached to the *kippah* that my mother handmade for me for my *bar mitzvah* – stone-coloured linen with tiny beads embroidered on one side, and blue marbleised cotton on the other – I recognise that this sartorial choice is unlikely to render my time in Hendon easier, simpler or shorter. However, diving in and purchasing an enormous black-velvet *kippah* feels entirely unrepresentative of who I am, and as though I'd be cosplaying my way through the process – the equivalent of immediately growing a floor-length beard. Instead, I invest in a *kippah* that is small, knitted and dark blue. It feels like an appropriate step forward – and also, more so than my historic *kippah*, something that I could actually wear every day. Because that's part of it, now; my *kippah* goes on first thing in the morning after showering (and, in several tired instances, before and thus *during* showering – which, most ancient texts seem to agree, is a level of piety too far). So too, now, does my *tzitzit* – the white knotted tasselled garment worn under that day's outfit, the tassels emerging from my waistband and tucked into my pockets.

When I first wear both items out into the world, the act feels intensely strange, and I am hugely self-conscious. Riding the Northern Line from Hendon down into central London, the carriage filling with more non-Jewish travellers at every stop, and I feel myself flush hot with embarrassment. When I first get changed at the gym, I take elaborate, time-consuming care to hide my *tzitzit* within my shirt as I take everything off, so that the full extent of my tasselled apparatus goes unnoticed.

This feeling stays with me until I sit and address it properly. Why is this new mode of dress giving me a sense of discomfort? Partly there's the oddness of it, certainly – the knowledge that, had I not begun this conversion, I would not otherwise be wearing these items at 2.30pm in Soho. Far more than that, I realise, the thing I am finding truly difficult to deal with is the knowledge that I am now broadcasting my identity to the world. My Judaism, such as it is (or isn't), is no longer internal; it is clearly, definitively visible. But what am I worried about? That someone will see that I'm Jewish and . . . not like it? This, it becomes immediately clear to me, is a 'them' problem. That of all the reasons to not wear visibly Jewish clothing, the worry that I might upset 'people who dislike Jews' is absolutely the worst of them. At this, my perspective immediately shifts. I promptly relax about these new additions to my wardrobe – a *kippah* being something I've worn my entire life anyway, for goodness' sake, just not so regularly, and as for the *tzitzit*, so what? Should I not embrace another facet of a tradition I have always been connected to? Soon I come to wear them both entirely unselfconsciously, cycling through town with my tassels flapping in the breeze.

Despite this evolution in my personal style, and despite having packed only my more austere clothing into my suitcase, by the standards of The Cholent Pot I am still dressed flamboyantly. My *tzitzit* may be flowing, but they are emerging from some deconstructed cotton trousers and a knitted Cuban-collar T-shirt, not the grey or black or dark blue suit and white shirt that is the de facto uniform of the Hendon man. And my *kippah* may be adorning the back of my head, but it marks me out as someone whose sensibilities differ from the majority of those in the room – someone who has yet to ascend to the level of black velvet, and frankly may never get there.

And then, of course, there is my lack of tefillin. With each *shul* I attend on my shopping spree, my unadorned biceps and forehead – lacking as they are any hint of leather strap or wooden box – invariably draw attention. Most commonly, someone rushes over and proffers a hastily located spare set of tefillin, assuming I have forgotten mine in the morning rush. So, each time, I explain who I am and what has led me here. I receive umpteen warm welcomes, multiple phone numbers eagerly shared, and numerous fascinated questions about how I am finding the whole thing. And, every single time, there is the big question, which, via my *shul*-shopping, I am attempting to answer; 'Where will you be for the festivals?'

*

The cyclical rhythms of Jewish life adhere to a lunar calendar, and thus the dates of the festivals – or *chagim** – shift each year – but, generally, they arrive in in the months of September or October, and they come thick and fast. 'They' is actually a misnomer, as there are plenty of other festivals throughout the year, but when someone Jewish refers to 'the festivals', it's almost certain that they are referring to the autumnal rush that sees the end of one Jewish year and the beginning of another: Rosh Hashanah, followed by Yom Kippur, followed by Sukkot, followed by Shemini Atzeret and Simchat Torah – all of which are marked within a period of around three weeks.

Each festival comes with its own set of rules, prayers, traditions and ceremonies and – much like Shabbat – work is strictly proscribed on all of the key days of observance. The result is a packed, hectic, relentless annual schedule, which I heard more than one rabbi laughingly cite as irrefutable evidence of the Almighty's existence – given that no human would design an itinerary that is so spectacularly inconvenient.

We have been transported to Hendon for the express purpose of being immersed in religious Jewish life, and the festivals are when religious Jewish life reaches its zenith; the question of where we will be is a crucial one to answer. It feels hugely important to find a community that is warm, inviting, and that we connect with. Also, given the amount of time we'll be spending there over those three weeks, they would ideally have comfortable chairs.

In the end, it is Eliana's tutor who points us in the right direction. We want somewhere friendly, welcoming, musical? She knows just the place. Only trouble is – they're all booked up. But either way, the thing to do is introduce yourself to the rabbi.

---

* There's that soft 'ch' again.

And so we make an appointment with Rabbi Weissman, the presiding rabbi of Ohr HaTorah synagogue, and, sat in his office, bearing gifts of *rugolech* (aisle six of you know where), we present ourselves to him and explain our story.

'Thank you. I am very moved by your journey', are the first words he says to us, once we have finished speaking. He has a kind face, and he talks to us with warmth and sincerity. About the fact that we have uprooted our lives in ways he will never know, and about how calmly and unitedly we are tackling the challenges ahead of us.

He oversees a huge, thriving community – amongst the largest in The Area – and they are long overbooked for the festivals, and massively so. But, nonetheless, he welcomes us. He is certain they'll find a way to squeeze us in – and, promptly, he walks us down the corridor and introduces us to the (all-powerful) woman who controls the seating plans. Unflappable, she assures us that she'll sort something out. Rabbi Weissman thanks us for meeting with him. 'So good to meet you! You'll come to ours for lunch, of course?' say three separate people we pass on the way out.

And so the festivals begin, and Eliana and I turn off our phones and are plunged into a whirlwind social calendar we are in no way prepared for. Rosh Hashanah is simply a case of:

Night one: *davening* at Ohr, followed by dinner at my tutor Rav Dov's. This is followed by Monday morning at Ohr, followed by lunch with the Bernsteins' eldest son and his wife and children, followed by afternoon and evening prayers at Ohr, followed by Monday dinner with the Bernsteins themselves, and all their family, followed by Tuesday morning prayers at Ohr, followed by lunch with the Bernsteins' friends the Feldmans . . .

Each meal a new house, a new group of people, a torrent of new names and faces.

As we make our way uncertainly around the neighbourhood,

desperately attempting to remember directions we have been given, or clutching scraps of paper with inexpertly drawn maps, in search of our next meal, I am struck by the extraordinary interconnectedness of communal life here.

I examine the crumpled paper in my hand, attempting to read my own awful writing. 'Oh – I think we're on the wrong side of the road – we need number forty-six . . .'

'Forty-six? The Kleins,' says a woman walking past. 'It's that way.' She doesn't even look up.

Another occasion, having tried and failed to remember either the location or name of the road we are seeking, the young men we ask for directions insist on walking us to the door – knowing not just the names of our hosts, but having been babysat by them and later taught by them. 'Give the Feldmans our regards!' they say, as they vanish off into the night. *'Chag sameach!'**

When we attend Rabbi Weissman's *shul*, we find it categorically impossible to leave without more lunch and dinner invites than there are weeks in the year. So populous is the *shul* that regular seats are an impossibility – one merely squeezes in where one can – but I end up befriending a tall genial man, who asks about my story, and talks freely and amusedly about his own on-off relationships, with Judaism and with women, over the years.

'When it works, the support of a functioning Jewish community is unmatchable,' he says, looking around the room fondly. 'Unmatchable. It's the matrix of all human life. And it's all contained in the Torah. All the strangeness, everything. It offers something for everyone – even me, a total *lobbus*†.'

---

* Happy holidays!

† The wonderful thing about Yiddish is that more or less every word sounds exactly like what it means. So the brilliant *lobbus* is a somewhat affectionate term for a lazybones, urchin, or good-for-nothing. But you sort of instinctively knew that, just from the word alone.

The service ends and the room-dividing *mechitza* is removed, so men and women can mingle once more. 'Anyway, you must find your good lady and enjoy the *kiddush*. I'm off to see if there are any grandmas I can marry.'

Forget every nonsensical nostalgic Facebook meme depicting an imagined 1950s England in which everyone left their doors unlocked and 'looked out for each other'. In Hendon there is community in its most active and functional sense; roads and roads of houses whose inhabitants all know one another, and take an active and practical interest in the welfare and wellbeing of their neighbours.

There is a *safeness* I have experienced nowhere else.

Looking back – and this can't be true, but this is how I remember it – over the course of the festivals we attend no fewer than twelve lunches a day. Each family we visit has their own trademark type of meal – their signature dishes, the things they always serve and never serve. Needless to say, these secret formulas are a mystery to Eliana and I, dining as we are at each home for the first time, and so any attempt at pacing ourselves becomes a total impossibility.

'Oh, today is just a one-course wonder,' says Eliana's host Sarah Green, dismissively, when we join her for meal #473 of the festivals. This is true, as long as you define a 'course' as 'as many dishes as can be fitted onto a large table at one time'. If, like me, you go by '*number* of dishes' . . . well, she is serving fifteen courses, minimum. We eat, we pray, we sleep, we repeat.

We are in Hendon's warm, inescapable embrace.

CHAPTER 23

A Walk in the Park

It is the strangest thing, to be rendered entirely helpless. To be uprooted from your life, and the trappings of reality as you have come to understand them, and to find yourself in an environment that is utterly other. Transported to some new world, for an unknown period of time, at the whims of an unanswerable authority.

Here at the Bernsteins', I am born entirely anew. I am a man in my thirties and I am a baffled infant – far slower and simpler than the Bernsteins' polite children. I am their idiot eighth son who lives in their attic and can barely get out of bed properly. In the days that it takes me to learn not to concuss myself each morning, the Bernsteins' children have collectively run and cycled the length of the country, and studied the entirety of the Torah inside and out, all before breakfast.

It is blindingly clear why the Beth Din seek to move people here. In these streets, Judaism is manifest. Here, a tiny diaspora is not just preserving but building upon centuries of unbroken tradition. A way of life underpinned by the study of an ancient text, the importance of which shapes every element of life – the physical environment, the atmosphere in the streets, the very passage of time.

There is much to wonder at: the way that, because nobody has any free time, they make exceptional use of it, maintaining friendships and conducting business transactions in the spare seconds it takes to walk from the *shul* to their car on a weekday morning; the unaffected manner in which parents speak to their children, engaging with them as intellectual equals, encouraging them to join in with any and all conversations, challenging their logical fallacies and celebrating – learning from, even – the ideas they contribute; the hunger for study in all its forms, with men and women eagerly attending lectures and talks and *shiurim** late into the night or first thing in the morning, seven days a week; the colossal importance that is placed on family life, which is deemed every bit as important as professional success – it being understood that the latter is only ever in service to the former; the way in which the indivisible combination of family, *shul* and geographical proximity conspires to create a safety net which means young parents are supported, the elderly and the infirm are integrated, strangers are welcomed, no one is left behind or unnoticed.

The total directness and closeness is protective, almost exhilarating – but it is also stifling.

And, as the festivals engulf Eliana and I, and I feel myself dragged beneath a tidal wave of religion, the groggy confusion that first greeted me upon waking is now being replaced with a state of increasingly acute distress – the feeling that I am drowning.

When Eliana and I walk together in the small park near our houses, or take the ninety-minute walk to her parents' house on the rare Shabbatot that we dare leave The Area for fear of not being seen, our arguments bubble up with increasing regularity, and become ever-more heated.

'The Beth Din don't owe you anything, OK?' snaps Eliana, midway through another of my miserable rants. 'They didn't ask you to convert.'

---

* Lessons in rabbinic texts or Jewish concepts.

No. That's true. But, from another perspective: 'I didn't ask to have the nature of my soul called into question, did I? To be deemed a non-person. To have my traditions and my history and my identity nullified. I didn't ask for any of that.'

I am set off by small things.

'Like the wine! Do you know how that makes me feel?!' There are rules about wine, you see (there are rules about everything, obviously, but there are *more* rules about wine). Wine is generously offered at approximately 100 per cent of the gatherings we attend and, *within* the sphere of kosher wine, there is a type that is permissible for non-Jews to pour, and another type that they – and I'm using the royal 'they' here – cannot touch.

The complications are numerous. For one thing, the difference between 'pourable by me' and 'do not touch under any circumstances' relies on a single word, which may or may not be printed somewhere on the bottle, in text which could well be microscopic in size. Thus begins a silent game of label studying and attempted psychic communication between Eliana and I, in a bid not to inadvertently upset our host. There is further confusion to be found in the fact that not all of the families who invite us to eat with them adhere to this rule – some of them happily passing me theoretically unpourable bottles in the full knowledge of my spiritual irregularity. Do I accept the bottle, knowing that in doing so I am rendering it unkosher, which might perhaps upset other guests around the (inevitably packed) dining table? Do I reject it, embarrassing the host? Generally I try and fumble my way through by having both of my hands occupied – lunging erratically for whatever's near, on one occasion grabbing two plates, both containing schmaltz herring (a dish I also happen to find completely inedible), and serving myself pointlessly from both – whilst Eliana attempts to intercept the bottle.

And for those instances when it *is* a rule our hosts adhere to?

'Aha – let me,' the husband might say, heaving himself from his chair at the head of the table and making a light jog past sixteen other guests in order to pour me a glass of the red wine that is inches away from my hand. Faced with his kindness – and it really is kindness, from his perspective – I sit powerlessly, and I feel myself wilt.

Across the table, Eliana, who is reading my mind, will nod imperceptibly. 'I know, my love. I'm sorry.' Such a tiny thing. And yet it is enough to launch me ricocheting into another litany of grievances.

I am still set off by the big things, too.

'Like the fucking circumcisions! I ended up at another one this morning. Practically every other week I end up having to watch babies get bits of their bodies removed – it's not pleasant!'

'I'm sure it's not, and I can't imagine how stressful it is for you, but if it *is* something you're going to have done, wouldn't you rather it was when you were a baby than—'

'And d'you know the reason they happen?'

'There are lots of reasons—'

'Sure. Well, d'you know what Maimonides says? "To weaken the member"! I don't *want* my member weakened! Are you nuts? Let's just say, for a second, that this wasn't an ancient, millennia-old tradition, and I came up with it, just now – would it sound like a good idea to you? Really?'

In a turn of events so unbelievable that any good editor would dismiss them from a work of fiction, I stumble across a piece on the website of the *New Yorker* called 'Dear Max: Contemplating Circumcision'. It is a short animated film about a concerned Jewish narrator weighing up the pros and cons of circumcising his son, Max. 'Was I really going to inflict such outlandish barbarity on another human being?' the father asks himself. Is this something one should really do 'because God slash your grandparents told you to do it'? In the end, he does give his son a *brit* – but it's a decision he is deeply conflicted about, and something he describes as 'the worst day of my life'.

'Oh – and did you know that the actual nature of the procedure itself has changed?' I say, having emerged from my laptop freshly disturbed by another bout of research. 'That, because Jews in Greece in the year 300 BC started tugging on what was left of their foreskins to make it look like they weren't Jewish to try and avoid persecution, the rabbis *made the surgery more invasive*! So the thing everyone does isn't even the original thing! And now it's going to be done to me! WHAT IS GOING ON?'

And, perhaps more than anything else, I am set off by regular things.

'Going to synagogue three times a day! Do you have any idea how many times a day that is?!'

'I know, I know, it's a lot. But you also knew what you were signing up for—'

'Intellectually, sure, but I didn't know what it would *feel* like! It's everywhere! It's a constant countdown!'

And then there is the biggest thing of all. There is my father. And this I bring up less, because I can barely stand to bring it up at all.

As I lash out, and wallow in my misery, I am painfully aware of how much of it stems from my own self-disgust; at how badly I am dealing with this experience I had deluded myself into thinking I would sail through. Acutely conscious of how pleasant and kind and welcoming our foster families are – how supportive our *actual* families are – how much is in our favour, and yet how difficult, how close to impossible, I am finding it all.

In the end it takes a softly spoken therapist on Zoom to pull us back from the brink. His large, kind, pink face fills the screen, and he nods calmly as I rant and vent and Eliana speaks passionately, until we are both exhausted.

Even the fact of his presence is a help. A reminder that we are trying to solve something together, not extinguish one another with the heat of our righteousness.

The therapist listens unjudgementally, and then he speaks gently and practically.

He encourages us to structure our conversations, compartmentalising the difficult topics of the day into one clear window of time, so that we might focus on it, address it, and move on.

So that's what we start trying to do. We decide to call the window of time in which we air our grievances 'the cloud', and we funnel our worries and fears, discomfort and rage into these conversations, and purge ourselves, and it does begin to work – the world begins to feel a little more manageable.

As the chill of winter descends, we walk around the small, slightly ragged Hendon park together, as close to one another as we dare. Unable to hold hands, in desperation we resort to each holding on to one of the other's gloves. It's such a pitiful arrangement that we laugh at our own misery. Eliana has been given a pair of vintage kid gloves by her grandmother, Lion. I interlace the glove's fingers with my own, I feel the soft fabric in my hand, and I hold on for dear life.

CHAPTER 24

Pure Hendonism

Life, it feels, is nothing but a succession of 'new normals'. I am forever off-balance, constantly seeking equilibrium as I am flung between ever-changing worlds governed by ever-changing rules.

And, because I am always deep in the midst of finding my bearings, I seldom realise how far my journey has taken me. When, at the very start of the process, I first visited Eliana's family's *shul*, Beit Shalom, it had seemed a mysterious, daunting location – now, when returning there from Hendon, it feels reassuringly comforting. It is curious, the way one adjusts, the way the foreign becomes the familiar.

Eliana and I come to Beit Shalom for a handful of the many days of the festivals, walking the four miles or so along the Finchley Road, in order to celebrate with her family. When we are here, we are welcomed by the community of Eliana's childhood. I am waved back in by increasingly recognisable, increasingly friendly faces, and I am hugged and greeted as a roving pilgrim, bringing tales of the mysterious north.

But for the most part we spend the festivals, and our lives, in Hendon, participating as fully and as keenly and as consistently as possible, though we presume the all-seeing eye of the Beth Din perceives us wherever we might be. Whilst I am yet to fully adjust to the intensity of this newest new normal, I am finding ways to attempt to regulate my response to it all.

I vent judiciously into 'the cloud' with Eliana, when walking in the scrubby park, or speaking to her on the phone at the end of another endless day, lying in bed and looking up at the eaves. And I have started keeping a diary. Up in my bedroom, I sit on the end of my bed, with an ironing board for my desk, and I write into the night, until my mind is clear, or exhaustion drags me to sleep.

My *shul*-shopping is now more or less concluded, and I have alighted on the places that feel least alien to me; weekends are spent at Ohr, where, on days when I am feeling emotionally robust, the musicality of the densely packed congregation can feel powerful and uplifting – a little like Beit Shalom on steroids. And on weekday mornings and evenings (if one times it right, the daily afternoon and evening prayers can be done together in one sitting) I attend a small nearby *shul*, somewhat sparse and utilitarian in design, but overseen by a supremely warm and welcoming rabbi. I even manage to attain something close to a 'regular seat' most days.

With this gradual establishment of coping mechanisms and daily routines, a rhythm of sorts emerges. I begin to settle into Hendon living.

More evenings than not I find myself sat at the Bernsteins' kitchen table, eating the supper that Ronit has somehow prepared whilst simultaneously working and volunteering and swimming and attending *shiurim* and seeing neighbours and hosting relatives from overseas and reassuring Joel that no, the slight sore throat he has picked up is very unlikely to be a terminal condition.

If I am back late, I might sync up with Joel, who will rush back in from a long day at the office and swiftly inhale whatever food is on the countertop, before retreating to his study to work late into the night. And if I'm back earlier, I'll often eat supper with some of the many Bernstein children, who will be sat variously doing their homework, or reading, or browsing YouTube, or, occasionally, thumping one another and running away, as siblings must.

It is via this amicable window of evening socialising that I fall in with one of the Bernsteins' sons, Nahum, who, via the surly grunting of a teenage boy, invites me to hang out with him at a local fast-food joint.

'We can go Slice if you want,' he mutters one day, whilst staring into the middle distance.

He'd clearly heard me discussing the place with Eliana, having become fascinated by it. Slice, which claims to serve both sushi and pizza, is somewhere I now walk past on multiple occasions each day, yet have never once seen any indication that its doors have opened or lights been turned on at any point in the last fifteen years. I am of the opinion that Slice is, essentially, a myth – the building itself either a long-forgotten film set, some sort of obscure tax dodge, or the quasi-haunted location that an excited child breaks into at the start of a Studio Ghibli film, before finding themselves in a magical alternate universe and completing a quest alongside an anthropomorphic slice of stuffed-crust margherita and a wise old giant tuna. But Nahum assures me that Slice does open, and that it's actually something of a local hotspot – it's simply because I've been leaving the house early and working long hours that I've missed out on this Italian-Japanese-north-London kosher fusion dining experience.

'Sure thing, Nahum,' I say. 'I'd love to go to Slice.'

Via my time in The Cholent Pot, I have discovered there is a unique style of service particular to the majority of London's kosher restaurants, and although I have diligently scoured the thesaurus searching for an appropriately evocative literary descriptor, the most suitable word is, simply: 'bad'. There are the restaurants whose proprietors seem visibly dismayed that you have entered, despite their premises being entirely empty. There are the many types of service: indifferent, incompetent, sullen, openly hostile – often a potent combination of all four. There are printed menus that diverge wildly from the food actually on offer, unaccountable wait times of upwards of ninety minutes (often, mystifyingly, in the restaurants that are empty), and there is the scientifically calibrated lack of anything approaching a 'vibe'. On the plus side, no two restaurants offer the *same* terrible hospitality experience, which adds a frisson of mystery to each excursion.

And so, when I rush back from working with Ivan, rush to *shul* for evening prayers, and then rush towards Slice – seeing its signage, yes, illuminated, and people inside too! – I'm not sure exactly what to expect. I am thus unprepared for what does happen when I walk into the strip-lit room, which is that I am promptly refused service by the fourteen-year-old boy behind the till, who appears to be Slice's manager, on the grounds that he's 'had enough'.

It's a disarming statement, and one I'm not sure how to deal with. I've arrived at the allotted time set by Nahum, and according to Slice's signage the premises is very much open, and should be for another hour or so. Further to that, the place is absolutely rammed; a sea of *yeshiva bochers* – feral teenage boys clad in white shirts and black fedoras – are crowded around the tables and crammed into the red and blue faux-leather banquettes, chattering away at a deafening volume.

It is the act of managing this chaos that the manager appears to have had enough of. Fielding orders, granting refills, turning down audacious requests for free food – it's clearly got too much for him.

'Oh,' I say, nonplussed. 'So, you're definitely closed?'
'Yeah.'
'Elective mid-shift closure' is a new addition to my kosher

restaurant bingo card. Not knowing what to do, I text Nahum. 'Apparently they've stopped serving!'

Seven seconds later, Nahum – who was next door at a delicatessen with some mates, attending to who knows what crucial business – comes tearing in through the door shaking his head, his eyes lit up with a sense of purpose.

He makes a beeline for the till and, in an urgent hushed yell (honestly, there's no more accurate description than that), he conducts a furious argument with the young manager – also his schoolmate, it turns out – who, after a few seconds of deliberation, throws up his hands in resignation and agrees to serve us.

We order two signature oversized slices of pizza, and some tuna uramaki rolls, both of which – to my disbelief – turn up instantly and are . . . delicious.

Nahum's act of negotiating has also had a knock-on effect, in that the floodgates have now reopened for our fellow diners to swarm back up to the till and order yet more slushies and iced coffees and pizza slices, tripping over their gigantic e-scooters and one another in their urgent, directionless excitement.

Nahum and I put the world to rights – we chat upcoming A levels (his), driving lessons (both of us) and the David Walliams BBC special *Gangsta Granny* (which Nahum has worked out, via diligent IMDB stalking, that I had a one-word cameo in, and quizzes me about at length).

In my peripheral vision, I realise a small boy is lingering by our table, furtively trying to attract my attention.

'Mhphn?' he blurts out, in a rapid-fire squeak.

'I'm sorry . . . ?' I say.

'He wants to use your phone,' says Nahum, with a sheepish grin, whilst making eye contact with the table.

'Oh! Erm . . . sure?'

The formally dressed eleven-year-old boy is holding out his hand with something approaching impatience, and so, uncertainly, I pass him my phone.

'Hi? Dad? Yeah, can you pick me up, please?'

At the sound of this conversation taking place, dozens of ears prick up, and word gets around: there's a bloke over there with a phone, and he lets you use it!

Suddenly, a stream of boys charge over and form an unruly line, each making the same request. I give up trying to keep track and they pass the phone between one another, summoning their various parents to collect them. Nahum grins and shrugs and turns a gentle shade of pink, embarrassed by his schoolmates and, as a teenager, the general act of existing, and talks me through his plans for once he's finished college ('Dunno').

'So what do you do?'

It's a fairly inevitable question in any dinner party situation – and Eliana and I are now in dinner party situations for approximately 80 per cent of our waking lives.

It's also a question with a host of possible answers. Because I do various things. Am I a writer who's also a comedian? A comedian who also writes? An actor who's appalling at auditions but is nonetheless an asset to any production and a delight to work with and should definitely get brought in for more projects without having to self-tape? The truth is, of course, that I am a combination of all of those things. But what do you tell someone you've just met? And further to that, what do you tell someone you've just met, in a house you've just entered, in a social gathering which has a delicate socioreligious balance that you are yet to quite work out?

Within the Hendon-verse, the infinite permutations of Orthodox socialising now reveal themselves to me still further. At the highest end of religiosity and formality, there are large-scale dinners at the houses of senior rabbis. On the most relaxed end, there are intimate meals with couples we have come to befriend from our time at Ohr, and a few other more freewheeling (albeit entirely Orthodox) communities we visit from time to time. And then there's a plethora of intermediary levels between those two extremes. In an odd way, I find it less challenging dining at the house of some formidable rabbi. In this setting, it is always abundantly clear that we are operating in a world that is not our own; the ceremonial formalities, the modes of conversation, the religious songs sung midway through the meal, these all serve as constant reminders of where we are.

Ironically, it is the more relaxed environments that prove the most stressful – because these are the moments when life feels so deliciously, flickeringly close to 'normal'. Eliana and I will be sat next to one another, chatting, drinking, laughing with those around us. And then, in a stab of jagged discordancy, I will remember; if I were to inadvertently hold my girlfriend's hand, place my arm on her shoulder, make any form of physical contact whatsoever . . . this could all be over. The bridge we are attempting to cross could disintegrate beneath us.

It's not that, at these meals, we are surrounded by anything other than kind, supportive, pleasant people, wholly sympathetic to our cause. But, if someone from the Beth Din were to ask them directly: 'Did you see this couple break any of the laws they are now governed by?' It's impossible to imagine that anyone would lie. And, more than that, we wouldn't dream of asking them to.

So as I pass someone the roast potatoes, and eagerly accept a third portion of roast chicken, I will quietly start to disassociate, my consciousness floating up to the dining room ceiling and gazing down in fascinated incomprehension at the environment

I have somehow found myself in; quietly suburban, yet dangerously high-wire. A casual, chatty dinner where, were I to unthinkingly rest my hand on Eliana's knee, then the life we are seeking to build together could be rendered permanently and irrevocably out of reach.

Most dinners, however, are not quite one thing or the other – neither the height of formality nor the loosest end of casual. And so, when I am asked the question 'What do you do?', I tend to begin with 'writing'. I have no wish to alienate or confuse whoever I'm speaking to – and, if they happen to be someone's elderly aunt, or a deeply religious young woman who's moved to the area for the purposes of finding a *shidduch*,* or just a slightly dull man who works in commercial finance, then looking them dead in the eye and leading with 'I'm in a narrative-sketch-comedy double-act' doesn't feel like a particularly sensible opening gambit.

Sometimes, 'writing' alone is an eccentric enough response for my conversational partner, who will smile blankly and politely and leave it at that. But more often than not they will ask further questions, and so I will explain as much or as little as they care to hear about exactly what I do – the different types of writing, and the fact that much of it is within the world of comedy, as I am also a performer. This softly-softly approach has the added bonus of mostly avoiding that most dreaded of interactions: 'I'm a comedian.' 'Oh yeah?! Tell us a joke!'

And the upshot is, at those moments when it feels appropriate to do so, the fact that I am a comedian bubbles up into the conversation – at which point people will invariably announce their personal favourites. Michael McIntyre is huge in Hendon (and I mean huge). *Little Britain* is very popular. Jackie Mason

---

* A *shidduch* (soft ch!) is the Jewish concept of matchmaking.

is name-checked regularly (absolutely everyone either saw him perform in their *shul*, or knows someone who did).

I had wondered whether those more conservative people I end up speaking to might have some issue with comedy itself, and they do – only it is the worry that freedom of speech is being curtailed. 'You can't say anything these days, can you,' says a man passing me some potato kugel. What exactly this highly religious accountant feels he might be prevented from saying is unclear, but he seems fairly certain of the fact. 'You can't say anything these days,' he repeats, shaking his head.

When it comes to Eliana's playwriting, however, we generally operate a 'don't ask, don't tell' policy. And, as playwriting isn't her 'job', when grilled about her work Eliana simply talks about her day job at a talent agency, or the jewellery company she started in lockdown. Other stuff.

Her play, *Anything with a Pulse* – which I first saw in Edinburgh – transferred to the Park Theatre shortly after the Fringe, and has now been brought back for an extended run at the same venue. The theatre is, geographically, thirty minutes away from Hendon, but it also feels like it's an entire universe away.

Until, one evening, at another dinner . . . 'Do you know,' says a woman at the far end of the table, who we've not properly spoken to yet, 'last night I went to the Park Theatre, and I saw this play.'

No. Eliana and I lock eyes across the table, screaming, silently. The woman continues.

'It was by this young Jewish female playwright . . .'

Immediately, my brain fills with intrusive thoughts, jump-cutting to various moments across the play: a montage of drinking and shagging and colourful obscenities. Is it all extremely funny and artistically valid within the context of the play? Yes! Would I rather calmly take my own life with the ornate breadknife on the table than explain any of this to the people in the room and have this information filter out into the community? Also yes!

'... And it was called *Pickle*!'

The relief hits us both with an impact that makes me feel like I might plummet through the floor. The theatre has programmed two complementary plays as part of the same season, and this woman has seen the *other* one.

The woman continues describing the play she saw, as Eliana and I silently decompress. It's completely possible that, had this woman seen Eliana's play, she'd have had a great time. So too everyone around this table. But the possibility of it knocking us off course, putting an end to our tenuous journey, is just far, far too great. It's farcical, ridiculous and chilling, all at once.

Near-disaster moments such as this one are now notable for their irregularity. Eliana and I have hunkered down, acclimatised as best we can to our new life, and – with another Beth Din meeting approaching – we're mainly focused on trying really, really hard to nail it.

On our long walks, around and around the little park, or down to Primrose Hill, we revise furiously, internalising the hundreds of Hebrew blessings and their appropriate usages, quizzing one another on the minutiae of what can and cannot be done on Shabbat and at festivals, and the specifics of obscure passages of Orthodox Jewish law, such as when one might be likely to spit in a slipper (whilst ceremonially refusing to marry your deceased brother's widow, as would otherwise be your obligation).

My notebooks are densely packed with writing on every page, and meticulously indexed with tiny pink labels which emerge like the tentacles of a particularly organised sea anemone. I feel more prepared than I ever have done for one of these meetings. And, by chance, I have an encounter that makes me feel readier than ever.

One evening I make it back to the Bernsteins' relatively early, and as I am about to ascend to my room and my ironing board, I am met by Nahum on the stairs:

'You *davened ma'ariv* yet?'*

Ah, no. I have not.

So I join him. We go to a *shul* I'm not a regular at – an old, grand, formal building, where attendees might even be seen in a *shtreimel,* the round fur hats worn by some Hasidic Jews, and a little exotic even in my new neighbourhood. We make our way through the blessings, the distant sound of the rabbi's voice echoing off the high stone ceiling as he begins the service, before we lapse into the Amidah, the silent standing prayer. A few minutes later, when the service is concluded, Nahum and I walk back towards the house, at which point he has a thought.

'Shall we go and see the Dayan?'

The Dayan – as well as being the founder of the Bernsteins' *shul*, and the rabbi with whom they have the most profound, personal relationship – is a towering figure in Orthodoxy. He is one of the pre-eminent experts in *halacha* in all of Europe, and was for many years the head of the London Beth Din. It is he who was responsible for establishing the unrivalled standards of the very conversion process I am now hurling myself at. Much of his way of thinking differs from my own – he has long stood against Orthodox Jews attending Limmud, a popular festival which brings speakers and educators of all Jewish denominations together, to learn from one another. To my mind, this cross-pollination is a laudable, essential act – to the Dayan it represents the corrosion of true Jewish values, allowing Orthodoxy to mingle with the pseudo-Judaism of lesser belief systems. But he is not strictly ideologically conservative – he has taken great

---

* 'Have you said your evening prayers yet?'

pains to improve the lot of Jewish women seeking religious divorces – and has long been a hugely respected and sought-after senior *posek* – that is, adjudicator – in disputes and community matters.

Having suffered an enormous stroke some years ago, the Dayan is now gravely ill – and the Bernsteins visit and support both him and his wife, the Rebbetzen, as much as they can. So Nahum's suggestion as we walk back home is instinctual – beneath his layers of adolescent furtiveness, there is an adult's sense of responsibility. 'Yes, of course,' I say, 'I would be happy to visit the Dayan.' Nahum promptly leads the way, knocking on the door of a nearby house. A smiling carer ushers us into the warm living room. Suddenly, I am face to face with one of the most significant Jewish authority figures of the twentieth century.

Having been told of the Dayan's stroke, which has rendered him bed-bound and unable to speak, I was prepared to meet someone with no faculties whatsoever, but it is immediately clear that this is not the case. He is sat up, in a sort of seat-cum-bed, and he is busy learning, reading from a dense Jewish tome – he is intently focused, and his mind is clearly alive.

Nahum says his hellos, and then he introduces me. The Dayan looks up, and acknowledges us – he is silent, but he reacts, he responds.

I explain that I am incredibly grateful to the Bernsteins, who have taken me in. And I explain my reasons for asking them to do so, and my journey. At this, the Dayan becomes animated. He nods, with a beaming smile, and with one hand he gestures to the skies.

I feel the force of his desire to communicate – and then, the force of his frustration. He taps at a piece of text in the book he is reading, and then looks at me, and then back at the text, but I am unable to understand him. With what seems like exasperation, he points again, from the text to me, and from me to the text. It is densely written Biblical Hebrew, and there isn't the slightest possibility I'll be able to decipher its meaning. 'I'm so sorry,' I say, 'I'm afraid I'm not able to read that, not yet . . .'

Then the Dayan changes tack; he starts to gesture towards Nahum and his carer – waving them both away from us.

'He wants to make a *bracha** for you,' says Nahum, as he moves to the edge of the room, giving us space.

I don't know how that would work. Ordinarily a rabbi would give their blessing verbally.

But the Dayan beckons me towards him, and then reaches his hand up to my head. He is a slight figure, and the bed is low, and so I crouch down onto one knee, by his side. The Dayan places his hand on my head. His hand is firm. I can feel that he wants it to be there.

I am acutely aware of how unlikely it is that the two of us would ever have met, let alone like this. I think of the coincidences and strange unknowable webs of cause and effect and chance that lead to life unfolding the way it does. And I sit in the silence with the Dayan, as he blesses me.

Surely, I think, I have been somehow supercharged by this meeting, this serendipitous encounter with perhaps the most senior Jewish figure in the country?

'Pshhhhhhh!' my tutor exclaims, nodding in respect when he hears the news.

It feels auspicious, and it further cements my sense that Eliana and I are accelerating on our path.

It's a feeling that I'm keen to hold on to, encircle myself in and project out into the world. Perhaps it's a feeling that's genuinely

---

* A blessing.

warranted, and perhaps it is something that I'm telling myself because I need it to be true.

It is my father's eightieth birthday, and so Eliana and I travel to Portsmouth, laden with presents (and Tupperware containers of kosher food).

My mum has a theory – which is as good a theory as any I've heard – that far too often people wait until after a loved one has died to say the things they truly wanted to say about them, and so people should take the chance to celebrate one another when they can. I couldn't agree more, and have long taken delight in organising needlessly elaborate celebrations for friends and family over the years, at any available opportunity.

For Dad, this first manifested in a large surprise party on his seventieth birthday – because why not? – in which Mum led him into their favourite theatre in Portsmouth, only for him to discover it packed with an array of relatives who'd flown in from across the globe, family friends, long-lost schoolmates, fellow university colleagues, all cheering his arrival and then fêting him with an evening of song, theatre, music, poetry, film and nonsense.

Now, for his eightieth, it is clear for so many reasons that an expansive celebration is in order once more and, led by my mum, plans have long been underway.

We walk as a family into the Portsmouth Guildhall, and Dad is utterly delighted as he finds it packed full of hundreds of those closest to him, standing and applauding. There are speeches; there are sketches; there is a truly ridiculous short film made by my brothers and me, referencing our dad's die-hard love of obscure late-Victorian ghost-story writer Oliver Onions; there is a fully fledged staging of a musical Dad wrote about the fools of Chelm, rehearsed in secret by university colleagues and devoted former students; and there is a *klezmer* concert. At the end, Dad stands and thanks everyone, and recites one of his favourite Robert Graves poems from memory.

Is the event a surprise to my dad? It's hard to say. In many ways my dad has long lived in a state of perpetual surprise, refusing to keep a diary or to plan his days. It's just that, perhaps, things are even more of a surprise to him, now.

Eliana and I return to Hendon. We work, we sleep, we study with our tutors, we revise on our own. And we meet, once more, with the Beth Din. It goes better than any of our meetings have gone before.

The encounter itself is no less gruelling, or rigorous, than previous meetings – but something feels different.

For one thing, it is with Dayan Landau, the head of the Beth Din, once more – the first time we have been granted a repeat audience with one of the Dayanim. This feels significant. What's more there is an air of finality to the lines of questioning. A sense that there is an understanding that this process is approaching its natural conclusion. At the end, I am even given permission to lay tefillin in the mornings – to begin presenting identically to every other Orthodox Jew in *shul*.

Nothing is ever said in the room. But we are certain it's gone well.

I shake Dayan Landau's hand and leave the room, quietly thrilled, in the knowledge that we are now on the home stretch.

It is possible that no human has ever been more wrong about anything in their entire life.

CHAPTER 25

Rosie Jones's Breasts (and Other Impediments to Conversion)

'The harder it gets, the closer you are to the end,' has been my mum's sage advice throughout, when she has seen me sat at the kitchen table late at night, strung-out and pale, gazing hopelessly at piles of Jewish books containing lifetimes of esoteric information, scrawling page after page of dense notes, and heaving myself onto the train back to London early the next morning, hurrying back lest my time spent with my family as opposed to being in Hendon somehow count against me . . .

Generally, I have used that philosophy as a North Star. As my world has become stranger and more difficult to navigate, I have pushed ever onwards, knowing that I am inching closer to the finish line, a world in which I can live in my own space, wake up in my own bed, in which Eliana and I are free to be together, free to be who we are, and free . . . well, just free, in fact. And, generally, it's a philosophy that has served me well.

As difficult as I have found this process thus far, bear in mind that – administrative hiccups aside – it has all gone exactly as it was supposed to.

But. Here's where things go properly off the rails.

*

I am stood in a wrestling ring in a draughty industrial unit in deepest southeast London, teaching comedian Ed Gamble how to deliver popular wrestling move 'the delayed vertical suplex', when my phone rings.

'I am calling from the Beth Din,' says a voice. And, for one blissful, completely misguided moment, my heart soars and I feel that I am being told I have completed the conversion.

'Don't panic,' says the voice on the phone. Helpfully. 'But some things have come to light about the nature of your work, and the Dayanim would like to discuss them with you.'

I feel my stomach lurch and my throat constrict.

I refrain from responding: 'Yes . . . I wrote about it in my first letters to you. Two and a half years ago.'

Instead I stammer and nod and agree, of course, to meet with them. Immediately? No. If only.

'Tuesday afternoon in two weeks' time? And until then, if you could reflect on what might need to change, given what you have learned . . .?'

My stomach tightens until it becomes a ball bearing with the infinite density of a black hole.

I ask if I might, possibly, perhaps, just get a sort of sense of, the sort of, well, is there anything in particular I should be thinking about, in terms of—

'Some things are best not put in writing,' says the voice, 'Better to talk in person.'

My heartbeat is so loud it shatters the glass in the windows of the cars around me. 'Oh – and no need for Eliana to come, we only want to speak to you.'

In a final, flailing Hail Mary (hail Moses?), I ask if, in fact, Eliana might join me anyhow.

A pause.

'. . . Sure. If that's what you'd prefer. See you in a fortnight.'

It is not a relaxing fortnight. 'Reflect on what might need to change,' said the voice.

In practice, this has involved scrolling mentally through my entire professional career, and, suddenly, finding myself disgusted with the lot of it.

Viewed from one angle, my work has primarily involved telling big, silly, warm-hearted stories about love and friendship. From another – it's a smut-fuelled, innuendo-laden hotbed of depravity.

With the help of one of our most supportive Supportive Rabbis, we have sat and combed through my *oeuvre*, highlighting such things as might be deemed problematic by a high court of the world's most serious men, and preparing our mitigating arguments – like lawyers prepping for a case. Which, in effect, we are.

'Some things have come to light,' said the voice. But what things?

Our sitcom is now out in the world, but it surely can't be that, can it? If anything, ITVX's marketing strategy seemed designed to ensure that the work sail under the noses of the Beth Din, and indeed the public at large.

Wrestling, we decide. It must be something to do with the world of wrestling. Which, to me, is a cherished performance art-form, a spectacular enactment of the timeless battle between good and evil, and a guiding passion fuelling much of my work. But, to unsympathetic eyes . . . well, it's a cornucopia of flesh and immodesty.

We assemble our defence. We discuss our strategy. Such is the gravity of the situation that a Supportive Rabbi arranges to join us, to sit alongside us in the room, as our advocate.

Dry-mouthed, I return to Barnwood Drive.

I am sat in the Throne Room once more.

Across the table, stern faces sit opposite me. Eliana and our Most Supportive Rabbi are next to me.

'We are here to discuss your work,' says a face. 'And, yes, maybe we should have looked into it earlier . . .'

Years. It has been over two years that they have known what it is that I do. It has taken them two years to Google me.

'Comedy,' says a face, with deep seriousness. 'Is that really a job . . . for a Jew?'

. . .

. .

.

Is comedy a job for a Jew?

Absolutely fair play to the Beth Din. They have said one of the funniest things I have ever heard, in an environment in which I have no possible choice but to respond with a poker-straight face. They've summoned me here, to this stifling meeting room, to end my comedy career, and they've done so with a joke. It's a twelfth-dan judo move – an absolute nine-dimensional checkmate.

I weigh up the notion of making an impassioned defence of the concept of Jewish comedy – its role not just as a job, not just as something that exists, but as an essential elemental life force in the world.

Of the work of the Marx Brothers. Of Mel Brooks and Carl Reiner. Of Joan Rivers. Of Jerry Seinfeld and Larry David. Of Andy Samberg. Of Abbi Jacobson and Ilana Glazer. Of the prose of Woody Allen and the early movies of Woody Allen and the nothing else of Woody Allen.

And then I look across the table into the impassive eyes of my interlocutors, and I realise that it would be not the faintest bit of use.

So, instead, with every molecule of self-control, I nod soberly, and I remain silent.

Then, they reach into a folder.

And slowly, solemnly, they reveal ... an A4 print-out of a photograph of me taken around 2 years before. I'm wearing wrestling tights and holding the comedian Rosie Jones on my shoulders. She wears a low-cut silver skintight leotard and holds her hands aloft, waving a championship belt. It is advertising a show taking place in a few weeks' time.

This, to us, is unacceptable, they say.

My face remains studiedly blank.

It's quite something. To know that your entire future, the narrative of your whole life, is held in the palms of the hands of men who care nothing for you. Who see themselves as arbiters of a tradition so infinite that your existence is as less than a mote of dust. And to know that your fate is, at that point, entirely predicated on their reaction to a photo of Rosie Jones's – in her own words – 'incredible tits'.

What I want to say, but don't say, is ... 'But ... Jerry Sadowitz??'

You may or may not be familiar with the work of Jerry Sadowitz, a man deemed by both fellow comics and the general public (two cohorts he by all accounts despises) to be the most offensive comedian in the world.

He's got a shock of unruly curls and the glower of a malevolent Marty Feldman, and he combines genuinely world-class close-up magic with pitch-black, utterly unrepeatable stand-up routines, delivered in a thick Glaswegian accent.

He's a man whom I have shared a Soho Theatre dressing room with, once or twice – but there, in the swift interchange between our shows, we barely swapped pleasantries. I know him only by his unrivalled, decades-long reputation for spewing terrifying filth.

And then, one morning, in Regency Square *shul* . . . I hear a deep, distinctive voice.

I look up, and I see the curls. Could it – surely not . . . ?

'Ah, hello, Jerry.' Dayan Horowitz smiles brightly and shakes hands with him.

With Jerry Sadowitz. With a man who once began his set at the Montreal Comedy Festival with: 'Hello, moose-fuckers. You know what I hate about this country? Half of you speak French and the other half let them', and was promptly punched in the face by an enraged audience member.

Jerry Sadowitz, the prince of darkness, a man who once told the joke: 'Nelson Mandela, what a cunt. You lend some people a fiver and you never hear from them again', is a welcomed, warmly greeted member of the *minyan*.

A man who makes a point of repeatedly saying the deemed-to-be-unsayable, specifically because, when it comes to comedy, 'there is no line to be drawn'.

'What about Jerry Sadowitz? Why have I been summoned to atone for my unimaginable transgressions, whilst Jerry Sadowitz is able to roam the world, terrorising audiences at leisure, before being welcomed with open arms, not just to any synagogue, but to literally *your synagogue*?' I don't say.

Instead, I sit contritely and, taking the greatest of pains not to lie, I present my vocation from the most pathetic of angles.

I reassure them that my sitcom won't be getting a second series (great). I explain how the precariousness of comedy means I often do other writing work (and I do) and how, as time goes on, it would make far more sense to focus on more stable employment. I accept that a freelance comedy career is irresponsible (clearly), frivolous (by definition!) – the sort of caprice that a married man might want to put behind him. That comedy and wrestling can only take a man so far (so true), and that I'm getting to the age where I'd need to think about stopping the wrestling nonsense anyway (of course) and that our producer has only one further show in the diary (they do) and nothing further is currently planned (there isn't).

I self-flagellate and I give voice to every shred of self-doubt I've ever had.

It has come to pass; I am a supplicant. I am their bitch.

And it would be infinitely easier for me at this point if I simply nodded and smiled and agreed to everything that is asked of me; namely, that I reject the world of comedy entirely. In many ways, it would be a relief. If I didn't make comedy, perhaps my life would be something along the lines of that of my schoolmate Joe, a supremely bright and capable man who, in the absence of an all-consuming passion such as mine, simply got 'a sensible degree' which he used to get a 'good job' in a 'stable industry'. It may or may not afford him the intermittent euphoric highs that I have experienced but it *certainly* exempts him from the negatives of my world: the total lack of structure or safety net, the perpetual financial uncertainty, the projects that flicker into existence and then back out again, the extreme difficulty in ever planning your life. So maybe the Beth Din are right. Maybe I should walk away from comedy.

The only problem is that this is completely impossible.

For as long as I have been able to formulate ideas, I have been compelled to arrange them in ridiculous shapes and present them to whoever is nearby.

I am drawn to the intoxicating hum of a theatre filling with people, to the extreme joy of being onstage in the middle of a comedy show that's in full flight – the feeling of conducting an audience with your words and your movements, and they in turn guiding you with the rhythms of their laughter, the hypnotic interconnectedness of everyone in the room, the sheer crackling *liveness* of it all . . .

And because of all of this, part of our careful, agonising planning for this meeting has involved not just preparing suitable apologies to atone for whatever transgressive work might be deemed to have taken place in my past, it has also involved carving out the space for me to make work in the future.

So, carefully, I map out the comedy projects I have ahead of me.

The faces are displeased. As we anticipated they would be. They push back. As we anticipated they would.

'Can you cancel these shows?' 'Can you break the contract?' 'Do you have to do them?'

I can't cancel them. I can't break the contract. Yes, I have to do them.

Eventually, after a decades-long silence, we move on. Whilst they've got me here, on the ropes, they turn their attentions to the remainder of my work. What else do I write about?

I'm ready to generalise – things to do in London – but Eliana gets there first; 'He's been writing a lot about theatre recently.'

Their faces drop further, and Eliana winces, realising she has – somehow – caused us further disfavour.

Theatres? Oof. Is that any place for a Jewish boy to be?

It is as though, to them, the act of simply watching a play is, somehow, a slippery slope to moral degradation.

We are far beyond *halacha* now. We are entirely in the realm of the members of the Beth Din's personal taste.

They disdain the arts. They look with alarm and discomfort at creativity.

If this process has been in any way about the soul, at this point I feel they are simply looking to extinguish mine.

Eventually, a billion years after the meeting began, it concludes.

I stand and nod and shake hands, and thank them politely for their bludgeoning.

I sit in another Hendon dinner, somewhere. An endless procession of roast meats passes by, and I gorge on them, thoughtlessly. Across the table is someone who we've met before, at a relaxed dinner, and so knows of my work.

'How's the comedy, Max?'

'Oh, he's a comedian?' says someone. 'I love comedy.'

'D'you remember *Little Britain*?'

'We love Michael McIntyre.'

'I used to love Jackie Mason!'

'I saw Michael McIntyre last year!'

'We went up to the Fringe, didn't we! Saw some amazing things! Crazy up there!'

'But it's gone woke, hasn't it. You can't say anything any more.'

It's true.

You really can't say anything any more.

'All that matters is being a good person,' says Shira, my driving instructor.

I'm sat in the driver's seat of her car, explaining my encounter with the Beth Din, and the scrutiny I'm under.

She's steadying my nerves before a test – sensationally, due to the backlog of tests, they are now only available every six months, and even then, that involves paying some sort of teenage hacker an ever-increasing sum of money to 'fast track' you.

'How often you go to *shul*, what you keep – that's between you and G-d,' she says. 'What truly matters is being a good person.'

I couldn't agree more.

It's the only time in months that I haven't felt compromised, or caveated, like I'm adrift in a world that isn't mine.

I thank her for her wise words, take a deep breath, and promptly fail my driving test, which feels appropriate.

CHAPTER 26

The March of the Living

At 4am one morning Eliana and I drag ourselves to Luton airport, where we are handed lanyards and literature and absorbed into an apprehensive mass of people travelling to Poland, to participate in the March of the Living. Here, over four days, we are to look at Jewish existence in Poland before and during the Second World War, visiting ghettos, forests, town centres and the concentration camps of the Holocaust.

I had always known that I would visit at some point in my life. But such a trip – worthy but painful, like giving blood – is easily postponed, kicked down the road for later. But, right now, the sediment of my identity has been kicked up and is swirling around me. If this awful pilgrimage is to ever be part of my Jewish journey then surely now is the natural time. There is also the matter of the event's name. The March of the Living is so called because each year it is attended by some of those who experienced the horrors of the Holocaust first-hand, and who survived. And, although there are still a number of remarkably vibrant survivors who are prepared to revisit these sites and spend their final years sharing the terrible truth about what took place, their numbers are dwindling. Soon there will be no one. And if visiting these sites feels important, hearing the testimonies of those who survived feels essential. So Eliana and I agree – we should go, now. We should experience as much as we can experience there, and hear from those who somehow lived through it, so that it is something that we carry within us.

Upon landing we join our sub-group of young professionals – who are mostly but by no means all Jewish – and we meet our guide, an educator named Angela. She is learned and empathetic, and she reminds me of my childhood rabbi, Orli.

That afternoon, Angela takes us to a beautiful ancient *shul* in the Kazimierz Jewish district.

'Let's all sing together,' she says.

'*Oseh shalom bimromav . . .*' In a soft melodic voice, she begins to sing the prayer for peace, and our group, who have barely met, all join in, uniting in a tune most of us have known all our lives. '*Ya'aseh shalom, ya'aseh shalom . . .*' Our voices ring out and reverberate around the high-ceilinged stone building. '*Shalom aleinu, v'al kol Yisra'eil.*'

Over two intensely long days we visit the Auschwitz and Birkenau death camps, the epicentre of the Nazis' programme of systematic dehumanisation and clinical, industrialised murder. Birkenau is an enormous, disparate site. We walk along train tracks, through dank, green fields with low industrial buildings stretching out against the empty grey sky.

We learn of the extraordinary acts of organised resistance from within the camps – such as the destruction of Crematorium IV. How a revolt was planned, and how women put to work in the munitions factory within the complex managed to smuggle tiny quantities of gunpowder under their nails, their food containers and their clothes – which they passed on to the men, who planned to blow up the Nazis and themselves. And how it all went disastrously wrong, how the prisoners were taken by surprise when the Nazis arrived earlier than expected, and so the plan played out chaotically, the crematorium set on fire, with three SS officers dying as gunshots rang out and 452 prisoners were killed. How the women deemed responsible were executed too. How 80 prisoners managed to cut through the camp's wire fence, and how perhaps 27 of those managed to survive.

Auschwitz is smaller, because the majority of the Jews transported here were murdered immediately after arrival. Within hours. It is an oddly familiar place, like the thing from the films. But we visit it with a well-dressed elderly man who rolls up his sleeve and reveals the number on his arm, and tells us of how he was taken there, how he slept in filthy dormitories on wooden boards, given one bowl that was both for his food in the day and a toilet at night, crammed alongside so many poor souls whose lives were extinguished, and how he was amongst the lucky ones – moved on, to a different concentration camp, able to cling on, survive until the end of the war. Somehow, he is able to return to this site to warn those who will listen about what happened, and what must never happen again.

In Auschwitz, there is the Book of Names. It is an enormous compendium of thousands upon thousands of metres-high pages, each page dense with tiny print. Millions upon millions of names of people who were murdered. The atmosphere in the room containing the Book is unlike anything I have experienced. Hushed, almost silent, but frantic. The room is crowded – there is only so much space, and only so many pages that can be accessed at once. But as people approach the Book, they experience an irrational sense of urgency – the desire to find their chosen names as quickly as they can. I feel it too, when I approach. I wait in the scrum and I push forward when there's a gap, and finally I am at the Book, turning the immense pages, searching hurriedly until I find them. Oleskers. Anna, Anna, Beylyla, Biba, Gersh, Gershon, Henia, Hilda, Iozha, Jakob, Leopold, Leopold, Leybish, Luchia, Marek, Marjem, Marjem, Markus, Markus, Meir, Mendel, Mendel, Meyer,

Pinkas, Rebeka, Regina, Ruta, Ruta, Saloman, Serit, Sime, Xetka, Visrael, Zigmund, Zindel. Thirty-five Oleskers, murdered in Czernica, Poland, or Opole Lubelskie, Poland, or Brody, Poland, or Maly Trostenets, Belorussia (USSR), or Wien, Austria, or, simply, place of death unknown. I wonder who they were, and who they might have been.

I am a prolific crier. I am known to weep freely at every wedding ceremony I attend and through most of the speeches. I had assumed that my time on the March of the Living would be spent ceaselessly wiping my eyes and rehydrating. But, at first, the tears don't come. Even stood amongst the buildings and the dull machinery of death, the fact that 1.1 million people were murdered here feels impossible to truly understand. It is only when I see the photographs that I begin to sob. We have seen images of prisoners, shaven-headed and reduced to their uniforms and their numbers, and they have been chilling and disturbing. But it is the photos of families – joyful gatherings of parents and children and grandparents, young lovers arm in arm, carefully arranged family photos of proud fathers and loving mothers, mischievous teenagers, chubby giggling toddlers, newborn babies. There is something about seeing these people at their best, as they wished to be seen and remembered, whilst knowing their fates, and standing in the spot where they were executed . . . as the dam bursts and I cry freely and angrily, I feel as helpless as I did when I first read *Rose Blanche* as a child, knowing that, no matter how desperately I reread the words, or flicked backwards through the pages of the book, there was nothing I could do to change the outcome of the story.

In the evening, wiped out from physical fatigue and emotional exhaustion, we sit at long tables in anonymous hotel spaces and graze on stodgy, bland kosher food.

The following day we visit Bełżec, a less 'famous' death camp, a place of mass graves, where corpses were burned on open-air grids until local residents complained about the smell, and had to scrub droplets of congealed fat from the windows of their houses. Today it has been transformed into an enormous memorial, almost a piece of art. There are two huge fields of pitch-black burnt rock, bisected by a stone corridor, topped with tendrils of wrenched, twisted metal that grow higher as you walk down them. It feels like a vision of hell.

We visit Bełżec with a 95-year-old survivor named Harry. This is the place where many of his family were murdered, he explains, and so there is something he must do. When we arrive, Harry walks unaided through the memorial site, to the very end of the corridor where there is space for contemplation, and here he recites the mourner's *kaddish*. The ancient words sap the poison from the air.

The trip continues. We speak constantly of unspeakable horrors. We visit a patch of woodland where children were shot dead, and babies had their brains dashed out against trees, as SS officers got drunk and egged one another on. Angela sings once more, a lullaby this time. It is all too much to bear.

At the end of the four days, we leave. I am relieved I have been, and relieved that it is over.

In the hours and days after I return, I reflect and unpack what I have seen and learned.

There are my most immediate, most inevitable reactions. Disgust at what took place, despair that humans are capable of doing such things to one another, and a chilling sense of the malleability of individuals. What feels most alarming is not the leaders of the pack – the keenest of the lot, the ideologues, architects of the whole repellent project, high on power and amphetamines – but their underlings, those people who allowed themselves to be swept along in a tide of fascism, and who suddenly found themselves uniform-clad and participating in the unthinkable, not because they truly believed, but because they were too weak and scared not to. Because it was easier to just go along with it all, to be told what to think, and do, and to feel part of something. How little it takes to shift the mood in the room. How quickly people fall into line.

But beyond that, the experience stirs in me another, more personal response.

I have spent these last days immersed in experiencing a tragedy that befell the Jews – something I have been informed, categorically, that I am not. So how am I to feel? On what level am I allowed to have engaged with that which I have seen?

During the trip, this was something I felt I couldn't address head-on. Not in an environment where we're being watched, constantly, by senior Rabbinic figures, shepherding other bus-loads of people, hovering around the communal gatherings in the evenings. And, also, not in an environment where my thoughts might upset others. Other people in our group speak proudly about their Reform and Liberal conversions. For me to raise the knotted problem of reconciling my own identity – it runs the risk of hurting them. And I don't wish to hurt anyone.

Furthermore, focusing on some personal sense of aggrievement when we're here to reflect on the injustices inflicted on millions of people – and not just Jews, but Roma and Sinti people, Black people, Slavic people, queer people, those with disabilities, and many, many more – feels wrong, and selfish.

It's not the time. It's not the place. Someone might disapprove. Someone might be upset. From every angle I feel boxed in, unable or unwilling to formulate a personal response. And so I swallow down my feelings when looking at the Oleskers in the

Book of Names. When encountering the town of Olesko listed on the outer perimeter of the Bełżec memorial site. When looking at photos of families – of boys who look like they could be my brothers, and men who look exactly like my father. I remain silent when we hear, on numerous occasions, speakers discuss the importance of one's name – knowing that this, too, is to be taken from me, my connection to my father severed.

It is only when we have returned to the UK that I allow myself to react to what I have experienced. And my reaction is one of furious indignation.

The Jewish people were almost annihilated. Almost erased. And yet, on the other side of this atrocity, one group of Jews cannot bring themselves to acknowledge, to accept, another group of Jews. I am astonished at the shortsightedness.

The common rebuttal to the notion that one should accept someone as Jewish just because they would have been deemed so by the Nazis, is that 'they' don't get to choose. No. Of course they don't.

However. If a community of people live lives that they consider to be Jewish, and they are persecuted by others for the fact that they are Jewish, in some cases put to death for the crime of being Jewish, it feels truly bleak that the only people on the planet denying them their identity . . . are Jews.

With burning clarity I perceive this entire conversion process to be nothing more than a trite game. An extended power play, from which G-d is entirely absent.

Humans are idiots. Idiots. We have such alarmingly limited time on this planet, and we insist on tripping ourselves up.

A post-March of the Living survey email arrives in my inbox. I am amazed to discover that it asks attendees to rate the experience out of . . . five yellow stars.

Are we incapable of learning anything at all?

CHAPTER 27

Having a Laugh

And so, somehow, to comedy.

As I explained to the supremely unimpressed Beth Din in my last meeting, Ivan and I have a venue and time-slot confirmed at the Edinburgh Fringe, and a show to write. In the context of all that has happened, creating a new comedy show seems both an impossible thing to do and an impossible thing to *not* do. And, as I discover on our first day of throwing ideas around together, there's really nothing quite like the sheer freewheeling creative joy of writing jokes with the spectre of the world's most serious men staring disapprovingly over your shoulder.

We start to write a show about our fathers. It's something we'd been discussing for a few years, both of our dads having lived colourful and hugely eventful lives, in very different ways – Papa Olesker having floated through misadventures across the globe led by an instinctive love of theatre and poetry and the ability to embrace whatever was directly in front of him at the time, whilst the ambitious, swashbuckling Papa Gonzalez spent a number of years [REDACTED] before [REDACTED] and finally ending up [REDACTED] in [REDACTED] and thus [REDACTED], meaning he spent a year in a Romanian prison.

I am determined that this show won't be about my father's condition, but about his approach to living. All four of us, I feel – Ivan, me, and both our dads – have taken very different paths through life, and the show becomes an attempt to map out those differing philosophies. It's a meditation on fatherhood too – on our own fathers, on Ivan's status as a confused, sleep-deprived new dad, and on my desire to one day have children.

I go down to Portsmouth and I speak to my dad. It happens to be Father's Day. Once again I am sat with a learned, bearded Jew in a book-lined study, only the shelves of this particular study have sections of books about puppetry, and the history of film, and music hall, and 'Art and the Imagination', and 'Brain and Memory and Hypnosis', and obscure languages, and self-proclaimed messiahs, and philosophy, and Yiddish jokes, and words and wordplay, and Judaica, and limericks, and witchcraft, and mythology, and utopias and dystopias, and short stories and ghost stories and science-fiction stories and an A–Z of novels and an A–Z of poetry, and a shelf dedicated to different types of encyclopaedias (or, as my dad describes it, 'The essentials').

Having claimed to be apprehensive about being on camera, Dad proves to be a natural – leaping on a half-second pause when I start filming and immediately inverting the whole interview: 'Ah, you're probably nervous,' he says, 'because I'm sure you haven't been on the stage and all that, but stick with me for a while and you'll get the hang of it . . .'

He swiftly relaxes into his role, firing back irreverent, schtick-filled interjections – 'Dad, I believe it was you who introduced me to comedy—'

'Yes. Comedy, Max; Max, comedy . . .'

And he launches into a ridiculous monologue, effervescent with word-play, packed full of jokes, and quotes from his favourite authors ('It was George MacDonald who said, "The business of the universe is to make such a fool of you that you will know yourself for one, and so begin to be wise," ' he says), and knowing tangents and self-referential asides and extempore poetry recitals.

'. . . sorry, what was the question?' he eventually asks.

'Erm . . . I hadn't asked one yet, Dad,' I say. 'I suppose the question was . . . hello?'

At the same time, Ivan interviews his dad about life and fatherhood, and Papa Gonzalez delivers a series of effortlessly charismatic responses in his thick Argentinean accent, his answers generally variations on the theme of 'You know those things I did? Yeah, don't do that . . .'

Armed with this patriarchal wisdom, Ivan and I meet up in London to write, and the beginnings of something start to come together. The first time we stand on a stage and perform a scrappy chunk of the show, it feels like coming up for air after hours trapped underwater. At the end of the gig I walk back through Soho, high with adrenaline and woozy with an almost-forgotten feeling of relaxation – of being able to exist, for just a moment, in the manner that makes most sense to me.

It now seems clear that pushing through and making the show is the right thing to do on every possible level (other than financial, of course, but that is quite simply the hellish pact one signs up for when forming a comedy double-act). So Ivan and I keep writing, despite my awareness of the humming threat, the sense that a single misplaced joke could rewrite the narrative of my life.

On one occasion we perform a preview of the show in a venue just up the road from Barnwood Drive, metres away from the Beth Din. The show contains nothing that I would deem remotely 'inappropriate' under any normal circumstances (perhaps because, under normal circumstances, the concept of 'inappropriateness' in comedy feels very close to meaningless), and yet right now my mind pinwheels in panic, perceiving hideous immorality behind every punchline. As people filter into the theatre I hurriedly cut joke after joke, lest halfway through the show a surprise rabbi stands up in the audience and delivers a Roman Emperor's thumbs down, and I am immediately excised from the conversion and consumed by lions. Ordinarily, the sensation of performing comedy is one that brings me a sense of profound calm (when it's going well, obviously), but on this night, as each joke lands, the audience's subsequent ripple of laughter hits me and induces a jagged spasm of fear. It is only hours after the gig has finished that I am able to begin to relax.

After any period of courtship, it eventually becomes time to stop messing around and start seriously planning the wedding.

Not for Eliana and me, obviously – who knows when, if ever, we will be granted such permissions – but for Adam, one of the Bernsteins' quietest and most studious sons, who reveals to his delighted and slightly stunned parents that he has met, started dating, fallen in love with, and subsequently proposed to a young woman, all within the space of approximately a month. The Orthodox truly don't mess about.

When I get back to the Bernsteins' house one evening, the family are gathered, and there's a new face – 'Max, this is Esther,' says Ronit, a smile on her face unlike any I've seen before (the added ingredient, I later realise, being 'mild shock'). I am introduced to a charming, faultlessly polite young woman sat on the sofa. Aha! I think – Adam's started dating! And, well, he has . . . but he's also finished dating, too. It takes me until halfway through my conversation with Esther to comprehend what's actually happened, and when I suddenly come to realise exactly why this particular gathering seems a little formal, a little excited, a little different... I experience a feeling of whiplash at the phenomenal speed of it all.

The concept of the *shidduch* – matchmaking – is hugely important in Orthodoxy. Not simply because adoring mothers wish to find the perfect partners for their genius sons and stunning daughters, but because bringing soulmates together is deemed to be a *mitzvah* of immense importance. At more than one Hendon lunch I hear the conversational refrain that 'If you set up three *shidduchs*, you go to the highest level of heaven!' The further up the spectrum of religiosity, the more formalised the matchmaking process becomes – a chaperone might be involved, and private conversations with the prospective partner's rabbi might be had. This delicate process is all overseen by the *shadchan* – the matchmaker – generally a respected woman in the community with an endless Rolodex of eligible singles, and a keen eye for any newcomer likely to prove a suitable match for those in her orbit. She will ensure that both halves of the potential couple are similarly religious (or irreligious), have similar values and ambitions, and personalities that seem likely to mesh. With those parameters established, dating can begin in earnest. And it really is in earnest; marriage is the headline goal for both parties, and so the immediate question both are seeking to answer is – do we truly align? Could we build a life together that we'd both want? If no, you swiftly move on. And if yes, and there's a spark of attraction, well...

It's a very, very different system to the, well, total lack of system I grew up with (not that someone walking furtively up to you in Portsmouth's 'vibrant' U18's club night and muttering, 'Will you go with my mate?' wasn't a noble *shidduch*-ing process all of its own). But I certainly see the value in the unflinching directness, the total lack of game-playing from both parties. Looking back, there were elements of this approach in the questions Eliana fired at me in our earliest conversations in Edinburgh; 'So do you want kids? Oh yeah, how many?' Questions that were sprinkled lightly across evenings, intermingled with cocktails and comedy shows, but which swiftly built a picture of who I was, helped her see me as someone it might be possible to spend her life with. Of course, there were questions that Eliana didn't ask me, too, but perhaps that was for the same reason.

I wish a hearty *mazel tov* to Adam, and Esther, and all of the Bernsteins. For them, there is much to be done. There is a wedding to be arranged, as swiftly as can be. There are dresses to be picked and a hall to be booked and relatives to invite over – a frenzy of activity is about to descend on Redwood Road. Which means...

'So, you'll have to move out in a few weeks, OK?' says Ronit with customary immediacy, when I arrive home the next night.

My time at the Bernsteins' is coming to an end.

Eliana and I are preparing for our next, non-emergency, meeting with the Beth Din. In the aftermath of our previous, devastating encounter, there have been cautiously positive signs. A follow-up letter from me, underscoring my commitment to pursuing serious and sensible employment, has been met with a response from the Beth Din that feels, tonally, like a return to our previous encounters (and, yes, the letter is addressed to a 'Max Olseker', but I have to hope that's not just an unfortunately similarly named man who's also attempting to survive the conversion and marry someone named Eliana). I am also granted permission to move out of the Bernsteins'. Though I've know I can't stay, I also dare not move out of my own volition, and so write an additional letter seeking approval to seek a change of address, meaning I will continue living in the Area . . . alone. It feels like a glimmer of autonomy, a tentative half-step towards independence.

There's another unexpected beacon of hope too. Rabbi Weissman, he of the Ohr community we became a part of when we moved to The Area, has taken on a new job. He has become a member of the Beth Din.

This feels like a surprise sliver of luck – it brings with it the prospect of a friendly face in the interrogation room, and a Dayan who already exists as a supportive figure in our day-to-day lives. Perhaps that will change now, I think, and he will need to withdraw from us, and become aloof and distant. But this proves not to be the case.

The week before any Beth Din meeting is always one of the great 'horrendous weeks' of all time – and, on this occasion, Eliana and I are blessed with a bonus one. An email appears, announcing that, for unspecified scheduling reasons, our latest meeting has been shunted back.

I have taken on as many additional forms of study as I can, beyond my lessons with my tutor, and my reading, and amongst them is a weekly *shiur* seminar with Rabbi – now Dayan – Weissman, expounding further on the weekly Torah portion.

On this particular evening, he is discussing the concept of *Tzara'at* – a Biblical disease that he defines as 'a physical manifestation of a spiritual malaise' (I can empathise with that concept, I think, as I sit taking notes, stress coursing up my spine and tingling down my leg).

When the *shiur* ends, I thank the Dayan as I leave, and I offhandedly mention that we were due to be meeting the Beth Din soon, but that the meeting has been changed.

We part ways, and start walking in opposite directions down

the narrow road between two of Ohr's *shul* buildings, and then Dayan Weissman does something extraordinary.

He doubles back, and calls my name. I spin back around and walk towards him – and suddenly we are stood, facing one another, in a children's play area.

'I wish I could hug you,' he says. 'I know it's terrifying and difficult,' he continues, 'being sat and having people judge you, and obviously *halacha* is what *halacha* is, I understand, and it's difficult doing it – that's my job – but I'm moved by you – my heart goes out to you, and these people I sit across the table from transforming their lives, upending their lives in extraordinary ways, going on journeys we've never had to do – and I just want to say you're good people and it's going to be OK.'

In ten seconds, Dayan Weissman has offered more support and kindness than I have received from the Beth Din in the entirety of the preceding two years.

I am taken aback, shocked and delighted – beaming with gratitude, overwhelmed, almost to the point of tears.

'Thank you, Dayan,' I manage. 'Thank you so much. That's an incredibly meaningful thing for you to say.'

And then I turn and almost trip over a child's plastic scooter.

CHAPTER 28

The Weight of the Wait

Inspiringly, despite the many constraints on my time, I still somehow find a moment to write the world's most self-pitying diary entry:

> Hi, I'm Max. I'm 36, and my hobbies are:
> - Not having a job
> - Trying to convince some old men to let me get circumcised
> - Failing my driving test.

The location in which I write this wretched passage is as responsible for my sense of despair as all the reasons I listed above; I have moved out of the Bernsteins', and into a genuinely repulsive bedsit. And the reason for *that*, well . . .

The Orthodox conversion process is, amongst other things, eye-wateringly expensive. Lessons with tutors alone would make the whole arrangement prohibitive for many – and by many, I absolutely include me. Left to my own devices, I would have drowned in the financial obligations of the process long ago.

However, from the off, Eliana and her family – mindful that I would have been unlikely to find myself on this path had it not been for them – have been insistent that they absorb any and all conversion-related expenses. This is immensely generous, thoughtful and considerate, and has the side-effect of making me quietly ashamed of my own financial instability. As a result, I am beyond keen that any amount Eliana's family contribute to the process be minimised wherever possible – and this change of address represents a prime opportunity for cost-cutting.

'Darling, just find somewhere comfortable and let us know,' says Eliana's mother.

'Firstly, thank you, again, so much,' I say. 'But it's just me, and it shouldn't be for long – so I'll find the absolute cheapest place I can.'

My trawling of Hendon's most reasonably-priced bachelor pads begins with a nerve-shredding near miss that almost derails the entirety of my journey. I go and view a room that looks ideal – a self-contained outhouse in a garden, pleasantly furnished, in which I could live an entirely painless (if sensationally weird) solo existence during this latest iteration of whatever my life has now become. Only there's an issue.

'Oh, my friend!' says the landlord, spotting my *kippah*. 'I don't know if I can rent this to a fellow Yid?'

The issue is that, being in the garden, the plumbing system is powered by electricity. And on Shabbat – when all such technology is forbidden – to use a tap or flush a toilet would either be an impossibility or constitute an unacceptable transgression.

'I'm so sorry, my friend – it was almost perfect!'

'Well, actually . . .' I begin, my eyes lighting up in hope.

You see, there is a school of thought that suggests that because a non-Jew is not *allowed* to keep Shabbat, a prospective convert should deliberately violate one of the laws governing Shabbat each week, as a mark of their not-yet-Jewish status – whilst otherwise maintaining full observance.

'. . . in other words,' I explain, 'that electric boiler could actually be ideal for me!'

'Aha, fantastic!' he says. It seems we've got ourselves a deal.

I am proud of my dextrous *halachic* negotiating, and explain my ingenious solution to Eliana that evening. Then I receive a phone call.

'Ah, you know, my friend, I just want to be totally sure this is kosher,' says the landlord. 'So I've called Dayan Landau at the Beth Din.'

Yet again, I have the sensation of my universe collapsing in around me. I am retching with panic, Eliana is fighting back tears, suddenly we're arguing:

'Why did you make such a risky choice?'

'It didn't seem "risky" at the time! It's perfectly valid!'

'But what if he phones up and says, "This guy Max is saying he can break Shabbat"?!'

'But that's *not* what I was saying! If anything I thought I was being *more* observant . . .!'

Once again I can feel the future I seek on the verge of being flushed away, like a cistern full of illicit, electrically powered toilet water. I am beside myself with fear, but it's like the saying goes: that which doesn't kill you simply makes you incredibly miserable, and puts an almost intolerable strain on your relationship.

I desperately email the landlord, pulling out of the deal, announcing I don't think it's right for me, but he's already made his own enquiries. Wincing and powerless, Eliana sits silently and we await news of my fate. We can't look at one another.

Finally, a call comes through.

'My friend, it's not to be – he says that because you're near the end of the process, you should be somewhere you can keep Shabbat.'

And . . . that's it. There was nothing to worry about – what's more, there's even a sense that we're 'near the end of the process'! It's all, actually, totally fine. But, as this misfire has demonstrated, 'fine' for Eliana and me is a fragile state of being right now. We are run down, perpetually on the brink of hysteria.

I lunge for the next-cheapest, guaranteed-Shabbat-compliant room in The Area that I can find. I immediately say yes on the basis of a grainy WhatsApp video sent by the agent, I bid farewell to the Bernsteins, trying and failing to find the words for their monumental kindness, and I move, once more, to a new home.

I had envisioned moving out of the Bernsteins' house as a step towards freedom – a world in which I was no longer an awkward adjunct to a family's life, but had a space all of my own. In taking this view, I neglected to consider a number of things. Firstly, their house was delightful; it was spotless, well appointed, and entirely comfortable. The space I have moved into is a single room containing a small bed, with a flimsy cupboard, sink, microwave and washing machine all crammed, sweatily, on top of one another. The 'hob', such as it isn't, is a portable device plugged into the wall, which sits, alarmingly, on top of the microwave. It's a weird room, which makes weird noises. There is a loud intermittent bubbling. There is shouting from nearby rooms. Even though I am, technically, indoors, I feel oddly exposed – a constant sense of the hectic, thumping, dark-shadowed chattering of city life rattling onwards all around me. Sounds of scurrying beneath the floorboards and clattering in rooms above. Unseen voices of men struggling, shouting, coughing.

The 'flat' has no plates and no cutlery, and I never work up the willpower to buy any. My reusable coffee mug becomes my all-purpose drinking cup. I hastily eat takeaway fast food or pre-packaged sandwiches. It is accessed via a back door that doesn't lock, which is reached via an alleyway in which constant indeterminate building work is taking place (or, at the very least, in which building equipment is regularly abandoned – it's hard to tell which). My bedsit-mate across the landing is a person I never physically meet, but whose commitment to playing hard techno music at all times cannot be disputed. It is an eerie, dripping, gurgling, wafer-thin-walled indignity of a place.

And the other terrible thing about living alone is: I'm now living alone. Solitude, my great nemesis, has never felt quite so powerfully solitudinous as during those evenings spent in my bedsit – which Eliana is categorically not able to enter, for all the reasons we're not permitted to live together – sat on the one flimsy plastic chair at the small 'kitchen' counter, watching YouTube on my phone, eating Kosher Kingdom sushi and endless bags of kosher sweets, and more or less mainlining depression.

I am, in short, in desperate need of a win. To my surprise, it comes in the form of our next meeting with the Beth Din.

It simply couldn't have gone better. That much we are certain of.

The build-up was the same – the pressure cooker of stress, the revising with our notes and our cue cards and our Post-Its, the final lessons with our tutors. ('Don't think of it as an exam,' smiles Rav Dov. 'Even though . . . it is.') Then the day itself: the careful process of getting changed into what has become my Beth Din suit, Eliana driving us there, us both sitting in the car and letting out cathartic screams, vowing that whatever happened in the room we'd be there for one another on the other side, the slow walk from the car to the door of the building, the centuries-long wait in the various antechambers, the uncertainty as to who we'll actually meet . . .

But then we're in, sat with Dayan Landau once more, who is sunny and affable. The stresses of our last meeting are acknowledged and brushed aside. That's been dealt with. Onwards!

In previous meetings, we have been asked about the *brachot**

---

* Blessings – *brachot* being the plural of *bracha*.

for different foodstuffs until we have tripped up, reached the limits of our knowledge. This time, we are asked if we know our *brachot* – we do, we say, gearing up to be rigorously tested – to which the response is: great! And we move on . . .

We skate across the main subjects swiftly; our competence and learning is clearly not in doubt.

This, surely, is what one's final meeting feels like.

Eliana is asked about the intricacies of kosher kitchens – she answers fluently about the home we will surely soon be building.

We are asked where we will live.

'Northwest London,' I say confidently (as if there were any other answer).

But where? Where exactly, we are asked.

Eliana and I look at one another, cautiously.

For the most part, the question of where we might live next isn't something we've allowed ourselves to expend energy on. It feels too distant and implausible. But in those moments we've discussed what life might be like on the other side of all this, the general principle has been: as close to Primrose Hill as we can afford. It gives us proximity to Eliana's family, to Beit Shalom, the *shul* she has grown up being part of, which has welcomed me more enthusiastically than any other, and to the beautiful leafy urban village, with central London on our doorstep. That said, as neither Eliana nor I had the foresight to become oligarchs, the prospect of a family home in Primrose Hill feels almost certainly unattainable. So perhaps we'd live further north – and perhaps Eliana's siblings would too, and, in fact, perhaps Eliana's parents would as well, if all the kids ended up in a different neighbourhood.

So we ramble slightly, discussing the various spots we might live – 'Somewhere between Primrose Hill and Hendon' – I venture, at one point, an answer which is met with a flicker of concern. You're not going to live in the Cholent Pot, that's unrealistic, he says. But it's clear that Primrose Hill doesn't feel suitable either. Uncertain, we blabber on about neighbourhoods in a mid-point between Hendon and Primrose Hill – Cricklewood, anyone? – and about the many friends we've made in The Area, and how we'd love to ensure we live somewhere that means we can still visit them on Shabbat, but also about Eliana's parents, and about Lion, of course, and about wanting to find a place to call our own.

Eventually Dayan Landau nods, and we move on. Phew. He brings the meeting to a close. I'll need to talk to my colleagues, he says, but I'm satisfied.

I'm satisfied.

What words to hear.

It is time, clearly, for Eliana and me to activate our 'if-it-goes-well' gameplan. I give a tiny nod to Eliana, turn to Dayan Landau, and ask if he and I might have a word in private.

Eliana leaves the room, allowing me to discreetly raise the subject of . . . the circumcision. Before the meeting, a Supportive Rabbi advised that it's possible the Beth Din might not have noted down my specific surgical requirements; the fact that I'd need not the ceremonial drop of blood but the full works – a procedure which would entail, no doubt, *many* ceremonial drops of blood, not to mention an extended healing process, something which could impact the eventual date of a *mikveh* and, ultimately, a wedding.

Without using the phrase 'just reminding you', or inferring in any way that the conversations from our first meeting might have been forgotten, I delicately address the delicate matter of my delicate matter.

Once more I am asked if I am prepared to go through with it. Once more, with solemnity, I explain that I am afraid, but that, yes, I have committed to this process and to the inevitability of the procedure.

Dayan Landau references the Soviet Jews under the Communist regime, during which time circumcision was banned – as the government began to ease its control during *perestroika*, they were begging to have their *brits*, he explains, and when they were finally able to, they felt so happy, it made them feel connected . . .

My surgical requirements are duly noted. Everything we could have possibly hoped for from the meeting came to pass. Freedom is on the horizon.

I meet Eliana outside, both of us exhilarated. The world has suddenly become a more positive place. The crushing blow of having failed my driving test once more fades away to less than nothing. It feels like the first day of summer. We drive off back towards Hendon together, tingling with happiness, cackling with excitement, singing to each other and the passing cars.

And then we wait. Which is normal. It should be a week until you hear back, Eliana's tutor says. There's a formal process to be followed. And so, as per the formal process, time stops for us once more.

We've lost all sense of time, Eliana and I. Since all this began, and we have been locked in stasis – waiting, waiting, waiting to be given permission to exist – months and years have ceased to have meaning in the way they used to. We are dimly aware of the seasons changing, but the only timeframe that has any meaning is the perpetual countdown to the next meeting, the next letter, the next stage.

It's only by looking to those around us that we get a sense of how much time has actually elapsed.

Lion has celebrated her ninetieth birthday – hosting a grand gathering of her extended family over a long glamorous weekend in a country house hotel (obviously), in which many toasts are given and speeches made, and the common Jewish blessing 'May you live to 120' is constantly in the air.

Both of Eliana's siblings and their partners – everyone else who found themselves on that impromptu night out in Edinburgh, a lifetime ago – are now married. At Julius and Tamara's beautiful ceremony, Lion leans over to me. 'You'd better get a move on,' she says firmly, 'because if I'm not at yours I shall be furious.' I am, I promise her, doing what I can.

Michael and Talia are expecting their first child. Julius and Tamara, now the besotted cat-parents of Cleo, their perpetually alarmed Scottish Fold, have acquired a *second* cat, Gus, an adorable himbo of a Ragdoll, and celebrated the joint birthdays of both (truly – there's an actual party, involving costumes).

Ivan and Andrea have gone from expectant parents to parents, and now their son is here in the world, constantly growing and learning and talking and questioning – developing in a million ways in the time it takes for Eliana and me to receive a single email.

Baz and Arielle, our friends undergoing the Sephardi conversion process, have lapped us – they wrote to their Beth Din, had their first meeting, were rejected from the process, had another meeting, and were accepted on the process – all in the time it took for us to receive a response to our initial letter.

That's not to say it was easy for them, or swift; one evening, Arielle, congenitally unflustered and master of the archly delivered pronouncement, declares: 'Ugh, I'm so sick of waiting. I've decided I'm getting married in the summer, with or without the Beth Din, and with or without Baz.'

'Yep, fair,' says Baz, with a shrug. (When asked *who* she'd marry, Arielle shrugs dismissively and says, 'Oh, come on, we've all got back-ups.')

But now they have reached the other side, and they promptly get married. Before we arrive at their wedding, I quietly wonder whether I'll find it difficult, knowing that they've finished their journey whilst we're stuck at some indeterminate mid-point, whether I'll struggle with jealousy or frustration. In the end, it is a pleasure and a relief to witness people on the other side of the conversion process. To see Baz and Arielle so happy, and relaxed, to hear jokes made about circumcisions, to spend the evening celebrating with them. To know that it can be done. It is only on the dancefloor, as Eliana and I stand awkwardly, not touching – instead we each hold the end of the same white napkin, swaying, the way we've seen *frum* couples do – that my teeth clench through the laughter.

Everywhere around us there are weddings and babies and landmark birthdays; for other people, life is happening.

And for me?

'Lovely moon out there!' shouts a man after *shul* one evening. 'Kiddush Levana?' As I walk outside, I am handed a laminated piece of card full of Hebrew text. 'Moon dance, anyone?' says the man to passers-by, drumming up custom.

The Kiddush Levana, I have learned in my lessons, is the Sanctification of the Moon, a ritual completed at night under a clear sky, when the moon is waxing and bright, at some point during the third and fifteenth days of the Jewish month.

'Sure,' I say, 'I'm in for a moon dance.'

A small group has been assembled in the *shul* car park, and I read from the laminated paper as best I can. One is required to greet and be greeted three times – so I, and the men, greet one another. 'Shalom Aleichem.' 'Aleichem shalom.' And so on.

And then the moon dance begins. I dance around the car park in honour of the moon with five strangers, linking arms and forming a circle. 'Lovely.' 'Cheers.' 'Have a good evening.' And then suddenly it is over, and people have dispersed.

I return to my bedsit and eat a kosher pot noodle in bed.

So, yes, life is happening for me. Just . . . very differently.

The only people whose lives seem more stuck in suspended animation than ours are other people attempting to navigate the same conversion process. We hear numerous stories of people whose conversion took four years, five years, seven years, or simply never ended. We have Friday night dinner with a couple whose fate I fear will be the latter. He's Jewish, grew up in northwest London, and historically deeply religious. She, a glamourous French woman with long jet-black hair, has keenly embarked on the conversion. She is enthusiastically building a Jewish life with her partner, keeping forensic levels of kosher in their small flat, studying all that she can.

Only there is a problem. They live together, and are unwilling to separate. There are a host of reasons – emotional, financial, and then there is the small matter that they are already civilly married. They would have been willing to separate for the period between the *mikveh* and the Jewish wedding (the Sephardi custom), but to split apart for an undefined period of time . . .?

'It's just unrealistic,' he says, 'We can't do it.'

The Beth Din, it seems, are impervious to their lines of reasoning. There is no meeting in the middle, no reaching out and seeking to find a way through.

In practice, the couple are being frozen out of the process. Meetings are scheduled even less frequently than ours, or not at all. And when they do occur, there is no sense of progress. No indication at all that they will ever reach their goal.

And, as a result, the man's previous love of Orthodoxy, his passion for studying the Torah, is fizzling out.

'I've just completely switched off, really,' he says.

It seems ludicrous that a loving couple seeking to live an Orthodox life will, ultimately, in all likelihood end up abandoning their goal, but given the circumstances it also seems inevitable.

It makes me think about how many other couples like them must have eventually given up, gone another way, due to the staggering inflexibility of the process.

In that sense, there is a dark irony – that the Beth Din, for whom 'marrying out' is an unthinkable violation of Jewish law, might themselves be responsible for people 'marrying out' on an industrial scale.

Other things mark the passage of time, too. When I am able to, I return home to see my parents. There are incremental changes in the way Dad interacts with the world. He is in many ways strengthened by his passions – the never-ending research, his fascination with the world and with ideas and with, yes, wilfully obscure authors – that fuel his inner life. None of that changes. But as his needs are slowly altering, so too are our responsibilities as a family, as we seek to accommodate them. The house is starting to change, too. One afternoon I arrive in Portsmouth and notice all the clocks in the house are now larger, and more clear-cut in their signage. One of them simply reads 'MORNING', or 'AFTERNOON' or 'NIGHT', at the relevant time of day. When I first see it, the sheer starkness of the large-format writing, and of its unavoidable implications, stops me in my tracks, and I feel my throat tighten. But, regardless, Dad is sat happily reading in his study, surrounded by towers of books, and he is as surprised and delighted to see me as ever, and soon we are singing at the piano together in a world that's close to normal if you don't examine it too closely, which neither of us do.

When I am in Portsmouth, I now also attend the local Orthodox *shul*, which it turns out is approximately five minutes away from our house. It is populated by a tiny, friendly, ageing community, delighted to see new faces, even though I am unable to provide the crucial strength in numbers their *minyan* so frequently needs. ('Part of the reason your father never went,' says my mum, 'is that he knew that once they realised he lived round the corner they'd knock for him every time they needed a tenth man and he'd never be able to escape.')

After the service, we gather and mingle over smoked salmon and crackers at the inevitable *kiddush*.

As ever, when I am sitting with a group of Jews greater than, approximately, one, I am entranced by the many and varied creative approaches there are to Judaism.

There's the American woman who professes to be non-religious – having travelled over on a ferry – but who is seemingly wearing a *sheitel*, and nonetheless identifies exclusively as Orthodox.

There is the man whose first wife was Jewish but they didn't keep kosher in the house, and whose second wife isn't Jewish but they do, and who is a devoted core member of the community dedicated to overseeing the upkeep of the *shul*, but who also works on Saturdays and doesn't care who knows it.

And there's the northern man in his sixties who explains he's on the hunt for a good Jewish girlfriend of around his age – only he doesn't want anyone religious – 'Wouldn't want them to keep Shabbat, and all that,' he says, casting his eyes hopefully around this Orthodox *shul*. Perhaps the American lady is single.

It's a miasma of contradictions. Which is entirely in keeping with how Judaism – even Orthodox Judaism – exists in the wild. Which, presumably, is why the Beth Din don't want us in the wild, as the email we receive makes clear.

*

Our post-meeting week of waiting has come and gone. Pressure has built with each passing day – a sense of anticipation, and more than that, of genuine hope. It all feels so tantalisingly close.

And then the email arrives. It comes from Dayan Landau directly, not from any intermediaries, with the unpromising subject of 'more information please'.

It refers to the one dangling thread from that meeting. Where – exactly – we are going to live, following the end of the process.

The answer we gave in the room was unsatisfactory. More clarification is needed. We must be more specific.

And we begin to realise what an impossible situation we have been placed in.

'The Beth Din simply do not approve of Primrose Hill and Regency Square,' we are told, discreetly, by a host of Supportive Rabbis. 'The areas are deemed insufficiently religious. They don't want people to emerge from the other side of the conversion process and be "those sorts of Jews".' And the fear, clearly, following our last meeting, is that, left to our own devices, 'those sorts of Jews' is exactly what we might become.

This means that the only acceptable answer to the question of 'where are you going to live?' is . . . Hendon. Except, in our meeting, that notion was dismissed out of hand by Dayan Landau himself as being unrealistic. Meaning that we will have to present an answer that is, somehow, not in Hendon yet not *not* in Hendon.

There are a number of issues at play here.

The Ashkenazi Beth Din is part of a charitable organisation known as the United Synagogue, a name which I'm fairly certain isn't intended to be ironic.

The primary synagogues in the unacceptable areas of Regency Square and Primrose Hill are also part of the United Synagogue. So the Beth Din is actively trying to avoid us becoming members of . . . their own organisation.

Furthermore, as is blindingly obvious to everyone involved in this discussion, the *shul* in the apparently insufficiently Jewish area of Regency Square is overseen not by some subversive hippy rabbi seeking to introduce shellfish to the Shabbat *kiddush* before whipping off their fake beard and revealing they've been a woman all along – no, Regency Square *shul* is led by Dayan Horowitz, one of the senior members of the Beth Din, and has been for approximately thirty years.

I am dumbstruck.

Yet again, we find ourselves in a situation that seems well beyond the realms of *halacha*.

It is clear that there is an internecine civil war playing out within the United Synagogue, and we are trapped in the middle of it. As a result, we are being compelled to commit to moving somewhere that has no bearing on who we are, where we are connected to, or where Eliana's family actually lives. It represents an outrageous moving of the goalposts.

Eliana and I are locked in thunderous arguments once more. My rage isn't directed at her, but it so clearly points in her direction – at Orthodoxy, at the conversion, at the concept of religion as a whole at this point – that it might as well be.

I feel so deeply furious with it all.

We compose an email, miserably, thanking Dayan Landau for his email, and giving him what has become blindingly clear, by process of elimination, is the only acceptable answer. 'The area that makes the most amount of sense to us is South Hendon/ Brent Cross,' we say. And, in terms of visiting Ohr, the friendly community we would happily maintain ties with post-conversion, we could and would do it, if needed. It just isn't where we, you know, actually want to live.

Eliana is away for the weekend, and so I am at large in The Area for a rare solo Shabbat. Being without Eliana underscores how strange life now is. The extent to which the ground has shifted beneath me and my world has become unrecognisable from three years ago. On Friday night Ronit takes me under her wing and brings me along to the dinner she and Joel are attending. The warmth of the community here – welcomed as I am immediately into the house of yet another stranger, made instantly at home, urged to come back any time – feels so at odds with the flinty sharpness of the way the process is overseen.

In between rounds of singing *zemirot*, talk turns to my conversion. 'We're all rooting for you, you know,' says Ronit, in a rare display of emotion, following a rare consumption of alcohol. I am deeply touched.

The next afternoon, I make the long walk down the Finchley Road in the rain, to visit Lion.

En route I stop in on Bernard and Erica. Bernard always has an air of Saturnalian festivity about him, but on this occasion his grandson has just got married, right here in the beautiful communal gardens, and so there is particular reason for celebration. We drink coffee and Bernard plies me with books I must read and exhorts me – as he frequently does – to follow my true calling and become a classical actor. 'Come and see me again some time!' says a happy, addled Bernard, as I leave.

I walk on, to Lion's beautiful flat, and she welcomes me in with a flurry of *mwah-mwahs*. She already knows absolutely everything about the latest conversion fiasco, of course.

'Oh, darling, it's just unbelievable, trying to tell you exactly where you should live,' says Lion. 'It's simply wicked.' And she rings a bell, and cake is brought in.

All going well, the next step is the final letter. That's what we've been told, by both of our tutors. By Jake, my trusted adviser, the man who made it to the end and lived to tell the tale. The final letter will mean that our lives will snap into motion once more. It will confirm my *mikveh* date – meaning it will also greenlight the procedure which must take place in good time prior to my *mivkeh*. It will be, effectively, a letter telling me I must book my circumcision.

All of this means many things at once because, as ever, Eliana and I are inhabiting multiple realities simultaneously, and one of these realities involves planning a wedding.

The moment I emerge from the *mikveh*, the pendulum will immediately swing from 'Under no circumstances may you make even glancing physical contact with one another', to 'Get married, already!' We will have escaped from our current purgatory and landed squarely in Adam Bernstein territory; where weddings are arranged at bullet-train speed so that couples can get on with the business of being fruitful and multiplying.

That in itself isn't a problem for us. Of all the various adjectives that might adequately describe my and Eliana's relationship, 'casual' doesn't feature. We are, though it frequently gets lost in the mess of it all, keen to get married to one another. What is more of an issue is the sheer thundering impracticality of the situation we are currently in; of there being no concrete means of organising something which, by the time the conversion process has concluded, will need to have long been organised.

Or will it? The concept of 'organising a wedding' means different things for different people. Generally, the men of ultra-Orthodoxy are not inclined towards matters of domesticity or hospitality. This is the domain of the woman (most of whom simultaneously work). What's more, if one were to get married in The Area, there are function halls which cater to the local Wedding Industrial Complex, and little more thought need go into it than that. To the Beth Din, then, the notion of 'organising a wedding' is a non-issue. 'Pffft, how long do you need?' says my tutor with the shrug of a man who has almost certainly never organised a wedding. 'Four weeks? You book a room . . .? Eh?'

There is another view. Some people might, for instance, see a wedding as a once-in-a-lifetime opportunity to create a truly special event reflective of two unique individuals, and their lives, their families, and loved ones. They might have guests in, say, other countries around the world who might appreciate a degree of advance notice to book their travel. According to this view it might actually – whisper it – take longer than four weeks to organise a wedding.

Thankfully, there is quiet support for this line of subversive thinking, even within the highly Orthodox community – Eliana's tutor explains to her that many of the women she teaches, both Jewish and non-Jewish, have long-held fantasies of their dream wedding, and she is entirely sympathetic to their desires. She understands that there is often far, far more to the occasion than simply booking that hall down the road. So what happens in practice is, as Eliana is told by a confidante, this: people discreetly plan those details of their weddings that they can – those select elements not bound by timings, or other unknowable logistics – far more than four weeks in advance. Because . . . because of course they do.

Throughout this process, what Eliana and I have lacked in 'personal freedom and the ability to relax' we have made up for in 'an excess of time in which to overthink every element of our futures'. And so, as a defence mechanism, a reflexive means of keeping the darkness at bay and illuminating our passage through the endless tunnel of the conversion, we have escaped into our imaginations – plotted and dreamed, telling one another stories of how things might be when our lives are our own once more. A natural by-product of that is The Spreadsheet. It developed gradually and organically from when a slightly drunken Sunday afternoon conversation about what a hypothetical wedding of ours might look like generated a host of detail (Who exactly would be there? What sort of venue might it be in? What would we *eat*, for goodness' sake?) which it suddenly felt crucial to capture in a document of some sort. And beneath the frothiness of our planning – of our burbling on happily about who might make speeches (my area of focus), and what forms of dessert might be served (Eliana's undisputed domain, with a 'shortlist' of seventeen dishes being carefully considered) – there is a pent-up energy and sense of meaning.

There is an understanding that this event, as well as being a wedding, will mark us being able to take ownership of our lives once again. It will be a celebration of having survived this period of stratospheric instability, and of launching into the next chapter of our lives. And whilst, currently, our ability to make decisions is approximately nil, from our wedding onwards, we will once more be masters of our own destiny. So, with that in mind, let's start with a bang. Let's come roaring out of the gate and create an occasion in which every facet feels entirely representative of who we are. Let's throw a *simcha** for the ages. So, as the months go by, The Spreadsheet spirals in size and scope, accumulating our every wedding-related hope and desire across a dozen carefully ordered tabs.

'Make plans, but don't actually confirm anything', is the general guidance from those in the know. Plan your wedding. But

---

* A celebration.

don't. But do. But don't pay for anything in case it all falls apart. But pencil in the booking so you can secure it if all goes well. But don't think about it at all until you finish the conversion. At which point you'll need to have thought about it fully already. We exist in a paradoxical quantum state, our hypothetical wedding flickering, translucent, before us.

The thing about living within a paradox is that you still have to make decisions, in the full knowledge that they won't totally make sense.

It is now the summer. To the best of our knowledge, the next step in the process is the final letter. There's no way of knowing when it will arrive. But we can take an educated guess as to when, broadly, we might find ourselves on the other side of all this. 'The end of the year,' come the whispers. 'You could do something at the end of the year.' And so we take the paradoxical step of speaking to venues.

Have you ever tried to book a wedding venue? The current standard lead time to organise a wedding in the UK is, it appears, twenty years. Venues are booked up, somehow, decades in advance. Not that Eliana and I are booking a wedding venue. To be very clear, we are simply having conversations with various beautiful events spaces about the possibility of hiring them for an unspecified gathering, at a slightly unspecified time – just like so many converting couples before us. Of course, none of the spaces are even available ('Sorry, the end of *this* year?!' is the inevitable, incredulous response), but even the act of exploring brings with it a tingling thrill.

And then we discover a glasshouse in Devon. Its walls are a fantasia of vines and huge green leaves and trailing flowers, and it has an immense triangular glass-panelled roof of breathtaking theatricality. It is, definitively, the most beautiful place in the world. And, by some miracle, there happens to be one free weekend in late autumn.

We commit, in as much as we can commit, which is not at all. But we spend hours on the phone with the owners, explaining that we would absolutely love the opportunity to commit at an unspecified point later in the year – hopefully not too long! But also, to be clear, we really have no idea – and that in the meantime we *can* absolutely commit to the concept of committing at the point that it's possible for us to commit. Which is something, no?

Despite us only being able to communicate with the venue via a series of riddles, a tentative pre-commitment agreement is reached. Although it is clear that, as things stand, this unspecified event may or may not happen, in the event that it *were* to happen, a venue and a date have both been, tenuously, secured. For Eliana and I, our light at the end of the tunnel becomes the glinting reflection of the glasshouse roof.

But in order for the event to happen, a series of things must first take place. The final letter must arrive. Then I must speak to Dr Strasser once again, and my date with destiny, and his scalpel, must occur. And then my body must recover – a process of at least six weeks. Only once I am fully healed will my longed-for final immersion in the *mikveh* be permitted. And only when I have emerged from the *mikveh* will our day at the glasshouse become a possibility.

Now add to this equation the following: I am going to perform at the Edinburgh Fringe for the entirety of August – a month during which a trip to Dr Strasser would be entirely impossible. So from my vantage point in early July, this much I can at least say for certain: my circumcision, if it is to happen at all, will take place *either* before I go to the Edinburgh Fringe or afterwards. If it were to happen beforehand, then I now have a period of approximately three weeks in which to receive the letter, book in my surgery, and then will my body into healing enough to allow me to travel to Edinburgh and spend a month performing a comedy show. And if, say, it were to happen afterwards, then that leaves an extraordinarily precise window of time in which I would need to firstly undergo the procedure, secondly heal, and thirdly attend the *mikveh*, in order to make it to the glasshouse. I would more or less need to dive-roll directly off the train back to London and directly onto Dr Strasser's surgical table.

The notion of the glasshouse is both important and entirely meaningless. Yes, should the wheels of theological bureaucracy turn too slowly, and this glimmering weekend in autumn prove an impossibility, then ultimately Eliana and I could get married in someone's back garden, or a local community centre. What does it matter?

But, at the same time, there is something incredibly nourishing about picturing this tropical oasis in the distance – it is a means of making real this event we are reaching towards. And, far more importantly, by pouring our energies into fixating happily on the glasshouse, we can push away the real reason we experience the passing of the seasons with ever-increasing agitation; the knowledge that, right now, Lion and my father are waiting for us at the finish line. But for how long?

I go to *shul*. I return home and revise the thirty-nine *melachot* – the actions prohibited during Shabbat. I have a meeting with a costume designer, to discuss whether a potential quick change in our Edinburgh show would be possible if I have been recently circumcised.

It feels fairly unlikely that this specific combination of circumstances has ever befallen anyone before.

We have been assured, by those in the know, that when Wednesday comes around we are likely to hear a response.

It is now Wednesday.

I am wired with tension, barely able to think. Also, I happen to be spending the day dressed in a sequin ensemble as a circus ringmaster for a BBC children's comedy show. In between takes, I sneak my phone out of my pocket and desperately refresh my email, message Eliana, message her parents . . . has anything arrived in the post? Anything at all? No? Is there maybe a second post delivery due today? A third? No? No . . . No?

The day drips by. Nothing.

'I'm not sure why you haven't heard,' come the whispers. 'You normally would have, by now.'

With every passing day, the silence of the Beth Din grows louder.

The words we heard in the meeting room replay themselves in my head.

I'm satisfied.

If the head of the Beth Din is satisfied, if we've eased their concerns about where we might live as a couple . . . what more can there be to do?

The available window of time in which I might have a piece of my penis surgically removed becomes ever more narrow and immediate, whilst simultaneously remaining completely unknowable and abstract. Edinburgh approaches. Another week passes. Then, somehow, another. My skull feels like an ever-more over-inflated balloon. I am increasingly certain that I will pop.

The stress bleeds into . . . everything. My concentration is shot. When spoken to, I end up staring into the middle distance. When speaking I, oddly, find myself slurring my words – like my bandwidth is so used up that I barely have the focus to prevent myself even from dribbling.

It is now one month since the 'I'm satisfied' meeting. Since the first Wednesday came and went, we have existed on tenterhooks.

An additional 504 hours of waiting – that time only interrupted by the appearance of the 'Where will you live?' email.

And now it is Wednesday again. There is a profound absence of post on the doormat. My inbox is resoundingly, disdainfully empty.

Somewhere in the world, cogs are slowly turning that will decide our fate. Or else they aren't. Either way, it's destroying us.

Sick with worry and unable to get any work done in our respective homes, we gather together at Eliana's parents' house and fail to get any work done there, as we count down the hours.

And then, at the very, very, very end of the day, a phone call comes.

I hurriedly answer the phone, place it on speaker. I look to Eliana and, once again, I naively allow myself to feel excited.

'Hello,' says the emissary of the Beth Din. 'There are some concerns about exactly where you'll live . . .?'

And the floor crumbles beneath me once again.

'We'd like you to arrange a meeting with Dayan Weissman, which I will attend. The next date we are both free is in a few weeks' time . . .'

I curl my lip. My teeth grind into dust. My jaw clenches. Heat radiates from behind my eyes and boils through my skull.

Eliana is shaking, tears streaming down her face. 'I can't . . .' she is saying, under her breath. 'I just can't go on like this. I can't.'

I attempt to gather myself, to find the right tone and mode of address for this phone call, to remain a supplicant. I address the voice on the other end of the line. 'You can appreciate, I'm sure, the distress this is causing . . .'

I feel close to throwing up. Eliana, drenched with tears, is typing frenziedly on her phone, firing off messages to her closest friends, who had been wishing her luck for today.

'This is reaching a point that it is really, severely, impacting our lives, it's affecting our mental and emotional health . . . a few weeks just isn't possible.'

'Tonight,' Eliana mouths to me. 'We need to speak to him tonight.'

'Look,' I say. 'If you'd like us to speak with Dayan Weissman, can we just meet with him directly? Tonight?'

The voice senses, perhaps, our level of urgency.

'Well, I mean, perhaps you could – if you reach out to him directly . . . I'll call you back . . .'

And the voice is gone.

I can barely look up. The air is thick.

We sit with Eliana's parents and explain what has happened.

Her mother is shaken by what this has done to us. Her father is, as ever, determined to see the positives.

When I speak, my voice shakes. I am white-hot with fury.

'I am so incredibly close to walking away from this process. This has to end. Now. *This has to end.*'

'You've done everything right,' an exasperated voice says on the phone. Eliana is speaking to a confidante experienced in the ways of the Beth Din, and pacing frantically. 'You've done things by the book,' the voice continues, 'maybe a little too much. Maybe it's time to push back. Maybe now's the time.'

What is this nonsense?

'This is unfair,' says the voice, 'You're a great couple.'

A pause. And then the voice speaks again.

'Reading between the lines, it sounds like this might be coming from Dayan Horowitz.'

Of course.

The final boss. The leader of the very first place I walked into. Somehow, hellishly, also the guardian of the door to my freedom.

We are at a loss. What more can we possibly do?

Finally, the Beth Din's emissary calls back. Yes, we are permitted to reach out to Dayan Weissman.

We leave missed calls and send messages and stew in the silence. Dayan Weissman, eventually, responds.

'Come to Ohr? Can you be here in twenty minutes?'

Eliana is in no state to drive, and I've famously never been in a state to drive, so Eliana's mother drives us, ashen-faced, to Ohr.

Here, we meet in the same room that we sat in when we introduced ourselves, and joined this community.

'Firstly, I'm so, so sorry,' says Dayan Weissman, immediately. He is empathy personified. A hugely intelligent man, bound up entirely in religion.

As we approached the *shul* together, Eliana had said to me, 'I'm not going to hold back any more. I'm going to let myself cry, and show him what this has really been doing to us . . .' But, in the event, when we start speaking it is I who fall to pieces first.

'My father is eighty years old,' I say, and as soon as I start the sentence I can feel my tears start to fall. 'Many months after I began this process, he was diagnosed with dementia . . .'

Dayan Weissman's eyes widen. He nods, earnestly, kindly. And it is as though his kindness unlocks some deeper place within me, and my weeping becomes unstoppable.

'That was now over two years ago. This is the man who taught me Hebrew, helped me learn my *bar mitzvah* portion . . .'

I can barely speak. I have never cried like this. Not since I was a child.

'And all I want is for him to have a meaningful participation in my wedding, but I don't – I don't know what to do . . .' I am in pieces.

And then Eliana speaks of Lion, her last remaining grandparent. She explains how central to family life Lion is, and of her fervent desire – and ours – that she be there with us.

In every prior encounter with the Beth Din we have been primped and contained and job-interview fresh. But today, all of our previous reserve and decorum is left behind. We present our unvarnished human selves. It's all we have left.

Dayan Weissman has been listening to us as the rabbi of our Hendon community.

But when he speaks, it is as a member of the Beth Din.

The message he is here to impart is this: if you can commit to living in Hendon . . . it's a yes.

We are asked: could we envisage living in Hendon for the next four years?

I could envisage anything, frankly. Yes, I could envisage it. I could envisage being press-ganged into being there against our will, in having been backed into beginning a life that neither of us truly consented to. But I could envisage being there with Eliana. And I could envisage that, if we were together, if all this was finally behind us, then we'd make it work.

'Yes,' I say.

There is, clearly, no other possible answer to give.

We walk back to the car, utterly, utterly, utterly drained.

If one could imagine a process designed, in elegant perfection, to bring someone as close as can be envisaged to G-d himself – to place them within a whisper of the infinite, to help them perceive the great outer reaches of eternity and the deep rolling hills of the universe – the London Beth Din Orthodox Jewish conversion process is the opposite of that.

'The sad thing,' says a Supportive Rabbi, shaking his head, 'is that there isn't a feedback form.'

CHAPTER 29

Suddenly, Everything Happens at Once

It is the day after our impromptu heartbroken appeal to Dayan Weissman, and I am in a car with Ivan, en route to the Buxton Fringe for a preview performance of our new show, when I see the words 'Finalisation of Conversion' appear in my inbox and I emit an involuntary scream that sounds like no noise I have made before or since. The final letter has arrived.

Feverishly I open the PDF and attempt to read every word of it at once. It's happening. It's all actually happening. I have been given a date for the *mikveh*. And I am hereby encouraged to book my circumcision, by calling Dr Strass—

I haven't got to the end of the letter when a withheld number calls my phone.

'Hello, it's Dr Strasser,' says a familiar voice.

He's already been informed. He's calling to make arrangements. Suddenly I'm reaching for my diary and looking at my calendar app and looking at the letter again – the *mikveh* date is mid-September. Which means if I am to both undergo circumcision, and be able to perform in Edinburgh, I genuinely need to book in my appointment, well . . .

'Not to sound over-keen, but do you have anything tomorrow?'

He doesn't. Which would leave the weekend. And not Shabbat, obviously, so we're actually just talking Sunday. The only way this will all actually work is if I can be circumcised this Sunday.

I explain my commitments in full, the total impossibility of 'nipping back to London' for the surgery mid-month. It really is now or . . . well, it's now. Please.

And that's that. Before I've even finished reading the letter, my circumcision is booked in.

I look back at my email. I read the letter again, properly this time, from the top. And that's when I notice the phrasing.

Dear Max,

I am very pleased to advise you that after thorough consultation, together with your meeting yesterday with Dayan Weissman, at which you and Eliana agreed to live in the 'heart of Hendon' for several years post conversion, the Dayanim are satisfied with the progress of your Conversion Application and, accordingly, have asked me to confirm their decision to finalise your conversion.

The '*heart* of Hendon'. The words are there, on the page. It's in quotation marks, even. But who said them? No one in the meeting.

This letter is, in many ways, everything that Eliana and I have worked for for the last two and a half years. But when I phone Eliana for what should be an elated, congratulatory, excited conversation, she is deflated.

Where there should be celebration, there is instead the prospect of years spent living away from her family, in a place neither of us have chosen. All happiness and sense of accomplishment has been systematically extracted from the process.

'My love,' I say. 'This is what we wanted! This is great! This is really exciting!' But I know how she's feeling, because I feel exactly the same. Empty.

There's another thing, too. When I messaged my tutor, thanking him for all of his help, he didn't know what had happened. Ordinarily, he explained, he would be informed before the prospective convert that the process has reached its conclusion. Something unusual has happened.

I will never ever know what took place. But I know exactly what I believe: that at least one of the voices in the throne room advocated strongly for me to be accepted. And at least one of the voices fought until the last for me to be rejected.

An irregular conversion for an Irregular Jew.

It is very clear that a bedsit is no place for a man to convalesce (or, indeed, for a man to do anything that isn't 'pack up and leave, never to return'), so my recovery, thankfully, is to take place in Primrose Hill. At Friday night dinner we sit with Eliana's parents, all of us exhausted by the week. Champagne is poured.

'Please, G-d,' says Katy, 'this will all be over soon. And there will be a wedding.'

Amen to that. But before that, another ceremony must take place.

CHAPTER 30

D-Day

7am.

I wake up to an unthinkable reality; later today, a piece of my penis is going to be cut off.

It is the fear that has woken me up in cold sweats, it is the intrusive drumbeat that has derailed my waking thoughts, it is my nightmare; my actual, recurring, relentless, nightmare.

And yet... my morning is dreamlike.

Which is not to say it's 'dreamy' – instead, my actions seem to take on the smooth, surreal clarity of a dream – frictionless, quiet, lacking shadows and sharp edges.

The world is eerily calm. I rise. I bathe. I eat breakfast. I feel a strange, settled centred-ness – nothing around seems to cause stress or difficulty. I barely hear any ambient noise around me. I feel as though I'm gliding. 'Gliding', of course, being a particular sensation that I'm aware that a part of my body will soon be unable to experience, ever again.

11am.

I feel the anxiety began to settle, like an invisible dew – on me, the invisible Jew – and I realise that my time with my body, as I currently know and understand it, is running out.

And so I suddenly find myself compelled to take a blizzard of photos of my unsuspecting member, from every conceivable angle, in every possible state.

This urge is entirely new to me. When I was in the first flush of adolescence, mobile-phone technology mercifully didn't extend to photos – although the occasion that Stephanie Payne texted me the suggestively arranged punctuation marks (.)(.) was an experience so profoundly and formatively erotic that if I close my eyes I can still feel the heat of the Nokia 3330 in my hand, and picture the light of its green screen illuminating my euphoric face.

The photos I now take of myself are, of course, uniformly terrible – blurry, ill-focused, poorly lit – but I capture them with the solemn urgency of an archaeologist documenting a fragile fossil deemed likely to disintegrate at any second. It seems, somehow, an important thing to do. An act of remembrance, before my de-memberance.

I shower. I trim. I get dressed.

Time ticks forward.

1pm

Lunchtime.

As we eat, Eliana is very quiet, and so am I. And of course we aren't allowed to hold hands, so of course we don't. But if we had done, perhaps a benevolent G-d might have forgiven us.

We leave the house. It is a beautiful day.

2.11pm

Steve Coogan is to accompany me to my foreskin-removal appointment, it has been decided.

Not physically – we've only met twice, firstly in the streets of Edinburgh shortly after Ivan and I were nominated for the festival's Comedy Award, and secondly later that same day, when he sat in the audience and witnessed us perform our show, which was so poorly received by our audience that I can only presume he wrote me off as a deviant with a humiliation fetish – but he is to join me in audio form.

Eliana and I are sat in the back of the car as Eliana's father drives us towards the surgery, and we are urgently, frenetically, game-planning 'mid-circumcision distraction strategies'. We have settled on the idea that I listen to an audiobook – specifically, *Alan Partridge: From the Oasthouse*, Series 2.

Reasoning: There are few purer joys in life than discovering wonderful comedy for the first time, and the first series of that show was transcendentally brilliant. What better counter to a miserable experience than something nigh-on guaranteed to be hilarious?

I take slow, deep breaths, and busy myself with preparing cables and battery packs for my elderly phone, whilst Eliana tackles the byzantine, pyramid scheme-like interface that is Audible, a company whose business model is surely less 'people love audiobooks' and more 'a hefty majority of our users simply lack the willpower to navigate our riddle-based cancellation process'.*

Thusly we distract ourselves as the car moves through the oddly empty streets (although I know this can't be the case, it felt to me as though there wasn't another vehicle on the road that

---

* NB: Audible, if you're interested in this book, let's talk.

day). Eventually, we pull up outside the surgery. Cranwich Road, Stamford Hill.

All sense of calm has now retracted (like a beautiful, functioning foreskin) and I feel only a sense of mounting pressure.

As I walk from the car to the surgery, it is as though the sky is bearing down upon me and the floor is pressing upwards. From above, I feel the enormity of reaching this peri-climactic point in my Jewish journey – the hushed, massed voices of three thousand years. This is actually going to happen.

3.02pm

Maurice opens the door to the surgery, and we walk in. Contrary to the space I am desperately attempting to manifest into existence – some sort of gleaming, spotless, spa environment, in which gentle sitar music plays in the background as I am welcomed in by smiling employees who look like they're part of a benign cult, and I am laid down, possibly on a giant lily pad floating in an impossibly beautiful pool of water, and my body is augmented purely via some holistic method, potentially a gong bath and/or being fed some sort of delicious 'elixir', and no actual physical intervention occurs at all – we are immediately greeted by a sweaty, leathery man brandishing a sharp-bladed power tool.

'I'm here to cut your penis off!' he gleefully shouts in my mind, before sanity prevails, the horror-film narrative I have immediately conjured up dissolves, and it becomes clear that he is actually a builder. The whole reception is a building site, in fact – a hectic blur of workers and sawdust and wood shavings. It is, perhaps, the exact diametric opposite of my utopian wellness-retreat fantasy (in which, at this point, I would be being draped in some sort of shimmering iridescent gown, and for some reason being fed fresh mango). It is loud, chaotic, and the buzz and whirr of machines is upon me.

And then, suddenly, so is Dr Strasser. Diminutive and bespectacled. He is slightly fervid, a little manic, a little 'up'. He shakes my hand (his grip mercifully steady) and, as he does so, I notice that he is wearing a disposable plastic apron and – there is no real way of *not* acknowledging this fact – there is some dried blood on it. I mean, he's at work. He's busy. It's just a fleck of someone's penis blood, probably. No biggie.

We thankfully move to his office. Here, the sounds of sawing and chopping are at least somewhat muffled. They instead act as a sort of faint, horrifying background muzak, as Dr Strasser briefs me on what is about to happen.

'Morty is a paramedic for Hatzolah [the Jewish ambulance service] and Aaron is a trainee *mohel* who will be joining us.'

Two men I hitherto did not notice step forward and shake my unprotesting hand.

'Now. You will receive a local anaesthetic via injection in the base of your penis...'

I do my best to suppress what feels suspiciously like an oncoming panic attack.

I attempt to ground myself, to focus on something simple, to clear my head, to—

'Maurice? I think we've met...? I'm Morty Steinberg.'

Astonishingly, the paramedic has chosen this moment to break into a parallel conversation with Eliana's father.

'Steinberg, you say? You know, I was just thinking I'd seen you before! Are you part of Norrice Lea *shul*...?'

'No – though my cousin is. But did you do any projects in Edgware...?'

'Hmm, not Edgware, although – let me see...'

Jewish Geography is a time-honoured custom. It is the

compulsion Jews have to work out if or, inevitably, how they are connected to one another – and nothing, it seems, not even a detailed medical briefing prior to a surgical procedure, will stop this ritual from taking place.

Maurice and Morty are getting deep into it. In one ear, I hear snatches of Dr Strasser discussing recovery times, and possible risks, and potential losses of sensation. In the other, I hear Morty and Maurice chat and schmooze and joke about business rates and Westminster Council. It turns out, you see, they were once both involved in a deal related to an office block! And here they are again! A small world, no?

I give a strained smile, and suppress the urge to swallow my fist. I desperately want all of it to stop.

Dr Strasser has finished his briefing.

'You'll want to go to the bathroom, I expect?'

I nod, dumbly.

'Very well. We'll be up the hall.'

3.12pm

I am in the toilet cubical, drunk on the unreality of it all. I stand, trousers round my ankles, *tzitzit* flowing by my side, and I look at myself in the mirror.

What on earth is going on?

I clothe myself, leave the cubical, and stand for a moment in the corridor. I feel the acute sensation of being stood at a crossroads in my life.

At this exact moment, I am entirely alone, and I am the master of my destiny. I could do anything. I could turn right. Run out of the GP practice. Leave it all. Leave my life with Eliana. Run back to the Docklands. Or further back – to Portsmouth. To the old familiar childhood bed and the musty smell of books, and the puppets and paintings and the stories, and curl up and dream my way out again, dream some alternate future into existence.

The temptation is vast.

. . .

I turn left. Towards certain surgery, and uncertain physical sensations for the rest of my days, and the sure and certain hope of a life full of happiness and joy, if only I can just get over my hang-ups about letting a bloke cut a bit of my body off.

I push open a door, and there they are.

There's Dr Strasser, a fresh plastic apron on now (thanks), the best dick guy in the business. And there's the paramedic who sold Maurice the office building once (good to know, good to know). And there's the trainee *mohel*, assisting Dr Strasser. And then there's also another bloke I've not seen before, who shakes my hand – 'Hi, I'm Shmuley.' Turns out, Shmuley is just there to watch! So that's nice.

There must be witnesses, you see, because this isn't a medical procedure. Or rather, it *happens* to be a medical procedure. The fact that my foreskin is due to be sliced off with a razor, and the weeping perimeter of ruptured flesh then manually stitched back onto the base of my shaft – this is deemed, comparatively, inconsequential. As my tutor made abundantly clear to me in our lessons, what is truly happening, the nub of it all (ach – my poor, defenceless nub) is an ancient and profound *religious ceremony*. It is the covenant that Abraham made with Hashem. It is a binding symbol of what it is to be Jewish. It is fundamental, it is undoable, it is deemed the greatest of the *mitzvahs*.

And, as such, it must be witnessed by a Beth Din. Confusingly, this isn't *the* Beth Din, those fun-loving custodians of my soul, but *a* Beth Din; a convocation of any three Jewish men.

Hence, Shmuley. This is a man I have never met before and will likely never meet again, who got word of this procedure by means unknown (is there a mailing list?) and has shown up ready and raring to witness something most people would enthusiastically pay not to see. Also, not to split hairs, which is presumably a party trick Dr Strasser is more than capable of, but he is actually the *fourth* witness in the room. So there is an argument that Shmuley is sat by the side of the surgical bed, ready to watch an adult circumcision . . . purely for a laugh. Talk about an 'observant' Jew, am I right, folks? OK, have a great night. Try the fresh mango.

3.20pm

It's showtime.

'Right,' says Dr Strasser, briskly, as he turns towards his scalpels and needles, 'if you'd remove your trousers and your underwear.'

Off they come. I am flying far too high on fear and adrenaline to be self-conscious.

My foreskin is pre-retracted, like I've been practising. I've been waiting for this.

I lie on the bed, and feel my mind's eye looking down at this scene, zooming out, and further out, up and out into space.

Is any of this real? Do I really, truly, understand that this is actually about to happen? To what extent am I prodding and tinkering with the parameters of my existence, just to see what happens?

It transpires that Dr Strasser has been talking, breezily, as he prepares his equipment, and that I have been chatting back to him, animatedly. We appear to be getting on swimmingly, which is nice.

'And what happens to my foreskin?'

'It'll be buried in the garden. Ha – unless you want to keep it.'
A pause.
'. . . Can I?'
'. . . No.'
'Right, sure. Of course.'

It becomes immediately apparent that the bed is uncomfortable and narrow, and I am not sat up – I am more or less lying down. Secondly, there is no separating curtain, no *mechitza*, between me and the gory blood-letting taking place on the front line. Instead, a long tube of white sheeting, like a super-sized kitchen roll, is placed on my chest, to act as a makeshift divider. It is secured in precisely zero ways – so, in order to precariously hold it in place, I have to awkwardly tense my chest and my upper arms. It might, perhaps, be more comfortable to sit up. But if I do? Well, I will see the unthinkable.

As for listening to a laugh-a-minute audiobook? Whilst technically possible, I swiftly realise that it's also supremely ill-advised. The merest twitch of my body carries with it immense risk; placing myself in a situation liable to cause convulsive laughter is earth-shatteringly (amongst other things) stupid.

So, instead, I shakily fire up some music. 'Relaxing Classical'? Why not. As loud as it can go. I lie back, and the surgery begins.

3.21pm

A needle is plunged into the base of my penis. This is the moment I was dreading most of all, so I have arrived psychologically prepared, as much as I am able, to receive this injection. Sadly, there are in fact about twelve of them.

I attempt to focus on the positives. The uncertainty is gone, at least; this is actually happening, right now. Whilst I am in deep, morbid discomfort, I am not panicking. I am, at last, after all the uncertainties of recent months, dealing with a definitive certainty. I am able, almost, to relax.

...

Until, a few seconds later, I feel the unmistakable sharp 'tang' of a pair of scissors slicing into the tip of my foreskin.

My nascent stoicism evaporates. I convulse.

'Ah, he felt that,' comes a amused voice from somewhere in the region of my crotch.

I am suddenly flooded with terror. A paranoid, irrational, notion that...

Perhaps painkillers just... don't work on me? Maybe I'm a one in a million case? What if my physical make-up is unique? Am I about to experience every single—

'Right, give him a bit more...'

Another piercing sensation in the base of the shaft. Another cool silvery dose of foreign fluids coursing through my body. Good stuff.

And then, after that, I can't tell you exactly what happens. Because, of course, despite the sparkling uniqueness I delusionally ascribed to myself, it transpires that, eventually, painkillers *do* have an effect on me.

And as a blessed numbness spreads across my crotch, and I close my eyes, the men go to work – a hurried succession of hands, prodding, slicing, stitching. Exactly what they do, I will never know.

Though the ultra-violence is being masked by the strains of old Ludwig Van, I periodically still hear snatches of conversation, which I silently contribute to:

...

'... yes, we do that because of *hiddur l'mitzvah* ['beautifying the mitzvah']...'

Thank you, Dr S, for whatever you're doing! All beautifying gratefully received.

...

'... risk of penile necrosis...'

Ah, splendid. The most horrifying combination of two words I have ever heard. Please don't say that again.

...

'Hmmm, it's all folded over.'

...

With the procedure in full flight, I am suddenly hit with overwhelming nausea. Whether it's the mother lode of painkillers swirling through my system, or the stress, or just queasiness, or a combination of the above, I realise I am fighting the pressing urge to vomit. I am desperate for a glass of water, but am too weak to speak – finally, via nodding and croaking to Morty the Hatzolah man, I acquire one, and he helps me drink it.

The nausea subsides, the bile in my stomach retreats, and I begin to find a sense of internal equilibrium. I retreat into myself – allow a whiteness to envelop me – and let whatever is happening, happen.

And then the quiz occurs.

'Why are you doing this?'

Just as the circumcision isn't just a medical procedure, Dr Strasser isn't 'just' a doctor. He is a *mohel*. And it is in this form that he comes out of the mist.

What if I get the answer wrong? Does he sew my foreskin back on? I mean, you're good, Dr Strasser, but are you that *good...?*

'To become Jewish according to Torah law...?' I manage.

'And do you understand what that means? It means taking on every single one of the *mitzvot*. From *kashrut*—'

'All the way to the red heifer.' I give a weak smile and – insanely – a wink.

That seems to satisfy him. 'Very good.'

And he retreats into the distance, and they continue.

??pm

I am dimly aware that these men are praying around me. I don't know the words that are being said, but I feel them, hear them in the distance.

3.47pm

It is a testament to human beings' inherent ability to adjust to the new and the strange that, forty minutes into my lying half-naked on a bed receiving irreversible genital feng shui whilst a friendly bearded stranger watches on and occasionally smiles encouragingly, I have not only fully relaxed, I have managed to become almost . . . bored.

I'm feeling, basically, fine – it's now just a question of distracting myself.

Dr Strasser leans over. 'We're almost done.'

My heart leaps. It's nearly over?

'Yes, the religious component is almost complete.'

The remaining medical procedure – the afterthought that is sewing me up, rendering me fit for purpose, that has a way to go.

Sure. Fine. Great.

I need to kill time. Focus my mind. And then it hits me.

I should write a Post-Circumcision Speech. A few words that I can say back at the house.

Is it a great idea? Absolutely not. Is it a *good* idea? Again, almost certainly no. But it's the idea – fuelled by adrenaline and fatigue and painkillers – that I have, and I run with it. Or at least awkwardly lie with it.

My phone is about to die – the cable has fallen out. I scrabble to plug it back in, and realise it is now covered in fine speckles of blood, something I decide to completely ignore. Instead, as has been the case at innumerable points throughout my life, I attempt to make sense of my existence by writing jokes.

'*Whichever way you slice it . . .*' I type, '*when it came to marrying the love of my life, my foreskin was a drawback.*'

In the hinterland of my understanding, my penis is being sewn back together, but I'm busy – I have work to do.

4.07pm

The cutting and sewing has abated, and there is a sense of things slowing.

A liquid is tipped onto me, flooding my thighs. When it touches my skin it is cool, but, via some mysterious chemical reaction, it gathers in warmth until it feels like it might boil. I have no idea what it is, but it feels clean. Like it has scoured away the viscera and excess bits of human being, and left something fresh, ready to heal. I almost wish I'd seen what it was, and what it did.

I sit up, and Dr Strasser shows me the immediate aftermath of his handiwork.

It is purple, bloated, angry, but the main feeling I have is of relief – that nothing went wrong, that my brave, innocent frenulum survived the onslaught, and that the ordeal is over.

An endlessly long bandage is slowly wrapped, again and again, around my wounded penis.

I gingerly raise myself up from the surgical bed, and – in a process I can't vividly remember, but can only presume took several months – put my trousers back on.

4.36pm

I tentatively make my way to the office in which it all began, where Dr Strasser raises a glass of grape juice and delivers the blessing affirming the successful completion of my *brit milah*. Maurice films on his phone. His eyes are moist.

Dr Strasser and the witnesses wish me *mazel tov*, congratulating me on what I have undergone. Kosher Kingdom biscuits are passed around.

I am the oldest eight-day-old baby in the world.

I waddle out into the sunlight, less – or more – of a man.

Eliana leaps out of the car, tears in her eyes, and waves at me as I walk – very, very slowly – across the road to her.

The procedure took seventy-six minutes.

I have been circumcised.

CHAPTER 31

A Healing Experience

For the first time in a very long time, I am able to make plans . . . and then act upon them. (Beginning with my post-circumcision speech, written on the surgical table and performed some thirty minutes later to an impromptu gathering of friends and community members at Eliana's parents' house. Look, a gig's a gig.) The world exists in colour again.

Also, for the first time ever, I have a bandaged penis and I wake up in agony three times a night. You can't have everything.

I stumble on some stand-up from Ed Gamble, in which he talks about being circumcised as an adult (phimosis, classic), and realise he's likely to be a man with some answers.

'How soon after getting circumcised do you think one would be able to, say, perform a high-kicking song and dance routine?' I ask Ed.

'It's a great question,' he messages back. 'At least three weeks, I think – but to be honest it was over fifteen years ago, I can't really remember.'

'Thanks,' I reply, 'there's a choreographer coming round later today, so I'm just trying to work out what my limitations will be.'

'Oh,' says Ed, 'and there's me assuming you were using a weird subtle way of saying sex.'

'No, no. There's a genuine high-kicking song and dance

routine at the end of our show. Just trying to work out if it will kill me.'

Yes, to the disbelief and mild horror of our producer, one week after my circumcision, I head off to the Edinburgh Fringe to perform for a full month.

Tanked up on painkillers, I step, incredibly gingerly, from the train carriage onto the Edinburgh Haymarket platform, wincing as I manhandle my oversized suitcase.

My relief at having had the procedure pre-Edinburgh is twofold. There's the aforementioned race to the *mikveh*, and the fact our hypothetical glasshouse weekend can now become a glittering reality. And then there's also the incredibly essential matter of needing to be distracted. It has been made very clear to me, on websites, medical pamphlets, and via the good people of *r/circumcision* (honestly, guys, no need to keep 'checking in' to see if I've 'made my decision and are happy with the results' – really appreciate it, though!) that the absolute minimum time required to heal is four weeks. The sober, conservative estimate is six weeks. And in this matter – perhaps this matter more than any – I am prepared, determined even, to be conservative.

I set a non-negotiable alert in my calendar. Six weeks of monastic abstinence. Of course – for a man who is unmarried (yup) and Orthodox Jewish (nearly), there is simply no other state imaginable. No other state at all. But, also, the most daunting challenge I face is this: six weeks of *trying not to think about it*. About the fact that, as it currently stands, the only thing I have done is had a perfectly functioning part of my body surgically removed.

So I am overjoyed at the opportunity to place myself in a situation where I won't be compelled to think about it. Performing for a month at the Edinburgh Fringe is the most all-consuming, distracting thing in the world. It's also, quite possibly, a greater act of self-harm than an elective circumcision. For the duration of my time there, I will be compelled to obsess over line-tweaks, carefully calibrate sound cues, fret about choreography and harmonies, and bury myself in imperceptible adjustments to the word-order and delivery of all of our stupid jokes.

I am, clearly, replacing one form of navel-gazing with another. And, as we arrive at our flat by the Meadows, and Ivan gallantly hoicks my luggage up the stairs as I cautiously follow behind, I am beyond grateful for the timing of it all.

The act of sleeping is now a delicate assault course. Getting comfortable enough to sleep in the first place is one challenge (the winning technique ends up being something akin to the foetal position, with ice packs wrapped in tea-towels nestled in my crotch). Warding off nocturnal stirrings is another. Try as I might, I am jerked awake by the searing, agonising pull of nighttime erections. In desperation, I resort to Googling images of rotting fruit, or maggots, in a bid to disgust myself into a state of detumescence.

I stop drinking water long before bed in a bid to stop myself ever needing to pee in the night – but still, sometimes, I am forced to perform the slow, brittle roll that allows me to shift my body out of the bed and place my feet on the floor, and then perform a delicate walk that is somewhere between a waddle and a shuffle to the toilet. Fortunately, I had secured the bedroom closest to the bathroom.

I wake up each day in the knowledge that blood will have seeped through the gauze bandage.

By sheer chance, the flat we are staying in contains, thankfully, a large bath.*

---

* Edinburgh Fringe accommodation is an extraordinary lottery, and over the years my stays have featured both soaring highs – the beautiful Victorian house with stunningly appointed double-bedrooms for all – and crushing lows – the month in which I discovered upon arrival that I would be sharing a bed with a large, bearded spoken-word poet I'd never met before, who slept in his shoes and snored at a volume most people reserve for screaming for help.

Soaking in the oversized tub each morning (and here I use the Edinburgh Fringe definition of morning, meaning 'any time before 6pm'), the bandage is gradually and delicately removed, and I am subject to a hideous reveal.

There is angry inflammation. The newly stretched skin is now a grotesque sphere beneath the head of my penis. And beneath that, the scar line: a pus-filled trench of depthless horror.

Eventually I rise, ponderously, from the bath, and I am subject once more to the sharp sensation of gravity pulling cruelly at my unhealed body.

I dry myself incredibly slowly and, loosely draped in a towel and cradling myself gently for protection with one hand, I slowly shuff-waddle back to my room, fervently hoping that nobody sees me. Dignity, always dignity.

There is a small desk in the nook at the end of the room, and this becomes the station at which my intricate daily routine's essentials — bandage, scissors, Vaseline, a mug to contain boiling water, hand sanitiser, painkillers — are carefully stored. Here, I master strange new rituals, and attend to my suppurating wounds.

Behind the desk, the window looks out directly onto a beautiful garden, where residents of the block gather to tend to their flowerbeds and chat. Out of deference to their quality of life, my curtains are very, very, very rarely open.

When I left Dr Strasser's practice, he told me to message him if I have any concerns. Though I am not prone to hypochondria, I find literally everything about the state of my penis extremely concerning, and, as such, the good doctor is bombarded with hellish close-up photographs on a near-daily basis. Is this OK? Surely this isn't what it should look like?

Inevitably, seconds later, I receive a call back from No Caller Id.

'Everything's fine', he invariably intones. 'Everything's totally fine.'

Anyway, I don't think about all of that. Genuinely, I don't. As soon as I am dressed, and I have left the flat, all doubts and fears are blessedly cast away, replaced with far more pressing concerns.

The seventy-two hours between arriving in Edinburgh and the first performance of a new show are uniquely and spectacularly fraught. Inevitably, lines are rewritten, stoned eighteen-year-old technicians fail to show up at your venue and turn on the lights, props are discovered to be broken, flyers have gone missing, the one large-format poster you ordered for £1,000+VAT turns out to have been stuck at the very edge of the city on a billboard halfway up a mountain that is only visible to passengers on low-flying private aircraft.

So, as the first night approaches, these are my concerns. And, on top of that, Eliana is coming to town.

With a frenzied burst of exertion, Ivan and I perform our new show for the very first time. What began as a spark of an idea, something then nurtured and refined in supremely inopportune circumstances, is now a living, breathing thing. And whilst our first-night performances may lack in polish, when our dads appear onscreen they steal the show (and, unlike us, they know all their lines). With the help of four pairs of supportive underwear and a dance belt, I am able to participate in the show's ending, the fabled high-kicking song and dance routine – a duet of duos, sung by Ivan and me and our fathers, reflecting on the choices we've made and the possibilities yet in store for us all.

> *Life is an adventure,*
> *You can't tell where you'll go,*
> *Don't wait too late to celebrate,*
> *Cos what comes next, who knows . . . !*

After the show, I take Eliana for dinner.

'I've made a booking,' I say.

And we walk from our venue, down the road, back towards the Pleasance Dome.

On Edinburgh's Clerk Street there is a small strip of shops that performers have visited since the Fringe was formed.

These shops sell ... everything. Irons. Lamps. Silly string. Scented candles. Bertie Bass singing fish. Mugs. Shortbread. Lighters. Hoodies. Kettles. Lightsabres. Honestly, everything.

Here, dewy-eyed sketch troupes and idealistically earnest political theatre companies have hastily purchased their props before a tech rehearsal. Avant-garde clowns have hurriedly wrapped themselves in tinfoil. Absolutely everyone has bought staples and staplers, to attach their latest round of quotes to their flyers before pitching their wares on the Royal Mile once more. On numerous occasions, I can personally confirm, folding chairs and metal trays have been purchased for the purpose of being swung by comedians at wrestlers, and vice versa.

They are as central to the ongoing existence of the Fringe as any venue, bar or performer. And on the afternoon of my first show, making full use of a non-existent window of time in between our tech rehearsal and the moment we're allowed into our venue, I return to these adjoining caves of wonder, and I secure all that I need for my particular mission.

I have sometimes felt that my and Eliana's relationship has been reminiscent of the Morecambe & Wise and André Previn piano concerto sketch – in that we've experienced all the right notes, but not necessarily in the right order (and, also, it's involved quite a lot of double-act sketch comedy).

We lived with one another before we formally acknowledged we were in a relationship. When we each said our first I love yous, it was in the midst of a row about Judaism ('Well, *of course* I love you, but . . .'). We discussed the granular specifics of our married lives whilst we were broken up. And although we've started planning our wedding . . . we aren't engaged. Up until very, very recently, the idea of being engaged was effectively a conceptual non-starter. How can one propose that which is practically impossible? Only now, with the *mikveh* ahead of us, can the event we've daydreamed about in forensic detail begin to be brought to life. All of which is to say, I am determined that despite the strangeness of our circumstances we shouldn't be robbed of that moment experienced by nearly all other married couples – a proposal.

So when, where, how? The moment I emerge from the *mikveh*, perhaps? It would be the first second we could be truly certain that a future together is possible. But perhaps that might be a moment we might seek to mark in its own right? And also – well, I look at the calendar and it feels like the fates have delivered a *fait accompli*. The first night of my Edinburgh show with Ivan coincides with Eliana's birthday. Which means it is also the anniversary of the night of conga-dancing at which our story began. And, as an elegant addition to these converging signs, it also falls on a Jewish holiday called Tu B'av, which is a celebration of love – effectively, Jewish Valentine's Day. I mean, come on.

The problem is, Eliana has already booked to come to Edinburgh to see me during the first weekend. This is thoughtful, sensible, and supremely unhelpful.

'Sorry, you'd like me to come up on the Wednesday too?' She is, understandably, sceptical.

'. . . Yes,' I say, aiming for straight-faced nonchalance that doesn't acknowledge the staggering impracticality of the request.

'Are you sure?'

'I just think – I'd really like us to be together for your birthday.'

'I mean . . . I'll look at work stuff . . . and I suppose I could get an early train back the next day . . . You'd definitely like me there on the Wednesday? Only I'll be back, like, two days later?'

'I know. But . . . look.' In mild alarm, I resort to some light emotional blackmail. 'It's the first night of our show, and I'd really like your moral support, actually.'

'. . . OK, my love. If that's what you need.'

And so Eliana – suppressing any visible signs of annoyance she may or may not be feeling – commits to another ten hours of train travel in the same week, and I – panicking slightly – commit to making her journey worth the *schlep*.

The 'when' of the proposal is so clear: on this clearly auspicious date, and in the evening – once the stresses of the show are out of the way. The 'where' and the 'how' are slightly blurrier – but, when I think about it, it all comes into focus.

I think about Edinburgh's glitziest restaurants, its swankiest hotels and its most dazzling cocktail bars – and how completely unrepresentative they are of my and Eliana's time in the city. And then I think about the place in which we first raised those warm, appalling Jägerbombs together, four years previously.

The bar is called Brooke's, and it springs up for the duration of the Fringe where it becomes, for four weeks, a booze-sodden nexus point of the festival. It is an 'Artists' Bar', where performers and venue staff gather after their shows have finished, to brag, bitch, flirt, have poorly concealed affairs, tell tall tales, toast their triumphs and drown their sorrows, until the main lights finally flicker on at around 6am and people spill out into the streets, to the even later-night bars, or to the McDonald's on Princes Street, or to one another's beds.

Sure, it's essentially a completely unremarkable room containing some sofas of varying degrees of tattiness in which people drone on insufferably at one another – myself loudly and categorically included – but even in its most fallow years it's never quite shaken the sense of being a place where Edinburgh *happens*. A room where, after the most incredible show has taken place somewhere in the city, word will have gotten round, and the performer themselves might have turned up for a drink, long before anything has reached the morning papers. As such, there is an addictive pull to the place, which draws people there against their better nature. When Ivan and I first scrambled to Edinburgh as students, performing scrappy shows in unloved venues elsewhere in the city, the mere act of talking our way into Brooke's – thereby denoting ourselves 'real comedians' purely by dint of being allowed through the doors – could be the focus of our whole night, if not our entire month. And, as the years went by, it grew into a natural place to unwind, to catch up with comedian friends not seen since some other previous gig or festival, or to slip in for a swift half and lose an entire night. If I added up the number of hours of my life I have spent there, the total, at least, would be sobering.

Brooke's is many things. Romantic, however, it is not. But, nonetheless, it will forever be the place that brought Eliana and I together. And also, I realise to my delight, on the first night of the festival, whilst the place has been prepped and set up, ready to be reincarnated for yet another year, it *isn't yet open*. Meaning, if one asked nicely, one could have the place to oneself.

As Eliana and I walk up the familiar metal staircase leading to Brooke's, the door to the bar is held open for us, and the venue manager – a young woman named Abby I will forever be grateful to – welcomes us with a smile.

'Your table is ready,' she says.

We are led past a velvet rope, through a curtain, and into our very own private 'restaurant'. The space is illuminated by the light of half a dozen lamps. The music of Nat King Cole plays. The table is set for two.

Brooke's Bar could never – ever – be romantic. But what about, as the sign on the curtain reads, Brookestein's Kosher Deli . . . ?

Eliana bursts out laughing and beams with delight.

'Wow,' she says. 'How did you manage to score a booking at this place . . . ?'

Other than the table and chairs, everything else comes courtesy of the Edinburgh All-Purpose Emergency Shops – from the plates and cutlery to the surprisingly robust and bassy Bluetooth speaker, to the curtains that form the walls of the space, to the lamps lighting our meal (two of which, full disclosure, are lava lamps, in deference to Eliana's inexplicable love of them).

We take our seats and are served kosher champagne, followed by one of the heaviest meals in human history, courtesy of the one and only kosher food delivery service Edinburgh has to offer. It is generally used by Jewish students, unfussy about what they are eating and mainly seeking fuel to help them work into the night. So our dinner consists of the unholy, yet by definition also extremely holy, combination of breaded fried chicken schnitzel on top of rice, pasta with marinara sauce, and roasted potatoes. That's carb-on-carb-on-carb, served at precisely 30 per cent of the temperature that would represent optimum edibility.

'It's perfect,' says Eliana, grinning.

The impossibility of our relationship thus far has meant that so much of it has been an act of collective fantasy – existing in spaces we are able to imagine into existence, in which we can be together – and this is just one more of them.

The kosher champagne gives way to kosher red wine. A remarkable quantity of the carbohydrate assault course is consumed.

And then, for dessert, two distinctively undrinkable 'cocktails' are handed to us – shots of Jägermeister floating in a sea of Red Bull, the very concoction that brought us together. We knock them back, for old times' sake. And then I get down on one knee . . . very, very slowly.

I ask Eliana to marry me.

Reader, she says yes.

As we tumble out of our gorgeously tacky, slightly camp makeshift restaurant, Brooke's is just opening its doors to its very first legitimate customers – exhausted venue techs dropping by for their hard-earned post-show (or pre-show) pint (or pints). The immense machinery of the festival is gradually shifting into gear.

We profusely thank our host, Abby, who unflappably accommodated my batshit requests in the midst of every conceivable opening-night stress, and Eliana and I walk off into the night together, delirious with the sudden realness of it – with having arrived, via all sorts of wrong turns and circuitous back roads, at a major relationship landmark of the most traditional sort: being engaged.

Words of congratulation come flooding in from our delighted-if-entirely-unsurprised families.

'*Mazel tov!!!*' message my brothers. 'Glad it went well.'

'But also – would have been hilarious if she'd said no! Amiriiiight?!'

'Yeah, big time. Hell of a prank, eh?'

'Did you expect me to propose?' I ask Eliana later that night, as we celebrate with friends.

'No, I didn't *expect* it . . .' Eliana says. 'But, also, if you'd made me come to Edinburgh for the day and you *hadn't* . . . I'd have been furious.'

Ivan and I ease into the run of performing our show, and Eliana and I tear into the gleeful business of planning a wedding. I float between these two double-acts in my life, exhilarated at my sense of new-found freedom, of a life lived in motion. The future is becoming more tangible. The glasshouse is no longer a tantalising maybe – it is now the inked-in, double-underlined, deposit-paid space in which we are to get married.

My mother creates a beautiful hand-drawn 'save the date' illustration, which we begin to delightedly distribute. When it comes to the granularities of wedding planning, what might present as stressful for other couples seems, to us, an absolute treat. The opportunity to be suddenly debating napkin colours and glassware, as opposed to the nature of my soul or the fundamental impossibility of us being together, feels like such an unimaginable luxury that it leaves me lightheaded.

This golden feeling extends to our Friday nights when, to the envy of many of our fellow performers, Ivan and I have a night off. There are lots of reasons people perform for the entirety of the month-long festival – the increasingly criminally prohibitive costs of getting there in the first place, for one thing – but one of the main ones is just 'because you're supposed to'. It is simply a piece of vestigial received folk wisdom, baked into the collective comic psyche. However, it turns out, you can just . . . not. 'Wow . . .' says a slightly awestruck comedian we meet on the way back to our flat, 'so you're just going to . . . relax? That's . . . amazing.'

And, as weird as it is to obstinately switch off from the festival as it begins to work up a head of steam, reach its full clamouring speed, it does feel somewhat amazing. I trawl the massive Tesco and discover its kosher aisle, stocked with the kind of dishes that I have become used to on a Hendon Shabbat – *chrain*, the richly purple horseradish dip; chopped liver; potato latkes. To my amazement, I feel a yearning for it all. And so each week, as the festival progresses, increasingly elaborate Friday night dinners are held. Ivan throws himself into the affair with enthusiasm, prepping food, dressing up smart, donning a spare *kippah*. We bless the candles, the wine and the *challah* bread, and we sit with our fellow comedian housemates, and others who come to join us, as word gets out about this oasis of calm, a respite from the ceaseless pressures of the festival.

After the first weekend, Eliana returns to London, but our planning continues in earnest. And there is much to plan. Have you ever tried to organise a certified kosher wedding in deepest Totnes? The answer, almost certainly, is no – because, as we swiftly come to discover, it seems extremely likely that no one has done this before, ever.

The traditional route – hiring a caterer – is, we soon discover, a no-go. 'Where . . .?' is a common, incredulous, refrain. 'Sure, I'll get you a quote', is another commonly heard phrase, uttered by people we never hear from again. But there's another way.

The glasshouse, it turns out, has its own in-house catering team – led by a terribly nice young man who gamely states that he'd be more than happy to work with us on making the food they produce kosher, whatever that means. And, thanks to our exhaustive lessons in *kashrut* – the Jewish laws pertaining to kosher food – Eliana and I are now acutely aware of what is required in order to serve kosher food. The ingredients, the equipment – what to use, where to source it, how to store it, how to serve it: the works. Meaning, if we could order all of the supplies ourselves, from the mighty Kosher Kingdom, and The Area's surrounding suppliers, and then find a *mashgiach* – a kosher food inspector – willing to come to Devon and oversee the entirety of the food production process, and take all the necessary steps along the way to ensure the food is kosher, then we'd be in business. As a solution it's fiddly, intricate and time-consuming – but, honestly . . . that's never stopped us before. If anything, it's in keeping with our entire approach to our relationship.

We spend the next few days having long and engaging conversations with a series of people around the country who on no account wish to come to Devon and render our entire wedding kosher. They all lack either the expertise, the confidence, the inclination or some combination of all three. But then we speak to Josef.

I actually know Josef a little – he is a relative of the kindly gentleman I sat next to in *shul* at the start of my journey. He also happens to be exactly the man we seek: a *mashgiach*, a role he fulfils in a restaurant certified by no less an authority than the London Beth Din themselves. He is an expert, the exact man for the job – and, astonishingly, he is willing to join us in Totnes to facilitate our wedding. 'It would be my honour! *Mazel tov!*' Josef is perhaps the happiest man I have ever spoken to. His religious practice seems to manifest itself as a constantly replenished outpouring of love and warmth towards his fellow humans. He immediately understands the nature of our enquiry, immediately agrees, immediately says he will spend as long as it takes to make it happen.

He is entirely confident in his abilities, he assures us, and the Beth Din are welcome to speak to him if they have any queries. But, he explains, he doesn't do his job to the very highest standard because of the Beth Din – he does it because he is certain it is the right thing to do. It is a living, breathing example of *yirat shamayim* – a Jewish phrase often translated as 'fear of heaven', but perhaps one that might be more accurately thought of as a sense of awe and reverence. It is his way of honouring the Almighty.

And so, on a series of lengthy Zoom calls, the wonderfully game Devon chef unites with the preternaturally unstressed Josef, who calmly explains exactly how everything can and will be rendered utterly kosher. Meat and fish and herbs and oils and vinegars all ordered in bulk from London and driven up in a van.

And as for the koshering of the kitchens themselves – Josef will turn up in Devon three days before the wedding, and transform the space; scrubbing and cleaning and wrapping surfaces in foil and demarcating and doing all that is needed. What an absolute *mensch*. Via a combination of modern technology and ancient theology, Totnes's first kosher wedding feast is being planned.

I'd thought that my hippy parents, somewhat marriage-indifferent in their own relationship – their eventual wedding having been a pleasant means of marking thirty years together, as opposed to an essential starting pistol to their shared lives – might be politely uninterested in our new world of prepping and planning. But no. Not only does my mum begin to generate acres of gorgeous wedding-specific illustrations – invitations, signage, thank-you card designs, artwork for the *benscher* pamphlets containing the lengthy blessing for bread, all overflowing with vibrant colour and beautiful detail – but she also begins to quietly exhibit signs that she might be thinking of this event as a special occasion. 'I thought I might get your father a bespoke suit . . .' she mentions, one afternoon, casually. I break out into a broad grin. I know exactly what this day will mean for Eliana and me, but the thought that it is meaningful to my parents too fills me with joy. I love that my mum takes Dad to Portsmouth's one bespoke tailor (Jewish, naturally), where he spends sunny afternoons being carefully measured up for his suit, whilst exchanging endless tortured puns and ridiculous one-liners. I love that my mum begins to plan her outfit with a spectacular two-word description of the style she's going for ('Punk Duchess'). I love the entire process of celebrating.

Josef's magnificence, it turns out, extends beyond the provision of food. As we are going to be in Devon over an entire weekend – from Friday through to Sunday – there is to be a Shabbat service on the Saturday morning, an occasion at which, if at all possible, one should hear a portion read from the Torah. And to that end, Eliana's father Maurice has an idea. Many years ago Maurice had a Torah written as a birthday present for his father, Max, which was donated to the Beit Shalom synagogue. For our wedding weekend, Maurice wishes to transport that same scroll – incredibly carefully – from London to Totnes, and for it to be read from on Shabbat morning. It is a beautiful idea, and a way of Max being here, being part of our wedding. But there is a problem: reading directly from the Torah is a highly specialised skill – more complex than 'regular' Hebrew – and it is one that few people are capable of without lengthy preparation. Often the one *parsha* people are comfortable reading aloud is their *bar mitzvah* portion. And if no one can read from the Torah then Maurice's plan is done for.

'I must tell you two things,' says Josef, when he hears of our latest logistical entanglement, 'Firstly, I know that Torah. I have only been to Beit Shalom Synagogue once, and on the day that I went, it was the day of the Torah being given! It was a huge celebration – and I remember it so well because it was the day I met my wife.' Josef seems incapable of bringing anything other than warm energy and happiness into our lives, and he's not done yet. 'And secondly – the *parsha* for the Shabbat of your wedding, it is the portion that my son read for his *bar mitzvah*. He knows it well. If you are happy for him to join us, he would be delighted to read it?' We are all more than happy for Josef's son to join us. Maurice is beyond thrilled. Grandpa Max's Torah will be with us. 'It's going to be very special, my loves,' Maurice says softly.

The festival concludes, and I return to London, where Eliana and I continue our planning.

We carefully arrange the Sunday ceremony so that, should people wish to, they can take the train from London in the morning and return in the evening. And for those Jewish guests attending who wish to travel up on the Friday, before Shabbat, we invite them to stay with us, and we organise a special Friday night dinner in the glasshouse itself – an additional challenge Josef and the team happily take on. With care and excitement, we build a weekend-long celebration of love as kosher as any wedding has ever been.

And, in a final piece of joyful news, our wedding ceremony is to be led by the rabbi we'd dared to hope might one day marry us.

'Let me look at my diary now.' A brief pause. 'I'll be there,' says Rabbi Avraham, the warm, thoughtful man who guided my earliest conversations, welcomed me into his community, and has been a figure central to Eliana's life since the day she was born.

'That's incredibly kind,' I say, 'but I have to tell you, the event won't be in London, it will be in Totnes, so I don't want to hold you to anything until you've decided whether you actually want to—'

'I'll be there,' says Rabbi Avraham, serenely. 'No idea how I'll get there, but in my experience these things have a way of working out.'

CHAPTER 32

It Ain't Over Until the Fat Rabbi Sings

It is a bright, sunny Monday afternoon in September when the Beth Din phone me.

I have, up until that point, been floating on a sea of endorphins. Over the weekend, Eliana and I returned to Portsmouth. My parents were hosting the Reform Jewish community for Friday night, and so we were welcomed and congratulated by the families I'd known since childhood. They were delighted to meet Eliana, thrilled for us both, fascinated by our tales of exotic Hendon. They showered us with cards and gifts and *mazel tovs*. My parents were – both – on sparkling form. It was a wonderful weekend.

I return to London, buoyed by an intoxicating sense of momentum. The next day, Eliana and I are set to travel to the bucolic glasshouse in Devon, and we're bringing our mums. We're going to do wedding-y things; pootle around, and make crucial decisions about the placement of dancefloors and *mechitzas* and types of flowers to request and optimum locations for the photos and all sorts of other frivolous nonsense.

And the day after that? My *mikveh*.

It is all so nearly tangible, and so joyful, and so close.

I am in the gym for the first time in a long time. I can feel myself growing stronger. Everything feels possible.

And then the Beth Din phone.

My stomach lurches.

'Hello!' I answer, as chipper and as brightly as I can manage, willing the call to be positive.

It isn't positive.

'There are serious concerns about your wedding,' says the voice.

I feel my eyes rolling back involuntarily. An all-consuming queasiness.

'The Beth Din want you to come in tomorrow, if you can.'

Frantically, desperately, I beg him to explain. He won't.

There's absolutely no point appealing to him on the basis that we've got a lovely day out planned and we've already paid for our train tickets, so I don't. I am pulled into the vortex once more.

'I can't explain on the phone. All I can say is the best thing you can do is come to the Beth Din.'

The meeting has to be tomorrow, I am told. This is non-negotiable.

And then another gut-punch of a thought hits me.

'. . . Will this affect my *mikveh*?' I ask.

'. . . It could do.'

For what feels like the billionth time, I feel my entire future melting into non-existence.

'I really feel for you. I'm honestly trying to help,' says the voice.

Desperation rising in my chest, I attempt to remain calm and measured, as I plead for some sliver of insight into what's going on. But no. Nothing.

'. . . It would be far worse for you if you don't come in,' says the voice.

Seconds later, the inevitable group phone call with Eliana and her parents. Patchy signal and urgent questions and panic and misery. Eliana is distraught. Katy is nervous. Maurice, as ever, seeks the positives. I am flung back in time to every other moment this process has nearly derailed. I am trapped, bouncing around the walls of an inescapable maze, constantly searching for the exit, opening doors that send me tumbling back to wherever I started.

I run out of the gym and take a long, sweltering bus-ride to Eliana's parents' house, for an emergency meeting.

I am sweat-soaked, obsessively checking and re-checking my phone, my jaw clenched, my feet compulsively tapping with anxiety. I look deranged – which I am. I absolutely am.

I arrive at the house. Eliana is tear-streaked. Katy is sombre. I have no words.

And then I think back to our time in Portsmouth and suddenly I snap.

'We just spent the weekend surrounded and supported by a Jewish community that might be from a different tradition, but they're just as good as any other. This is awful. This is poison.'

'You think I don't know that?' says Katy. 'You think I don't think that?'

We reach out to one of the Supportive Rabbis we are closest to, and explain what has happened. He's shocked. He suggests a new Supportive Rabbi we could speak to, one who is in the loop, who might know what this is about. 'I was expecting this call,' he says, when he answers the phone.

What has happened is this.

As part of the process of sending out wedding invitations to our guests, Eliana and I have done the thing that couples about to be married, increasingly, do: we have made a little website.

It's got, you know, all the bits on it. It explains how to get to Totnes – the train is easiest, honestly! – it emphasises the importance of booking one's taxis early and offers a carefully collated list of all the local cab companies, and it provides a similarly painstaking list of places to stay for the weekend.

And it's got the weekend's itinerary. From Saturday afternoon onwards, guests are welcome to come and join us – to delight in the escapist beauty of the site. There are gardens, greenhouses, a hidden lake, a ramshackle farm shop with an honesty box, there's a heated outdoor swimming pool if they're feeling particularly brave, there are secret corners and private benches, there's a manor house stuffed with antiquities, there's a pub somewhere at the end of a winding country lane, and there's the glasshouse itself, which will be loaded with food to snack on, board games, drinks – a place for people to congregate and catch up and schmooze. A big, beautiful *kiddush*, a precursor to Sunday's festivities.

And it turns out that this website (for reasons I will *never* understand) is something that appears at the top of a Google search, when typing in our names. Our private invitation is, for some reason, a public website. This is something that, had I been aware of, I would have firmly voted against, for the simple reason that having one's wedding plans publicly available is just incredibly weird.

But it also has had the supremely unwanted side effect of the Beth Din having discovered it, and – to my slack-jawed shock – responded with utter fury.

The tone, apparently, is all wrong – the chatty conversational nature, the lighthearted jokes, the ridiculous photos of Eliana and I as children in fancy-dress. Surely not. Surely if last time our lives were nearly imploded by a photo of Rosie Jones in a leotard, this time the culprit can't be a photo of me, aged seven, dressed as a wizard?

But there's more. There is the suspicion that, by having proceedings on a Saturday afternoon, we are urging Jews to break Shabbat.

Given that this is not the case – in fact, it couldn't be further from the case – given that, left entirely to our own devices, we have been immersed in constructing the most Shabbat-compliant event it is possible to have, a weekend steeped in Judaism in all the most positive ways – this intervention feels staggering.

So too does the way this message has been delivered; not at all, other than yet another imperious summoning, via an intermediary. A demand that we return to the nerve centre, to be subjected to more remorseless, unspecified interrogation, and for my soul to once more be dangled in front of me.

What constitutes cruel and unusual punishment? It is a question I ask the room at large, not expecting an answer.

The Supportive Rabbi continues to talk, and I can't bear it any more.

I leave. I walk out of the house and walk down the street, to nowhere. Pointless. I turn back, return to the house, to the doom-call.

Maurice has arrived now, too. Projecting as much calm as he is able.

Through gritted teeth I express the point – blindingly obvious to all of us gathered around the phone – that we're not asking anyone to break Shabbat, because all of our Jewish guests are joining us for Shabbat. The invitation is, explicitly, for the vast majority of our guests who aren't Jewish.

'They might want to know why you have so many non-Jewish friends,' says the Supportive Rabbi.

This is a point of view – if indeed it is one they have – that strikes me as nothing short of utterly, utterly wretched.

There are further back-and-forths. With the Supportive Rabbi. With the voice of the Beth Din.

It takes until 11pm that night to confirm what is happening.

A meeting, late tomorrow afternoon, in dreaded Barnwood Drive.

In a last-ditch bid to crawl over the finish line, we've asked if Eliana's father can attend, too. Up until this point, no matter how tense the situation, we've avoided involving Eliana's parents. The situation is ours to navigate. We are, though it's never felt less like it, adults. Pressing the emergency button, attempting to call on Eliana's father to help bail us out – to somehow cash in his good standing in the community, in a bid to drag us to the end of our quest – it feels like another layer of ignominy. But the alternative is impossible to countenance, and I swallow my shame.

Eventually, we receive confirmation. Yes, he may attend – but he's not permitted to join us in our meeting. He will need to go in first. And then our reckoning.

How could you, I think. You have cut me to pieces.

The next day, as we wait for Maurice to return from his summons, Eliana and I sit in the Beth Din waiting room. Opposite us, there is a sign from a Jewish charity. '*Have you been the victim of abuse?*' it reads.

Have we?

We wait.

Eventually, Maurice emerges. If he has experienced the slightest stress, if the conversation has been anything other than pleasant, he betrays no sign.

Into the room we go.

Four faces sit across the table.

One of the men is tapping away on a laptop.

The Folder of Incriminating Evidence is produced once more.

This time, our wedding website has been printed out. Pages are held up.

The website itself is loaded up on a phone. Look at this. What do you have to say?

How, as a supplicant, do you tell the people who hold your fate in their hands that the assumptions they have made are utterly wrong?

This is what we must attempt to do.

We are humble, apologetic, contrite, and we exercise the most extreme caution – taking care to give no sense, via intonation or choice of language, that those we are speaking to are anything other than the wisest and most correct of authority figures. And yet, misunderstandings have arisen – entirely due to us, no doubt, our fault, absolutely. But misunderstandings have arisen.

We gently point out that the website is designed, almost in its entirety, for our non-Jewish friends. That part of its purpose isn't just to invite people to our Jewish wedding, it is to explain what a Jewish wedding *is*. Central to Jewish weddings of all stripes is the *chuppah** – the four-poster canopy under which the couple stands, as they are blessed. Amongst other things, our website explains what this is. There just isn't a chance that this information would be required for anyone with even a smattering of Judaism in their identity. Elsewhere we clarify the sorts of blessings that will take place, we explain how boisterous the dancing will be, urging those who've never been to a Jewish wedding before to ready themselves (and to bring a change of shirt), and we point out when the famous 'chair bit' is likely to happen. Jewish life isn't something we're trying to encourage Jews to contravene, it's something we're inviting non-Jewish guests to be a part of.

The print-out of the website shows my mother's carefully, lovingly rendered illustrations. But the copy is poor – the colours are muddy and indistinct. So much of the care and positivity we have sought to pour into this event has been misread, or missed in its entirety, or disregarded.

Our words are absorbed into the dull air.

Now it is the Beth Din's turn to speak.

---

* Soft ch.

We have never done this before, comes the message, but we are adding further conditions to your conversion . . . after the *mikveh* . . .

Eliana and I daren't look at each other as these impossible sentences wash over us.

There are to be monthly check-ins, one on one, with a member of the Beth Din. Additional classes to attend. Ongoing examination of my 'progress'.

The message is blindingly clear.

This process will never end. We will control you forever.

I nod, emptily, at whatever they say.

We drive home in the most torrential rain I have ever experienced.

That evening, I lie in bed and I close my eyes, but I do not sleep. My body is molten hot, and I am levitating with fury.

I feel, keenly, the inadequacy of organised religion. How, whatever the originating message, the inaugural miracle, what remains is, inevitably, a power structure in which some human beings control other human beings.

There is a Jewish concept that I have been learning about in my studies. *Middot tovot* – positive characteristics.

One is expected to embody these positive traits. And one is expected to assume them in others. To think the best of people at all times.

It is not a courtesy that has been extended to us in this instance. Or at any instance, in fact, throughout the process.

If we can engage wholeheartedly, hit every single marker, obey every single law, deliver something entirely in keeping with the rules of *halacha*, and it is *still* deemed unacceptable?

What is the point?

What is the fucking point?

CHAPTER 33

The Mikveh

It is, possibly, the morning of my *mikveh* appointment.

Moments after waking, I receive a message from Eliana's father, Maurice.

Can I meet him for a walk on Primrose Hill?

The morning is bright and clear.

We sit on a bench, and he talks frankly, in a way we haven't before.

He talks of the stress he felt, in visiting the Beth Din yesterday. Who knows the exact balance of cause and effect – whether his presence was the thing that helped ensure that today's ceremony, so close to being called off, will actually take place – but, either way, the experience has clearly taken its toll.

'My stomach was in knots, I didn't sleep – I was actually internally bleeding, I looked in the toilet and there was blood and I thought what the hell . . .?!'

And then he talks about the importance of not bringing anger into a relationship. About how, at the start of his marriage to Katy, he resented her desire that he stay in London, when he wanted to go off to build a career in America, and that he held on to this anger for years, and that it ultimately hurt them both.

And he talks about how he and Katy understand what I've

put myself through. How, as far as they're concerned, I've done enough.

And how, if entering the *mikveh*, undergoing the final stage of the conversion, will only cause anger and bad feeling, then I shouldn't go. They'll accept me as I am.

It is as profound a gesture of love as Maurice is capable of offering. For a moment, I am dumbstruck. And then I start to speak.

'Thank you so much, Maurice . . .'

A world opens up before me. In which, on the day of my dunking, I become a *mikveh* refuser.

In which I walk away, triumphantly, from the Beth Din, and into the welcoming arms of Eliana and my in-laws.

And we are married – not by Avraham, of course – and we start to build our lives together. Happy. Connected. A different ending to that which we have planned and fought for together.

And I think about the tiny fractures that will form in our lives – the ways I will be unable to engage in the traditions Eliana holds dear. I think about the things that I would gain, and I think about the things that we would lose.

'Thank you so much, Maurice,' I say. 'I appreciate what it must take for you to say that. But I don't think it's the right thing to do.'

I talk about how it would have all been so much easier if I hadn't entered into this sincerely. How I could have just smiled and nodded and agreed and been laughing away in my head. But that hasn't been the case.

About how, in giving of myself, I have tortured myself.

I talk about how refusing the *mikveh* might afford me a subversive thrill, but how that would be passing, transient. How walking away feels like it would be a brief, hollow victory. Hardly a victory at all. That, ultimately, it would feel like the worst of all worlds.

Because the impetus for this journey came from something Eliana needed. But from the moment I committed to it, it became something I wanted for us both, too.

We stand at the viewpoint of Primrose Hill and we hug.

And then it is time, at long last, for the *mikveh*.

For the second time in two days, I put on my Shul Suit. I am frazzled. Worn thin. I look like shit.

As Eliana and I travel by taxi to this final waypoint on our journey, we sit in silence.

I don't know how I thought this morning might feel. Not like this, certainly. Any sense of accomplishment, of joy, has been sucked out of this moment.

Instead, I feel a sense of apprehension – that Dayan Horowitz might emerge at a traffic light and ask some unanswerable *halachic* question – or tap up some online example of my moral depravity, or produce yet another incriminating print-out, or decide to move things back, just a few more days, for just a little more conferring.

But we arrive at our destination – a new *shul* we've not been to before. Before the *mikveh* itself, there is one more meeting with the Beth Din. Because of course there is.

'Well, friends,' says Dayan Landau, brightly. 'We are here on the day of your finalisation. You are to become a fully kosher member of our community.'

Eliana and I sit opposite three faces.

Landau, Katz, Weissman. The friendliest permutation of the three. Horowitz is not there. A telling absence. And a relief.

They ask me questions – but they are formalities. They aren't designed to catch me out.

They again allude to their intention to have me check in regularly with Dayan Weissman.

I nod.

I am asked to recite the Shema. It is one of the most fundamental Jewish blessings, read at every service.

I find the blessing in my own *siddur*.

I stand. As I begin to recite it, Dayan Weissman subtly reminds me to cover my eyes with my right hand at the start of the blessing. I nod, in gratitude, and I raise my hand to my face.

I read it aloud.

Sincere. Sombre. Feeling the weight of eternity and a moment of stillness. As I hear the words ring out my voice begins to crack. The Dayanim are nodding.

And then I am ready for the *mikveh*.

Dayan Landau walks me through a doorway.

We walk out into the sunny morning, past an empty marquee.

'There is a discreet private entrance to the *mikveh*,' says Dayan Landau, 'but we're walking through the *shul* because we wanted to meet with you first . . .'

We reach the entrance. It's slightly shi-shi. A bit spa-like.

'It's beautiful,' I manage.

Suddenly I am face to face with a tiny elderly woman, the *mikveh* attendant. She wears a brown *sheitel* wig, giving her the sense of agelessness common to many Orthodox women.

'Let me just get the towels,' she says. 'It's been a busy morning . . .'

She clears away the damp towels on the floor of the changing room. Perhaps remnants from the last person whose soul was transformed, or replaced, or enhanced, earlier that day.

I am led into the room, and given my instructions.

'Shower down. There are brushes and combs in there [behind the mirror]. Comb your hair wherever there is hair. When you're ready, wrap yourself with a towel, *kippah* on, and knock on the door on my side. Then, like magic, the Dayanim will appear on the other side.'

She walks out of the room. 'Alice in Wonderland,' she says, as she leaves. I wonder what she means.

And the door shuts. I am in the antechamber. I remove my Shul Suit, and spot for the first time that there are holes in the trousers. It, too, is worn out. Exhausted. Close to disintegrating.

I shower. I dry myself.

I look in the mirrors, and pose – vainly, stupidly. Do I look hench enough for the Beth Din?! Is this a question that has ever been asked, by anyone, ever?

And I wrap the towel around my waist, place my *kippah* on my head, knock on the door. From the other side of the room, I hear a call.

I open the door and there they stand.

In a line, facing away from me. Looking to the side.

'Come forward, put your towel on the rail.'

I do. There's a pause. I'm not sure if I am to walk in. Eventually Dayan Weissman gestures. I am.

I walk forward, into the water.

It is a narrow pool, with steps and a rail. The water is warm.

I walk to the edge, and turn around. I am in the *mikveh*. Up above me, the Dayanim look down.

I am told to fold my arms.

The responsibilities of being a Jew are reinforced. The *mitzvot*, hard and difficult. The aeons of abuse, anti-Semitism. You take on all of these things. Inescapably. I nod. I agree. I aver.

I am told to remove my *kippah*, immerse myself, to come up for air and to be silent. To await instructions.

And I do. I submerge myself beneath the water. I am surrounded, suspended.

I clear my mind and focus entirely on the moment. And then I re-emerge.

I am silent.

Dayan Weissman recites the blessing. Word by word, I repeat after him. He goes quiet when saying G-d's name. I say it in its entirety.

I reach the end of the *bracha*. I am offered the chance to immerse myself once again. I gratefully take it, and submerge myself once more.

I go deeper. Longer. I hold my breath and exist beneath the water for a lifetime.

In my floating stillness, I reach out to Eliana's Grandpa Max, and those Oleskers in the Book of Names, and Eliana, and the *mitzvot* – all 613, every single last one of them – and the eternal forces that bind and shape the universe.

I try and purge the poison of this process and engulf myself in light.

And then I shoot back to the surface. *'Mazel tov!'* come the voices.

They leave, and I slowly walk out of the *mikveh*. Dripping. Exhausted. A Jew.

Irregular no more.

Once I am showered and dressed once more, I somehow manage to get lost en route back to the room I first entered. I wander around for five minutes, each anonymous door leading me to a different dead end. I seem to traverse the space three times before finding the room.

Eventually, I walk in through the correct door. There is Eliana, and there are the Dayanim.

Dayan Landau wraps me in a bear hug. And so does the next Dayan. And the next.

They each hug me, in turn, and my heart splinters.
I am elated. Connected. Relieved.
But at the same time, as they wrap their arms around me, I feel an emptiness. And I feel a cynicism to their embrace.
We did this because we love you.

We thank them. Say our goodbyes. We walk out of the *shul*, and into the dazzling sunshine. There is a message on my phone from Maurice. 'Katy and I are crying with joy.'
We phone them and they answer, unable to properly speak, just weeping with happiness.
'My darlings,' they are saying, through the tears, 'we are so proud of you both.'
Eliana and I weep back at them.

The next morning, at *shul*, I receive my very first call-up to the Torah as an Orthodox Jewish man. Eliana and her father have both come to witness it in person. This particular *shul* is a small room, not used to female congregants. But accommodations are made for Eliana, who essentially ends up stood in a cupboard-like space that's part of an adjoining industrial kitchen. It's not much, but she is able to pray, and to watch.
I place the *tallit* prayer shawl around my shoulders. I recite, falteringly, but with growing confidence, the ancient blessings. I stoke the engine of collective worship. I am a part of the tradition.
I have never, ever seen Eliana happier. She is laughing with happiness whilst weeping all at once – insensible with joy. I know that there is no other earthly way I could have given Eliana this sense of fulfilment. And so I feel certain, for the first time, that I have done the right thing.

CHAPTER 34

Who Judges the Judges?

One of the most promising things I hear in my final *mikveh*-day discussion with the Beth Din is a throwaway phrase one of them utters. 'After this, we will disappear.' At the time, I clench my jaw, take pains not to react. But I know Eliana hears it too. Perhaps it truly is all over?

Perhaps the London Beth Din are, as many admirers told me along the way, the best Beth Din in the world. Or perhaps they are, as many other wary Orthodox told me – often in the same *shul*, often at the same event – the worst.

But in a sense, aren't those two assessments functionally the same – speaking to the same unassailable authority? Isn't their fearsomeness and their total intransigence, when viewed from another angle, simply their rigour, their unflinching upholding of the highest standards?

Perhaps the Beth Din are akin to academics – in the same way as one might encounter a PhD student, wide-eyed and frenzied from too long locked away, studying some inscrutability about the bouncing of a quark or the evolution of anaerobic bacterium, and realise they have become so immersed in their chosen subject that they now exist at a remove, untethered from regular society. So too, perhaps, are the Beth Din. Walled in as they are by their books, and laws, and centuries of raging

Rabbinical debate which they must parse and process and try to build upon, perhaps it is inevitable that they lose touch with the real world.

The very first Jewish conversion can be found in the Torah, and it involves a non-Jew saying to a Jew:
'Where you go, I go.'
That's it. It is an act of one person following another in their way of life, and being accepted by them.
I cannot help but feel that that is closer to what it should be, than whatever this has become.

Eliana and I navigate the path towards our wedding with a jangling combination of frothy excitement and the poorly suppressed quasi-hysterical fear that it might all come crashing down at any given moment. Because the Beth Din haven't, quite, disappeared.
For instance, a man named Henry who we've never met is now involved in the planning of our wedding, for reasons unknown. Or rather, the reasons are absolutely known: the Beth Din have made it clear that, amongst the many elements of our wedding that they don't approve of, our approach to the catering is one of them.
This is mystifying to us, given that we have taken absolutely every precaution imaginable to ensure that the event is kosher, up to and including hiring the mighty Josef, a Beth Din-approved inspector. But (and why wouldn't there be a but) it transpires that, as Josef hails from the world of *restaurants* as opposed to *catering*, he is, somehow, unacceptable.
The solution, apparently, is a semi-retired caterer (that's Henry), who holds a Beth Din-approved licence, and under whose auspices our event can take place in an officially

sanctioned manner. Henry is perfectly nice, and perfectly knowledgeable, and is very happy to join a series of Zoom calls with our mercifully tolerant Totnes chef, and to consult on this strange project in exchange for 'a nice weekend in Devon' and 'some money'. But there is a lingering question – given Josef's surfeit of experience – of why, practically speaking, Henry is needed. It is, it seems, essentially for appearance's sake. 'You see, we have a *policy* . . .' says a voice in Barnwood Drive, smoothly. Henry's presence ticks a box. Keeps the Beth Din's grip on the event watertight.

So, as unnecessary as it feels, we accept – embrace, even – this solution.

Any arrangement acceptable to the Beth Din is acceptable to us, and this one apparently is. Until, for reasons which remain truly unknown . . . it isn't.

One afternoon Henry phones us mysteriously, to explain that the Beth Din have gone over his head and hired another catering employee – to be paid for by us and to attend the wedding – without telling him. He doesn't understand why, and mutters the phrase 'We are but pawns.'

My distress at yet another destabilising intervention by the Beth Din in our lives is only mildly ameliorated by my excitement at hearing someone genuinely use the phrase 'we are but pawns' in a phone call. Anyway. There's now *another* man involved, hired on our behalf as a *fait accompli*, causing even the previous guy who'd been hired on our behalf as a *fait accompli* to raise his eyebrows.

At this point, my feeling is that all questions of religion and spirituality have been stripped away. In the glaring light of day, it feels a lot like we are being held to ransom by the paramilitary wing of a food hygiene certification company.

*

And yet, after this final series of arm's-length interventions, the Beth Din as an entity, do seemingly disappear from our lives. As our day at the glasshouse approaches, we are tensed for more disruption, but there is silence. We have no further direct encounters with them. No more emergency meetings. No more terror-inducing phone calls or weeks of nightmarish waiting. Perhaps they are still taking an interest, shaping our lives from afar. Or perhaps they have moved on.

Either way they are still out there, somewhere, shuffling their files, dictating the fates of individuals, of couples, of families – of those seeking to connect with their heritage, with their partner, with themselves, with the universe, with the Almighty. They will forever remain guardians of the narrowest of openings, begrudgingly letting people through. One at a time.

But, ultimately, this isn't a story about the Beth Din at all. It's a love story. And it ends with a wedding.

CHAPTER 35

Totnes

On the weekend of the wedding itself, the only plot twist is that there is no plot twist: somehow, it all comes off with a natural, flowing rhythm, a vibrancy and a joy beyond anything I dared wish for in my boldest and most audacious dreams.

After a solid week of thudding, ceaseless torrential rain (honestly, I still have the screenshots of the weather app), on the weekend of our wedding the clouds part and the skies are immaculate.

It all begins with a Friday night dinner. Our two families, and all of our Jewish friends who have come for the weekend, rushing to be with us before sundown – confused and thrilled to be in Devon, many of them giving every appearance of having left London for the first time in their lives. In the exquisite surroundings of the glasshouse we assemble around a long table, and we feast.

I had forgotten, in the midst of the excruciating catering ordeal, that food can actually be a pleasurable experience. But, as the first plates come out, a ripple of urgent whispering spreads around the table. I am initially worried there is some disaster that the guests are trying to shield me from, but I eventually intercept a whisperer and discover the message being conveyed is: 'Have you tried the celeriac?' They're not wrong. It's truly phenomenal. And as kosher as any meal that has ever been served. The food keeps coming – huge platters of meat and vegetables and salad – all deftly spiced and scented – and our guests are in raptures. We might just have ourselves a *simcha*.

Josef, our saviour, has earned the open-mouthed admiration of the kitchen crew for his steadfast devotion to his meticulous duties – when they cheerfully bring in some fresh locally sourced herbs as an additional ingredient for a dish, Josef smilingly accepts them into the kitchen, explaining that there is just the 'small matter' of inspecting them according to kosher tradition – a task he completes by hand, in a painstaking process that takes an additional four hours, yet he does this with a song in his heart. Thankfully, he can be compelled to join us for Friday night dinner, where he and his son are guests of honour. *'Mazel tov!'* he says, grinning, refusing to take any credit. 'You must just enjoy the weekend – *mazel tov!*' I truly think he is one of the most impressive men I have ever met.

We eat, we drink, we sing, toasts are given, vodka shots are filled and refilled. My parents present to me one of their cards, a classic of the genre, featuring my mum's illustrations and my dad's lyrics – a rewritten take on Allan Sherman's 'Hello Muddah, Hello Fadduh', which I perform for the assembled relatives:

> Eliana, and her Max
> Will get married, them's the facts
> It will happen with no ruckus
> So we wish you joy and happiness and *nachas**!

Up and down the table, buoyed on by the never-empty glasses and the golden warmth of the evening, people stand and impromptu speeches are made.

I feel with such a soaring thrill the thing that I had always

---

* The pride and joy that a child brings a parent.

hoped and suspected I might one day feel – that this cavernous gulf between us was no more than an optical illusion. That if I could just make one immense leap across the divide, then we might seamlessly be together. Not just Eliana and I, but our families.

'Would you like to say anything, Lion?' Eliana asks, in case she might need to quiet the chattering table to allow her grandmother's voice to be heard.

'Oh, my darling, I would love to, but I just can't.'

'You can't?'

'I'm too emotional, my darling...' she lapses into silence and the tears in her eyes glisten like her spectacular diamond earrings. And so my father recites an important piece of Yiddish nonsense poetry instead.

Night is upon us but the feast continues – there is another wave of excited alarm surrounding the dessert, the ice cream being deemed so delicious that guests can scarcely believe it is dairy-free, which the laws of kosher state it must be (it is, everyone is relieved to discover, and so second helpings are immediately in order).

Eventually, we stumble off to our beds.

We awaken for Shabbat morning.

The Torah, carefully collected from Beit Shalom, has travelled to deepest rural Devon unscathed – hand-delivered by Eliana's uncle and aunt – and with much delight it is unveiled. In the kitchen of the country house adjoining the glasshouse, a makeshift service is held.

As promised, Josef's son, a terribly well-brought-up young man, masterfully fulfils his duties and reads the week's Torah portion, to great acclaim from all around him in our little Totnes *minyan*.

There is a particular joy to the fact that here, between us, Shabbat has somehow been created out of nothing. There is a sense of tranquillity to the familiar blessings – and, as our other guests start to arrive, filtering into the building as the service is finishing, they seem to feel it too. We are singing, and our friends join in, humming along intuitively to songs they've never heard before, delightedly donning *kippot*, picking up on the strange happiness of it all. And then, together, we spill over into the sun-dappled glasshouse, reimagined now as a space for the *kiddush* of all *kiddushes* – a series of glorious side-tables now laden with all the food one could hope for, ready to fuel a wedding's-worth of people through a full day of schmoozing and chatting.

As more friends trickle in delightedly from across the country – from across the globe! – Eliana and I greet the new arrivals, introducing pockets of our different friendship groups to one another, beaming with satisfaction at the cross-pollination of our worlds.

As dusk comes in and the sky fills with stars, Shabbat concludes. Eliana's father, to my surprise, hands me a microphone and invites me to perform the *havdallah* ceremony, which takes place at the end of Shabbat, on behalf of all the guests. I tentatively explain it as best I can – the way it serves a dual purpose, marking the separation of Shabbat from the rest of the week, but also as a means of encouraging the warmth of Shabbat to last a little longer, infusing the ensuing days with sweetness. I sing the melody, inhale the sweet aroma of the *havdallah* spices, and Eliana holds up the plaited candle so that the glow of the flame illuminates the faces of those around us.

I remember being a Portsmouthian teenager, sheepishly inviting friends to my *bar mitzvah*, and then celebrating with them afterwards, relieved at the kindness and gentleness with which they received me and embraced my differences. I see these same faces stood here again, all of us transformed by age and all of us exactly the same, briefly together once more as we pass through another chapter of our lives. Again, they listen to me delivering inexpert Hebrew, and singing melodies that I get a little wrong, and again they smile in support and it doesn't matter.

And then, for the finale of the evening, the glasshouse is transformed once more, into a theatre! It was the world of performance that brought Eliana and me together, and here we have a stage of our own – a private one-night festival of comedy and poetry and songs and sketches, hosted and performed and lovingly prepared by our friends and family. It is perfect.

I wake up on the day of my wedding, electric with anticipation.

I have made a plan for the morning – one I am not sure that I will come to regret. There is a custom that, on the day of his wedding, the groom immerses himself in a *mikveh*. Unsurprisingly, the nearest 'conventional' *mikveh* is approximately three hours away – however, as my studies have taught me, under certain circumstances a natural body of water can be used. And, on the grounds of our wedding venue there happens to be, tucked away through a secluded doorway, the world's most beautiful lake. So, I resolved, I would begin my day by immersing myself in the water, no matter how grim, frosty or otherwise unpleasant it might be.

Taking a deep breath, I open the curtains – and the late-autumn sun somehow shines through with the clarity and warmth of a crisp spring morning.

When I committed to my morning dip, some months previously, I extended the invitation to my groomsmen, should they wish to join me – not thinking for a moment that anyone would take me up on the offer.

But as I step out of my bedroom and into the courtyard, I am greeted by my friends and brothers, towels wrapped around their waists, ready to roll. Together, we stroll towards the lake, grinning in anticipation. What began as an impulsive, ill-thought-out escapade shows remarkable signs of working out.

As the journey begins, Michael, my future brother-in-law, suddenly doubles back to the house. I think perhaps he's changed his mind – but, seconds later, he returns, sprinting, brandishing a bottle of vodka and frozen shot glasses.

Cackling with laughter and excitement, we match his pace as he runs towards us, and break out into song once more.

'*Woah-oh-oh-oh ay-ay-ay-ayyyyy!*' It's the tune that has been sung raucously at every Jewish *simcha* ever – and if you think you don't know it, honestly, you do.

We turn the corner, now jogging down a slight hill towards the lake – and, in an event which has categorically never happened before in real life, only in cartoons and caper movies, at that precise moment, Ivan steps out of his car with two more of my oldest friends, John and Simon, and so they charge towards us, singing as they approach.

'*Ay-ay-ay-ay-ay-ay-ayay—ya-yayyy!*'

Pied Piper-like, they seamlessly join our throng. It's very much a throng.

Our group gathers in momentum and speed and giggling excitement, until we make it to the old blue chipped wooden door, half-hidden by vines and greenery, behind which lies what can only be described as a secret passageway. It is a narrow, winding covered path, an abundance of flowers and leaves on every side and above us. Single-file, we pick our way down until we reach the end, and it opens up to reveal our destination: a huge, secluded glade leading down to a clear, crystalline lake.

I walk across the grass and straight towards it, throwing off my dressing gown and kicking off my shorts as I walk, and step into the water. It is perfectly cool – and I keep walking, deeper and deeper, pushing off and submerging myself entirely in the bracing water for just a moment. It is a *mikveh* immersion of far more uncomplicated purity than the fateful final day of my conversion.

My head emerges back above the water, and I look up to see the rest of the group hurling off their shorts and following me into the lake. There are gasps and laughter (and, in the case of Julius, incredibly high-pitched shrieking) and suddenly we are in – waist-deep and naked. We wrap our arms around one another and dance in a circle in the water, singing and cackling and rejoicing.

'*Woah-oh-oh-oh ay-ay-ay-ayyyyy!*'

In yet another instance of fate smiling generously upon us this Sunday, the train required to safely deliver our celebrants is not delayed. Rabbi Avraham, our officiant, and Rabbi Yossi, who will deliver several blessings and read aloud our *ketubah* – the marriage contract, which is written in fiendishly complex Aramaic – arrive, happy and intact, and are whisked from the station to our venue in a waiting vehicle. The Rabbonim have come to Totnes.

I return to my room, and I change into my wedding suit. If ever there was a day for being overdressed (which, as established, is more or less my go-to setting), surely today is that day. After much enjoyable overthinking, I have arrived at the suit of my dreams: a double-breasted shawl collar tuxedo jacket in navy-blue velvet, with black tuxedo trousers and velvet loafers. I wear bow ties with a frequency that means I have always *just* forgotten how to tie them when I am next required to put one on. So, as is traditional, I take roughly six goes to correctly tie it, ultimately resorting to my time-honoured technique of 'closing my eyes and pretending I'm doing my shoelaces'.

There are a series of elements that are unique to a Jewish wedding. Two of them take place – or can take place – before the ceremony even begins.

The first is the *tisch*. At its core, it is the moment that the *ketubah* is witnessed, formally accepted by the groom, and signed. But, in practice, it is also a moment in which the groom gathers with his family and close friends (and, this being a Jewish wedding, some snacks) just before the wedding itself takes place. Having attended Julius's wedding, I was moved by the way he invited his non-Jewish friends to speak at his *tisch* – this struck me as a brilliant way to incorporate them into the day. And so I asked a select few friends if they wanted to say a few words, and passed their names on to Rabbi Avraham. This part of Totnes being a place where phone signal is never a guarantee, the messages never arrived – which, it transpires, is a wonderful thing. Rabbi Avraham simply opens up the floor to the entire group, calmly asking if anyone would like to say a few words, and a host of people speak – those I had asked and many, many others. My married friends offer advice gleaned from their experiences:

'Always be quick to admit you're wrong,' says Tom, 'even when you're not.'

'It's hard work, but it's the most rewarding work you'll ever do,' says Joe.

My unmarried friends share reflections on our friendship, wish me luck for the journey ahead, share jokes and offer words of encouragement. Papa Olesker – looking dashing in his tailored tweed suit – riffs freely and happily, and forms an impromptu double-act with Rabbi Avraham based around whose beard is better.

It is a unique moment, this quiet gathering of men, all being loving and supporting to one another, and I wholeheartedly endorse it being stolen and incorporated into weddings of all stripes.

At the appointed time, our guests are called to their seats, and I am left alone with my family. Because, before we join them, there is the *bedekin*. This is the moment where the groom sees his bride for the first time on their wedding day, and covers her face with a veil, before the ceremony begins. Sometimes, this happens in full view of the guests. We have opted to take a moment before it all begins, in private.

My father is starting to walk off with the other guests, so I intercept him, and take his hand.

Accompanied by my family, I walk into the *bedekin* room. There, surrounded by her family, is Eliana.

She is sat, resplendent and serenely beautiful, her veil above her head, and her white dress hand-painted with flowers which appear to have sprung up from the floor of the ancient manor house, like a vision from a fable.

I am holding my father's hand, and looking across the room at Eliana, and at Lion, who sits in an armchair, beaming, and I fulfil one of Eliana's primary wedding-related requests by immediately bursting into tears.

There is a texture in the air, a richness and a stillness. It is just us, all together, in the room, and there is nothing else to be thought of.

And then it is time.

A marquee is set up amongst the apple trees, and inside is the *chuppah,* the four-poster wedding canopy, adorned with autumnal flowers, where we are to be married.

As I walk out of the manor house with both of my parents, I notice my father's shoes on the floor. Which must mean . . .

'Mum,' I mutter, nodding at my father's feet, 'Dad's still wearing his slippers.'

'Never mind,' says my mother, quick as a flash, looking at my velvet loafers, 'so are you.'

And she's right, they look almost identical. Fair play, Punk Duchess. I shrug and we keep walking, into a space full of everyone I've ever known.

As I stand beneath the *chuppah*, next to Eliana, the sun shines magnanimously upon us.

I am in the centre of the room, and chapters of my life surround me. Friends whom I have known since I was an eccentric four-year-old in Portsmouth. Friends from primary school, secondary school, university. Writers. Wrestlers. Comedians.

In a room full of non-Jews, Rabbi Avraham effortlessly charms them with a beguiling, twinkling service.

'Sometimes, people take a shortcut that turns out to be longer, whilst others take the longer route that proves to be more direct. You have both taken the long short way.'

Seven times, Eliana walks around me. I look into the eyes of my new parents-in-law, and my mum and dad, and out at the loved ones surrounding us, and up at the *tallit* prayer shawl hanging over us which belonged to the Max who came before me.

Here, under the *chuppah* on this charmed weekend, we are finally married. I have never felt my face physically hurt from smiling before, but now it happens. I am beaming, and there are tears in my eyes, and as Eliana looks at me I feel a new chapter of my life beginning.

Rings are exchanged. Blessings are made on cups of wine.

Finally, I stamp the glass – and the whole place goes *nuts*.

Suddenly the band is playing, and I'm up on someone's shoulders, and so is my new father-in-law, and everywhere there are people dancing and singing in the perfect sunshine, and the apple trees grow around us.

We spill out of the marquee, and Eliana and I are danced over to what is known as the *yichud* room – a place where we can be alone together, for the first time. Here, in this pocket of calm, we share the first kiss in the history of our relationship that hasn't made the world seem infinitely more confusing. And then we dive back into the madness.

Together, Eliana and I enter the glasshouse, to a wild roar from the crowd. We walk beneath a series of white arches, held up by our friends, and then we part – to each side of the dancefloor, and a free-flowing world of chaos and exultation.

There is nothing on earth quite like the feral, heaving collective mania of a Jewish wedding at the height of dancing fervour.

For the infamous chair moment, we had carefully selected seats with arms that would safely bear us aloft – these are, of course, nowhere to be found, and instead we are held high on flimsy, horrendously unsafe, arm-free wooden chairs, bouncing around precariously, half slipping off and somehow clinging on. It is glorious.

I am pulled into a circle of men, and spun faster and faster – the blood rushing to my head and the sweat caking my shirt.

Through the *mechitza*, I see Eliana dancing with her mother, and my mother, and all of her friends. A glamorous blur of colour.

My father stomps stylishly and suavely, linking hands with the rabbis, with Uncle Daniel, with my brothers, and with a host of Ostros – brothers, uncles, cousins; my new in-laws, my new family.

We even deliver a modified – grounded, yet even more spectacular – version of the iconic chair moment for my father!

As he sits proudly on the chair, two of my friends and both of my brothers lie on the floor, their feet hooking inside the chair legs on each side, and another four of us stand between them and grasp their hands. Together, we rotate – like some enthusiastic but completely untrained synchronised swimming routine – with my dad spinning at the centre of this human kaleidoscope, spreading his arms out wide, grandly and triumphantly.

My friends stand face to face and link hands – I dive onto the hammock of their arms and together they fling me into the air. As I am launched upwards, I see the sea of blue *kippot* beneath me. I travel higher into the air – now, over the *mechitza*, on the other side of the room, I see Eliana twirling triumphantly, encircled by a multicoloured blur of whirling women. I soar higher still, and at the very apex of my flight – just for a millisecond – I am suspended in mid-air, and I see everything: the smiling sweaty faces looking upwards, the dumbstruck guests on the outer perimeter of the dancefloor, and, through the vaulted ceiling of the glasshouse, the rolling green of the Totnes countryside.

Speeches are made, toasts are given, and I weep freely and delightedly throughout.

Eliana, having agreed to speak only under duress (acknowledging, with a begrudging smile, that as it is my one request she feels fairly obliged to honour it), delivers a barnstorming speech: 'Max, what you have done is the greatest gift, and the most meaningful foundation for us to build our married life upon. But I don't need to go on more about it . . . I know I'm preaching to the converted here.'

Eliana brings the house down, and ends with a toast of, yes, utterly undrinkable Jägerbombs. (There is a saying that Judaism is a religion that involves laughing from one eye and crying from another – in our case, it is possible this relates to the experience of drinking Jägerbombs.) And Ivan, my best man (and, I must state for the record, organiser of a reciprocal surprise stag weekend which surpassed all possible expectations) speaks warmly and wittily, and sings a magnificent self-penned song with my brothers.

Totnes's first kosher wedding feast is served to the masses, and consumed with delight. My Uncle Daniel sits with my father, and they catch up on lost time and exchange stories and *schtick* and torturous puns.

As dusk settles, the band strikes up the tune for our first dance. Yes, we'd all danced earlier – but we've lived this relationship in reverse; why stop now?

Eliana and I take to the dancefloor. It was always this moment that I reached for, in my dreams – when I was striving to picture a world beyond the conversion.

And as we dance, I feel an exhalation deeper than any I've felt in three years. A sense of deep, deep contentment. Of having landed safely.

I lift Eliana, and spin her delightedly around in a circle, her dress making a beautiful arc behind her.

As we finish, the dancefloor floods with our loved ones, and we are swept into the night on a tide of happiness, my wife and I.

CHAPTER 36

Endings and Beginnings

No relationship is without its complications – these just happened to be mine.

With the signing of the *ketubah*, and the breaking of the glass, the things that divided Eliana and me are finally no more.

Our life is no longer seasoned with the frisson of danger – the ever-present precarity, and prospect of societal ruin and spiritual limbo – that marked our path towards one another.

We are a married couple.

We move, as the Beth Din's final letter required of us, deep into the heart of religious north London. It isn't where we'd choose to live, but we find a flat and we move in. We are together.

Aside from our strange final enforced displacement, the problems we face now move from the theological to the pragmatic. The purchasing of plates. The deep scrutiny of cutlery. What's the best tog-count for a duvet, and also what is a tog, and furthermore, if you're only permitted to handle a small corner of a duvet (which, it turns out, is how they let you test them in the shop) how can you *truly* tell what it would be like to sleep under it?

We have an argument about whether or not there's any point in buying an air fryer, and the fact that we now have the bandwidth to expend energy on something so thunderously banal feels truly exhilarating.

I even pass my driving test.

Sometimes, when I leave the flat, I see a bearded figure across the street and experience a jolt of panic, thinking it is a member of the Beth Din. Sometimes it is – this is their neighbourhood, after all – but most often it is just another Jewish man, going about his business. And the monthly post-conversion check-ins we have been assured of never quite happen – Dayan Weissman does reach out, with warmth and compassion, but then life rises up in ways one is always preparing for, but never quite prepared for.

Less than four months after our wedding, Bernard Kops dies, aged ninety-seven, at home, with his beloved Erica by his side. Even at his funeral Bernard, typically, manages to hold court and have the last word – the service ends with a recording of him reading out one of his most celebrated poems, 'Shalom Bomb'.

Less than six months after our wedding, Lion collapses to the floor of her beautiful flat. She cool-headedly calls for an ambulance, diagnosing herself (correctly) with an aortic aneurism, and is taken to the Royal Free Hospital. Over a long weekend she elegantly receives queues of her visiting family, who have flown in from across the world, and, as she grows fainter, each person has the chance to sit with her, and say the things they wish to say. Her last moments are spent singing and laughing with her great-granddaughter. Aged ninety-two, she has a full face of make-up and looks immaculate.

And less than nine months after our wedding, my father begins to struggle to walk. His mobility rapidly declines, and his famous appetite begins to wane. In a strange, dense, unreal period of time, he goes from using a stick to a frame, to a wheelchair, before eventually becoming confined to a hospital bed in the centre of our dining room. Communication becomes more difficult, and one side of his face begins to fall. My mother explains, rightly, to the visiting district nurses that Dad would be happiest and most content at home, surrounded by his books and records and films and family, and so that is where he stays; gradually growing more distant from us, but never, ever, entirely losing his sense of who he is. One Sunday my brothers and our partners all assemble in Portsmouth, and join my parents for a family meal. We sit around the table at which we've shared so many meals together, with Dad's bed as close to us as can be, and all chat and eat and bicker and joke together. On Tuesday morning, as our taxi arrives to take Eliana and me to the station, I sit with Dad and say everything I wanted to say. I thank him, and tell him I love him, and kiss him, and read him a poem that I have written for him. In the final thing Dad says to me, he asks me to read it again, and so I do.

That evening, as my mum prepares food in the adjoining room, Dad dies peacefully at home. We all return to Portsmouth and gather in the dining room to be with him once more, and with each other. Dad's face is even, now. His features sit calmly – no more lopsidedness, no more discomfort. He looks, truly, like he is sleeping. And he looks wise again. Together, we read the *kaddish*, and sing the songs and blessings that Dad loved, and, eventually the night-shift undertakers come to take him away. When we come back into the dining room, the hospital bed that Dad had been lying in has been neatly made, like it was a hotel, and a small black-and-white paper windmill – sourced from a nearby vase full of them, made by Mum for Dad's surprise seventieth birthday, some decade previous – has been placed, thoughtfully, on top of the pillow.

Dad's funeral is full – a sell-out performance – a warm gathering of people from all chapters of his life: family, friends, university colleagues, students he taught decades ago, a man from the local paper. The service is led by Orli, the rabbi who had overseen every one of our *bar mitzvahs*, and our parents' wedding. She speaks movingly, sings beautifully, and seemingly hasn't aged a day. As we leave the room and walk out into the bright sunlight, Dad's choice of music plays; 'Hello, I Must Be Going', by Groucho Marx.

Papa, I miss you very much. I miss your enormous kindness, and your relentless fascination with the world, and with ideas. I had so many more things to ask you, and you had so many more stories to tell.

These vast, tidal changes reshape the landscape of our world. Eliana and I inevitably spend a great deal of time away from The Area, because the area we have needed to be is closer to those we love.

We return to Primrose Hill to grieve with Eliana's family. And then to Portsmouth, to grieve with mine.

As, gradually, the tumult starts to subside, the prospect of returning to The Area, and building our lives there, is unrealistic. We have lived in the heart of Hendon, just as we said we would. But life has happened, and we are no longer supplicants. We are a married couple, and the choices that we are able to make are, finally, our own.

And so, over a year after our wedding, Eliana and I move, for the first time, into a place of our own, in a location of our choosing.

To our amazement, we find a flat in Haverstock Gardens, a few doors away from where Bernard and Erica spent so much of their lives together, with the miraculous secret green oasis at our doorstep. Here, we are within walking distance of the world Eliana grew up in, and we have the space to begin to craft a life for ourselves.

It is a place where we can be closer to Eliana's family, to my brothers, to everything.

A space in which to, slowly, rebuild my own relationship with Judaism, scorched by those ruinous final months.

A home in which we will – like every other Jewish couple in the world – build a life that works for us.

It's not The Area, I'm afraid. But it's our area.

After all – 'It's not all or nothing,' one of the Supportive Rabbis tells me, quietly, right at the end of the conversion process. 'The Beth Din won't want to hear it, but it's not.'

To misquote Shakespeare: some are born Jewish, some achieve Judaism, and some have Judaism thrust upon them.

In some ways, I feel like I've experienced all three.

There are many things that happened to Eliana and me along this process which caused me great pain. In recounting everything that happened, I have walked the corridors of my memory, relived things that choked me and outraged me and made me weep hot indignant tears. But they are all now in the past. What rage I once had has long cooled, and unless I focus on those embers and fan them into flames, it no longer burns within me. It is gone.

But the joy I have experienced stays with me, and it always will. I am a hoarder of happiness – of nourishing friendships, of wondrous experiences, of beautiful memories. I ingest them greedily, and relive them constantly. They are the world I choose to inhabit.

Whatever else happens in my life, a part of me will always be in the quiet stillness of the *bedekin* room, looking at Eliana for the first time on the day of our wedding, enveloped by the love of our families. Part of me will always be stood beneath the *chuppah*, as Eliana circles me, with our parents looking on. And part of me will always be suspended in mid-air – flung up into the heavens by people I love, a panorama of beaming faces beneath me, as far as the eye can see.

There is Lion, stood on the edge of the dancefloor, her diamonds glistening, her flame-red hair catching the light. There is my father, laughing and singing, arm in arm with my brothers. And there is Eliana, whirling and spinning in the centre of it all, the flowers in her dress intertwining with the greenery of the glasshouse, her smiling blue eyes the colour of the endless autumn sky.

Acknowledgements

I owe immense thanks to my brilliant agent, Georgia Garrett, who is astute, unflappable, supportive, and quite frankly everything one might dare to hope a literary agent could be. It was Georgia who introduced me to my publisher, the indefatigable Robyn Drury, my superb editor Jessica Patel, marketing and publicity genii Laura Nicol and Molly Maynard, and the entire team at Ebury/Penguin Random House, who warmly and supportively guided a skittish first time author through the process of bringing a book into the world. I am immensely grateful to all of them for their expertise and forbearance.

If I've written this book in any way effectively (and your mileage may vary on that front, obviously) then I hope that in many ways it functions from start to finish as an extended acknowledgement of the many people who helped both Eliana and me in so many ways as we attempted to navigate a process that pushed us far beyond our limits. But one can seldom express too much gratitude, and there are many, many people I will be thanking for as long as I live; the many people in Hendon who extended such immeasurable kindness to us on our journey – particularly the two extraordinary families whose homes we shared; the communities who have welcomed us; the rabbis who have supported us and guided us (and in some cases, married us); and the friends who have, against all odds, put up with us.

I must thank John Hunter, the greatest photographer on the planet, for taking my author photos, and Catherine Hayward, the greatest stylist on the planet, for being the sole reason I resemble something approaching an author in said photos.

Thanks to Andrew O'Hagan, for his wise and perceptive counsel over a series of crucial cups of tea.

And huge thanks to Deborah Frances-White, Tom, and all of the Chateauvians – beacons of creativity, pillars of practical support, wellsprings of advice, fonts of scurrilous industry gossip, and invariably superb, nourishing company precisely when it's been needed most.

Finally, love and thanks to Eliana's remarkable family, who welcomed me into their world with huge kindness. And to my family; my ridiculous and talented brothers, my exceptional mum, and my brilliant father, whose songs and stories I hope to teach to my children, one day.

To Ivan, my partner in comedy. And to Eliana, my partner in everything else.